THE OPERATION OF THE INITIATIVE, REFERENDUM, AND RECALL IN OREGON

THE MACMILLAN COMPANY
NEW YORK · BOSTON · CHICAGO · DALLAS
ATLANTA · SAN FRANCISCO

MACMILLAN & CO., LIMITED
LONDON · BOMBAY · CALCUTTA
MELBOURNE

THE MACMILLAN CO. OF CANADA, LTD.
TORONTO

THE OPERATION OF
THE INITIATIVE, REFERENDUM, AND
RECALL IN OREGON

BY

JAMES D. BARNETT, Ph.D.

PROFESSOR OF POLITICAL SCIENCE IN THE UNIVERSITY
OF OREGON

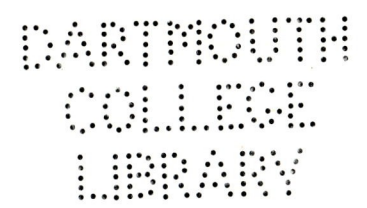

New York
THE MACMILLAN COMPANY
1915

All rights reserved

COPYRIGHT, 1915,
BY THE MACMILLAN COMPANY.

Set up and electrotyped. Published December, 1915.

Norwood Press
J. S. Cushing Co. — Berwick & Smith Co.
Norwood, Mass., U.S.A.

PREFATORY NOTE

IN the preparation of this book indebtedness to many persons, especially state and local officials, has been incurred for information on various matters. As is evident, extensive use has been made of the leading state newspapers, the *Oregonian* and the *Oregon Journal*. These have been supplemented especially by two of the local papers, the Eugene *Register* and the Eugene *Guard*. A bibliography of studies by observers of the Oregon System, consulted in this connection, is given in the appendix. For suggestions and corrections I am under obligation to my colleagues, Professor J. H. Gilbert and Professor R. C. Clark, who have read the manuscript and proof. The scope of the book is not as wide as the title would strictly indicate, for the operation of the initiative and referendum in the localities is not included.

JAMES D. BARNETT.

UNIVERSITY OF OREGON,
November 1, 1915.

TABLE OF CONTENTS

PART I

THE INITIATIVE AND REFERENDUM

CHAPTER I

INTRODUCTION

	PAGES
1. THE ADOPTION OF THE SYSTEM OF DIRECT LEGISLATION	3–5
2. THE PROVISIONS FOR DIRECT LEGISLATION IN GENERAL .	5–8

CHAPTER II

THE AUTHORS OF PROPOSED LEGISLATION

1. THE LEGISLATURE	9–12
2. THE EXECUTIVE	12–13
3. "THE PEOPLE"	13–20
1. Authors Concealed	13–16
2. "Every Man His Own Legislature"	16–18
3. Associations	18
4. Radicals and Conservatives	18–20

CHAPTER III

THE MOTIVES IN LEGISLATION . . 21–25

CHAPTER IV

THE PREPARATION OF MEASURES . 26–30

CHAPTER V

THE SUBSTANCE AND FORM OF MEASURES

	PAGES
1. THE MEASURES SUBMITTED	31–37
2. SUITABLE AND UNSUITABLE SUBJECTS	37–41
3. DECEPTION IN MEASURES	42–44
4. THE COMBINATION OF SUBJECTS IN MEASURES	44–46
5. CONFLICTING MEASURES	47–49
6. THE FORM OF MEASURES	50–53

CHAPTER VI

THE MAKING OF PETITIONS

1. THE PERCENTAGE OF SIGNATURES REQUIRED	54–58
2. THE GEOGRAPHICAL DISTRIBUTION OF SIGNATURES	58–59
3. THE PAYMENT OF CIRCULATORS	59–64
4. THE METHODS OF CIRCULATORS	64–74
5. SUBSTITUTES FOR CIRCULATION	74–77

CHAPTER VII

THE MULTIPLICITY OF MEASURES

1. THE NUMBER OF MEASURES	78–80
2. THE BURDEN ON THE VOTERS	81–82
3. THE CAUSES AND THE REMEDIES	82–85

CHAPTER VIII

CAMPAIGN ORGANIZATION . . 86

CHAPTER IX

FINANCE 87–90

CHAPTER X

THE EDUCATION OF THE VOTE

1. THE STUDY OF MEASURES	91–92
2. THE MEANS OF INFORMATION	93–99
3. THE RESULTS OF EDUCATION	99–100

CHAPTER XI
THE VOTE IN DIRECT LEGISLATION

1. THE INTEREST IN THE ELECTIONS	101–103
2. MINORITY *versus* MAJORITY	103–105
3. THE AMOUNT OF LEGISLATION ENACTED	105–107
4. THE RATIONALITY OF THE VOTE	107–125
1. The Confusion of the Measure with the Referendum	107
2. The Identification of Measures	107–108
3. Knowledge of the Contents of Measures	108–112
4. Attention to Legal Technicalities of Form	112
5. The Vote on Subjects Unsuitable to Direct Legislation	112–113
6. The Vote on Measures Submitted by Selfish Interests	113–115
7. The Vote on Conflicting Measures	115–117
8. Conservatism and Progressivism in the Vote	117–120
9. The Vote of the Uncertain Voter	121–123
10. The Vote as Protest	123
11. The Intelligence of the Vote in General	123–125

CHAPTER XII
DIRECT LEGISLATION AND THE EXECUTIVE 126–127

CHAPTER XIII
THE DIRECT AND THE REPRESENTATIVE LEGISLATURES

1. DIRECT LEGISLATION AND REPRESENTATIVE GOVERNMENT	128
2. THE TWO LEGISLATIVE BODIES	128–130

CHAPTER XIV
CHECKS OF THE LEGISLATIVE ASSEMBLY UPON DIRECT LEGISLATION

1. THE REGULATION OF THE INITIATIVE AND REFERENDUM	131–132
2. EMERGENCY LEGISLATION	132–144
3. THE DIVISION OF LEGISLATIVE MEASURES	144

CHAPTER XV
THE AMENDMENT AND REPEAL OF DIRECT LEGISLATION BY THE LEGISLATIVE ASSEMBLY 145–156

CHAPTER XVI
PUBLIC OPINION BILLS 157–158

CHAPTER XVII
COMPETITION WITH THE LEGISLATIVE ASSEMBLY 159–166

CHAPTER XVIII
THE EFFECT OF DIRECT LEGISLATION ON THE CHARACTER AND ACTIVITY OF THE LEGISLATIVE ASSEMBLY 167–170

CHAPTER XIX
THE REFERENDUM AS A SUBSTITUTE FOR CONSTITUTIONAL LIMITATIONS UPON THE LEGISLATIVE ASSEMBLY 171–172

CHAPTER XX
DIRECT LEGISLATION AND THE COURTS
1. The Interpretation of Direct Legislation 173–174
2. "The Recall of Judicial Decisions" 174–176

CHAPTER XXI
DIRECT LEGISLATION AND THE CONSTITUTIONAL CONVENTION . . . 177–179

CHAPTER XXII
DIRECT LEGISLATION AND THE STABILITY OF GOVERNMENT 180–184

CHAPTER XXIII
DIRECT LEGISLATION AND POLITICAL PARTIES 185–186

CHAPTER XXIV
STATE DIRECT LEGISLATION AND FEDERAL MATTERS 187

CHAPTER XXV

THE POPULARITY OF DIRECT LEGISLA-
TION 188

PART II

THE RECALL 189–218

PART III

APPENDIX

I.	BIBLIOGRAPHY	221–227
II.	CONSTITUTIONAL AND STATUTORY PROVISIONS	227–241
III.	THE VOTE ON INITIATIVE AND REFERENDUM MEASURES	241–253
IV.	A MEASURE AND ARGUMENTS	254–274
V.	AN INITIATIVE PETITION	274–275
VI.	NEWSPAPER ADVICE ON DIRECT LEGISLATION	275–279
VII.	RECOMMENDATIONS OF THE TAXPAYERS' LEAGUE	280–286
VIII.	ADVERTISEMENTS	287–288
IX.	A BALLOT FOR MEN AND MEASURES	288
X.	A RECALL PETITION	289–290
XI.	A RECALL BALLOT	291–292

INDEX 293–295

PART I
THE INITIATIVE AND REFERENDUM

CHAPTER I

INTRODUCTION

I

The Adoption of the System of Direct Legislation

THE state constitution of 1859 provided for an obligatory referendum on constitutional amendments proposed by the legislative assembly to the people, and, while prohibiting generally the referring of statutes to the people, it authorized the submission of local and special legislation to the voters of the district affected.[1] At the constitutional convention a proposal had been made to allow the legislative assembly to refer any statute to the voters, but this was rejected.[2]

The agitation for the present system of direct legislation hardly commenced before 1892.[3] Beginning with 1892, a campaign for the adoption of the initiative and referendum was carried on with tireless effort, under the remarkable leadership of W. S. U'Ren, aided by the Joint Committee on Direct Legislation, later broadened into the Direct Legislation League (the forerunner of the People's Power League), with the result that after ten years the system was embodied in the constitution.[4] Advocated by the granges, the labor unions, and the Populist

[1] *Constitution*, art. 17, sec. 1; art. 1, sec. 21 (1859).

[2] *Proceedings of the Constitutional Convention, Oregonian*, Oct. 3, 1857, p. 1, col. 6. See also G. H. Williams, quoted in *Oregonian*, May 27, 1902, p. 10, col. 3.

[3] For details regarding the adoption of the initiative and referendum see especially L. Pease, *Initiative and Referendum — Oregon's "Big Stick," Pacific Monthly*, vol. 17, pp. 563–75 (1907); L. Steffens, *U'Ren — The Law-Giver, American Magazine*, vol. 65, pp. 527–40 (1908); B. J. Hendrick, *Initiative and Referendum and How Oregon Got Them, McClure's Magazine*, vol. 37, pp. 234–48 (1911).

[4] *Constitution*, art. 4, sec. 1 (1902).

party, it had finally been indorsed both by the Republican and Democratic parties.

"The causes which led to its adoption are the same that are in evidence throughout the country generally. The people felt the government was getting away from them and they desired a more direct control, both in the making of laws and in their enforcement, than they enjoyed. More potent, however, than this was the failure of the legislature to respond to the demand of the people for the enforcement of laws respecting the control of corporations, taxation, and kindred subjects affecting public interests. Boss-ridden legislatures and councils were the rule rather than the exception, and the people were tired of coaxing and pleading to secure desired legislation. Legislatures and councils were too often more solicitous for special than for the public interests and the people wanted to secure some effective and direct method of making their influence felt and their wishes respected. The difficulty in securing the enactment of the Australian ballot law and the registration law are examples of laws the people wanted, and which were enacted grudgingly and after long-continued agitation. Other important measures failed repeatedly to pass. The combined effect was to create a sentiment (as shown by the vote) overwhelmingly in favor of the new procedure." [1]

---

[1] J. N. Teal, *Practical Workings of the Initiative and Referendum in Oregon*, *Cincinnati Conference for Good City Government*, 1909, pp. 309, 310. *Cf. Oregonian*, Nov. 28, 1902, p. 6, col. 1; H. W. Scott, *ibid.*, Oct. 16, 1907, p. 11, col. 3. "Although it was adopted by a majority of eleven to one, a great many people did not know what they were voting for. The friends of the measure had been working judiciously for it for years, had secured the endorsement of the newspapers, many of the leading men of the state, and had by shrewd management got possession of the political parties, to the extent, at least, that all candidates printed 'Vote for Initiative and Referendum' on all their election cards and bill posters and were all lined up to advocate the measure during election. . . . Many did not know what they were voting for, simply following the rest." H. Denlinger, *Arena*, vol. 38, pp. 83–4 (1907). Such statements are repeated by Oregonians again and again, both in regard to the members of the legislature and the people, and are widely believed to be true.

Some of the leaders have been interested in the movement chiefly as a means of securing the ultimate adoption of the single tax. "I went just as crazy over the single

Introduction

In 1906 the initiative and referendum system was extended by constitutional amendment to every municipality and district, as to "all local, special, and municipal legislation" of every character for the respective municipalities and districts.[1] For some reason the majority of votes received by this amendment was very much less than that received by the amendment which established the system for the state four years earlier.

2

The Provisions for Direct Legislation in General [2]

"There is a difference between the initiative and the referendum — a vast difference. . . . The initiative is an instrumentality of popular government through which the people propose and enact laws or adopt constitutional amendments without regard for any legislature or any other representative or delegated body. The referendum is a plebiscite by which the people as a whole approve or reject any measure previously adopted by the legislature, or referred to them directly by the legislature. All measures under the initiative are a demonstration of the original law-making function. All measures under the referendum are a demonstration of the law-approving or law-rejecting function." [3]

tax idea as any one else ever did. I knew I wanted single tax, and that was about all I did know. . . . I learned what the initiative and referendum is, and then I saw the way to single tax. So I quit talking single tax, not because I was any the less in favor of it but because I saw that the first job was to get the initiative and referendum, so that the people, independently of the legislature, may get what they want rather than take what the legislature will let them have. . . . All the work we have done for direct legislation has been done with the single tax in view, but we have not talked single tax because that was not the question before the house." W. S. U'Ren, *Report of Single Tax Conference*, 1910, pp. 21–2.

[1] *Constitution*, art. 4, sec. 1a (1906). [2] *Below*, pp. 227–40.

[3] *Oregonian*, Oct. 15, 1913, p. 10, col. 2. "There is a distinction . . . between the referendum and the initiative, in which latter legislation is initiated and the whole matter must be formulated just as it is to be submitted to the people, while in the referendum it is only a question of the approval or disapproval by the people of what the legislature has already enacted as a law." *Palmer* v. *Benson, Oregon Reports*, vol. 50, pp. 277, 279 (1907).

6   Initiative, Referendum, and Recall in Oregon

The original constitutional provision for a referendum upon constitutional amendments required for the approval of the amendment a majority vote of all the members of each house of two succeeding legislative assemblies, and the approval of a majority of the electors voting at the election for putting the amendment into effect.[1] This was changed in 1906 to allow amendments to be submitted after action by one assembly, and to require only a majority of the votes cast on the amendment for its approval by the voters.[2]

By the radical extension of the principle of direct legislation established by the constitutional amendment of 1902, "the people reserve to themselves power to propose laws and amendments to the constitution and to enact or reject the same at the polls, independent of the legislative assembly, and also reserve power at their own option to approve or reject at the polls any act of the legislative assembly." "The first power reserved by the people is the initiative." Any measure may thus be proposed by a petition signed by eight per cent of the legal voters of the state as determined by the votes cast at the last preceding general election for justice of the supreme court.[3] Initiative petitions must be filed with the secretary of state not less than four months before the election. "The second power is the referendum." It may be ordered, except as to emergency measures, by a petition signed by five per cent of the legal voters determined as in the case of initiative petitions. Referendum petitions must be filed with the secretary of state not more than ninety days after the final adjournment of the legislative assembly. The referendum may be demanded "against one or more items, sections, or parts of any act of the legislative assembly" in the same manner as against a complete act. The

---

[1] *Constitution*, art. 17, sec. 1 (1859).   *Below*, p. 180.
[2] *Ibid.*, art. 17, sec. 1 (1906).
[3] The substitution of the vote cast for governor in place of the vote cast for justice of the supreme court would remove a difficulty of calculation in cases where more than one justice is elected at the same time.   *Cf. House Joint Resolution*, 1915, no. 2, sec. 1.

Introduction

legislative assembly, formerly prohibited from submitting statutory measures (except local and special measures to the localities affected) to the voters of the state, may now so refer any statutory measures whatever. Statutes providing for the relocation of the state capital or for the location, away from the capital, of state institutions, or for calling constitutional conventions must be approved by the voters before they become effective. The vote upon measures submitted to the people is had at the regular biennial election, unless (except in case of statutes relocating the capital or locating state institutions away from the capital, or calling a constitutional convention) the assembly calls a special election for the purpose. A majority of the votes cast upon a measure is required for its approval.[1]

If two or more conflicting laws or conflicting constitutional amendments are approved at the same election, the law or amendment receiving the greatest number of votes is paramount in all particulars as to which there is a conflict, even though it may not have received the greatest majority of affirmative votes.[2]

The forms for initiative and referendum petitions are prescribed by law.[3]

Under the law of 1903 the verification of signatures on the petition was made by the county clerks, who compared them with the signatures on the registration records, and certified their findings as to the genuineness of the signatures and the qualifications of the signers to the secretary of state. The decision of the secretary of state as to these matters and as to whether the petition generally fulfilled the requirements of the

---

[1] *Constitution*, art. 1, sec. 21 (1859); art. 4, sec. 1 (1902); art. 4, sec. 1a (1906); art. 14, sec. 1 (1859); art. 14, sec. 3 (1908). A constitutional amendment of 1910 provided that no bill regulating taxation or exemption throughout the state should become a law until approved by the people of the state. *Constitution*, art. 9, sec. 1a (1910). But this was repealed two years later. *Constitution*, art. 9, sec. 1a (1912).

[2] *Laws*, 1907, ch. 226, sec. 7; *Lord's Oregon Laws*, sec. 3477. See below, p. 47.

[3] *Constitution*, art. 4, sec. 1; *Laws*, 1903, p. 244; 1907, ch. 226, secs. 1–2; *Lord's Oregon Laws*, secs. 3420–2; *Laws*, 1913, ch. 359, sec. 1.

law was reviewable by the supreme court.[1] Verification by the persons circulating the petition is substituted by the law of 1907, and the circuit court is authorized to review the secretary's action in mandamus or injunction proceedings.[2]

A person signing a name other than his own to any petition or knowingly signing his name more than once for the same measure, or who is not at the time of his signing a legal voter is subject to punishment by fine and imprisonment.[3]

The ballot titles, formerly drawn by the authors of initiative or referendum measures, are now drawn by the attorney-general, but appeal from his decision to the circuit court is allowed.[4]

Under the law of 1903, pamphlets advocating or opposing initiative or referendum measures, prepared at the sole expense of the interested parties, might be filed with the secretary of state for distribution to the county clerks for final distribution to the voters.[5] At present the state shares the expense of the preparation of the "voters' pamphlet," and the distribution is made directly by the secretary of state to the voters.[6]

---

[1] *Laws*, 1903, p. 244, secs. 3-4.

[2] *Laws*, 1907, ch. 226, sec. 3; *Laws*, 1913, ch. 359, sec. 2. The supreme court may, in its own discretion, take original jurisdiction in mandamus proceedings. *Constitution*, art. 7, sec. 2 (1910).

[3] *Laws*, 1903, p. 224, sec. 10; *Laws*, 1907, ch. 226, sec. 13; *Lord's Oregon Laws*, sec. 3483.

[4] *Laws*, 1907, ch. 226, sec. 5; *Laws*, 1913, ch. 36.

[5] *Laws*, 1903, p. 244, sec. 8.

[6] *Laws*, 1907, ch. 226, sec. 8; *Laws*, 1913, ch. 359, sec. 4.

CHAPTER II

THE AUTHORS OF PROPOSED LEGISLATION

I

The Legislature

WHILE the action of two legislative assemblies was required for the submission of constitutional amendments to the voters and a majority of the votes cast at the election was required for the approval of amendments, but few amendments were submitted by the assembly. But since the submission of amendments by a single assembly has been allowed and only a majority of the vote cast on the amendment at the election required for its approval, the assembly has been more active, and has submitted twenty-two amendments to the people since 1908.[1]

The shifting upon the people of responsibility which should be assumed by the legislative assembly is prevented by the provision of the original constitution which forbids that "any law shall be passed the taking effect of which shall be made to depend upon any authority except as provided in the constitution," but at the same time the constitution permits the assembly to submit special and local laws to the voters interested,[2] who generally should be better judges than the assembly in such matters.

The necessity of local legislation by the assembly has been reduced by the amendment of 1906 investing the localities with the power of initiative and referendum in matters of local

---

[1] At the next general election three constitutional amendments originating in the assembly will appear on the ballot.   [2] *Constitution*, art. 1, sec. 21 (1859).

interest,[1] and an amendment of 1910 has reduced the power of the assembly in the direction of local legislation.[2]

Although the amendment of 1902 permits the people of the state to demand the referendum upon legislation passed by the assembly, it unfortunately permits the assembly of its own accord to refer any legislation to the vote of the people for final determination.[3] This optional referendum not only encourages the assembly to shift responsibility for legislation upon the people,[4] but is a means whereby the assembly may prevent the operation of the governor's veto, since the veto is not applicable to the measures referred to the people.[5] "If the legislature would avoid the Scylla of a veto, it may steer its measures toward the Charybdis of the referendum."[6]

In view of the advantages which should accrue from further discussion of initiative measures, as well as from a hope that in this way action by the legislative assembly would often render unnecessary action by direct legislation, it has been proposed that all initiative bills shall first be presented to the legislature and that the legislature shall then either pass the bill without amendment, or substitute a rival bill and submit both bills to the people.[7] It would seem that the creation of any tendency toward shifting the legislature's responsibility by such an optional referendum would be at least balanced by a tendency to enact needed legislation without waiting for pressure from unofficial action.

[1] *Constitution*, art. 4, sec. 1a (1906).

[2] *Ibid.*, art. 11, sec. 2 (1910); art. 9, sec. 1a (1910, 1912).

[3] *Ibid.*, art. 4, sec. 1 (1902). "A bill adopted by the legislature may be referred to the people for their ratification. . . . When an act comes from the legislative assembly it may be affirmed, we think, under the clause of the constitution above quoted that that body cannot leave it to a vote of the people to determine whether or not it shall become a law, because the taking effect thereof is thereby made to depend upon an authority other than that provided for in the constitution." *Fouts v. Hood River, Oregon Reports*, vol. 46, pp. 492, 497 (1905). See also *Oregon Journal*, Feb. 12, 1913, p. 2, col. 2; *Oregonian*, Feb. 12, 1913, p. 2, col. 1.

[4] *Below*, pp. 169–70   [5] *Constitution*, art. 4, sec. 1 (1902).

[6] *Libby v. Olcott, Oregon Reports*, vol. 66, pp. 124, 131 (1913).

[7] *Below*, pp. 164–5.

In addition to the objection urged against the resubmission by the legislative assembly of measures enacted or defeated by the voters, as an unwarranted interference with the will of the people,[1] a more substantial objection lies in the fact that such a practice encourages the over-use of direct legislation. "If the legislature at this time establish a precedent of taking from the statute books measures passed by the people and resubmitting them, you will soon have every man with anything against a measure up before the legislature with resolutions to put it in the ballot again."[2] The same, indeed, may be said in regard to measures which have been *rejected* by the voters.

Of course all measures passed by the legislative assembly and referred by the people are, in a certain sense, "initiated" by the assembly.

In some instances the assembly has delegated the initiation of constitutional amendments or bills to committees acting under its authority. The important "rational tax reform" amendments and bills of 1912 were initiated by a "legislative tax committee" consisting of members of the senate and the house of representatives, acting in conjunction with the state tax commissioners. And a similar provision was made for the submission of tax measures in 1914. A commission appointed by the governor under authority of the legislature in 1911 was empowered to submit measures for the reform of judicial procedure either to the legislature or the people, but the commission decided in favor of the legislature.

Under such arrangements, of course, the legislature is shifting its responsibility for the enactment of legislation and neglecting to exercise even the *advisory* function of referring legislation to the people.[3]

---

[1] *Below*, p. 146.

[2] L. G. Lewelling, senate, *Oregon Journal*, Feb. 8, 1913, p. 14, col. 1.

[3] In 1911 the legislative assembly could not act finally upon taxation bills, and of course must still submit any proposals for constitutional amendments affecting taxation to the people.

The action of the "legislative tax committee" of 1912 was obnoxious to the supporters of rival measures, and it was doubtless for this reason that in a proposed constitutional amendment of that year there was included a provision to the effect that the legislative assembly should not "appoint or create any committee, board or commission to prepare or propose any measure by initiative petition," and should not appropriate any money for the making of initiative or referendum petitions.[1] This proposition was criticized as "a step to deprive the people, to a certain extent, of the right to call on their legislatures for preparation and submission of bills, which in the end would be submitted to the people."[2]

2

The Executive

Recently a quasi-official form of organization for the preparation of initiative measures has been developed. On account of the failure of enactment of "good roads" legislation at the legislative session of 1911, the governor, upon his own responsibility, appointed a "state-wide committee" who prepared several measures on the subject. These were later revised by a "harmony committee" similarly appointed, and were finally submitted to the popular vote. The "blue-sky" bill and the "millage-tax" bill, submitted at the same election, were prepared, both without legislative sanction, the first by the corporation clerk under the direction of the secretary of state and with the coöperation of the governor, and the latter by a "joint committee" made up from the governor's "special committee" and from the boards of regents of the university and the agricultural college (the institutions affected), working with the presidents of the respective institutions. The governor was also largely responsible for the submission of the anti-capital punish-

---

[1] *Referendum Pamphlet*, 1912, no. 362, art. 4, sec. 3f, p. 214. See *Oregonian*, Aug. 11, 1912, sec. 2, p. 7, col. 1.

[2] Reported in *Oregonian*, Aug. 11, 1912, sec. 2, p. 7, col. 1.

ment bill at the same election, and he was the real author of the bill for the consolidation of the desert land board and the state land board submitted at the next election.

Such procedure on the part of executive officials has met with objection. In regard to the initiation of the "blue-sky" bill it was said: "The sole question here is whether the executive department, through the secretary of state, or the legislature shall legislate for the people of Oregon. It is an unwarranted invasion by one branch of the state into the constitutional territory of another."[1] And it has even been suggested that it should be made unlawful for public officials other than the governor to prepare any measure affecting his own public service or employment.[2]

The objections asserted against executive interference in direct legislation of course apply to the proposal for appeal by the governor from the legislature to the people in case of vetoed bills.[3]

3
"The People"

1. Authors Concealed.

At times the real authors of initiative and referendum measures find it to their interest to conceal their identity from the public, and so the voters are at times confronted with measures the sources of which are unknown or uncertain. Thus, the origin of the attack on the corporation bill of 1903 was uncer-

[1] *Oregonian,* Oct. 20, 1912, sec. 3, p. 6, col. 3.
[2] Reported in *Oregonian,* Dec. 17, 1912, p. 10, col. 1. *Cf.* California *Laws,* 1913, ch. 196.
[3] *Below,* p. 126. A proposed constitutional amendment which authorized the governor to introduce bills and resolutions in the house of representatives at the same time authorized him to order a referendum on any of his measures which might not pass, and, in case the legislature passed a measure on the same subject, to order the referendum on both measures, so that the people might choose between them. C. H. Chapman and others, *Introductory Letter.* 1909, pp. 8, 33-4. *Cf.* E. L. Norris, *Strengthening the Power of the Executive, Governors' Conference Proceedings,* 1911, pp. 19-20.

tain, the authors of the "open-town" initiative bill of 1908 remained hidden, and the real authors of the referenda on the public utilities act and the university appropriations of 1912 have never been revealed. The authors of four out of the five referenda of 1913 are generally unknown or uncertain. In regard to the "open-town" bill it was reported: "The canvassers who are circulating the petition decline to tell whence it emanated or to give the name of anyone interested in the adoption of the measure. . . . The obvious desire of the sponsors of this petition is to keep in the background, and to escape public comment upon the proposed amendment."[1] The party who filed the petition against the workman's compensation act of 1913 declared that he himself did not know who was behind the movement.[2] Attempt was made to conceal the real authorship of several measures submitted in 1914.

Instead of simply hiding behind the party who filed the petition, sometimes the real authors of measures adopt misleading names. Thus the owners of the Barlow road, who initiated a bill for the state's purchase of the road, appeared as "A Committee of Farmers," a commercial club initiating an amendment to require a majority of the votes cast for the enactment of initiative measures appeared as "The Majority Home Rule League," and the opponents of the university appropriations of 1913 appeared as "The Oregon Higher Educational Institutions Betterment League." The interest of the single-taxers in the "home-rule" taxation measure was partly obscured by the fact that it was filed by the State Federation of Labor.

For many years "deceptive law-making" has been decried, and the necessity of reform in this direction emphasized. "The origin of measures when known, discloses much concerning their purpose and often leads to a closer investigation of the merits of a bill. Concealment of origin leads to deception of the people."[3]

[1] *Oregon Journal*, Nov. 1, 1907, p. 8, col. 1. [2] *Ibid.*, May 31, 1913, p. 17, col. 5.
[3] *Oregonian*, July 15, 1912, p. 6, col. 2.

"This evil should not be tolerated by the people of this state. The voters have a right to know the persons who are boosting every bill that appears on the ballots. The only reason for concealment makes this public knowledge necessary, for in each case some designing group of persons is trying to hoodwink the public by covering up the real purpose of the measure."[1] The remedy is not easy to find. "As in the case of bills in the legislature, ... it is not always possible to determine who prepared the measures and in whose interests they were filed. In some instances the real party in interest can be only guessed at. To determine who are the secret promoters of any measure must be more difficult than to ascertain the hidden interests back of a bill in the legislature."[2]

Until 1913 the law did not even require the secretary of state to keep a record of the names of the parties who filed petitions. But that year the legislature passed a law which provides that the ballot title shall contain the name of the party under whose authority the measure was initiated or referred.[3] However, this provision is very inadequate to stop the abuse described. Further, by the act of 1908, which aims to secure the publicity of campaign expenditures in direct legislation,[4] the statement of expenditures "is not demanded until after the issue has been settled at the polls,"[5] and the law as it is has generally not been well enforced.[6]

"Law says no man shall lobby among the ninety legislators at Salem for a bill 'without first truly and completely disclosing his interest therein' on pain of being deemed a criminal. Why not a penalty also for the man who, without disclosing his interest, lobbies for an initiative measure among the 100,000 law-making voters throughout the state?"[7] A meritorious bill which aimed to accomplish this purpose failed of passage in the

---

[1] *Oregonian*, Feb. 3, 1908, p. 8, col. 3. [2] *Ibid.*, Feb. 16, 1908, p. 9, col. 1.
[3] *Laws*, 1913, ch. 36.
[4] *Laws*, 1909, ch. 3, sec. 12; *Lord's Oregon Laws*, sec. 3497. See *Oregonian*, Feb. 3, 1908, p. 8, col. 3. [5] *Oregonian*, June 6, 1913, p. 10, col. 1.
[6] *Below*, p. 87. [7] *Oregonian*, Feb. 3, 1908, p. 8, col. 3.

legislature of 1913. "Before beginning to solicit signatures on any initiative or referendum petition for a constitutional amendment or a general law, or for any local law for a county or district composed of more than one county, the person, committee or organization proposing the same shall file ten printed copies thereof with the secretary of state, and also the name and post-office address of the person, the members of the committee, and of the organization, and the amount contributed or promised by every person contributing or promising to contribute towards paying the expenses of such initiative or referendum petition and campaign for the measure."[1]

2. "Every Man His Own Legislature."

The system of direct legislation, and especially the initiative, it is urged, makes "every man his own legislature."[2] "The initiative affords any citizen who has evolved a solution of a governmental problem an opportunity for demonstration of its merits. Under a system of delegated legislation only, his ideas would be, or quite likely would be, referred to some committee where further action would be prevented through the influence of selfish interest. Where the initiative exists, he may present his idea in the definite form of a proposed bill if eight per cent of the legal voters consider it worthy of consideration and sign a petition for its submission to a popular vote. The system encourages every citizen, however humble his position, to study problems of government, city and state, and to submit whatever solution he may evolve for the consideration and approval of others. . . . How different from the system so generally in force which tends to discourage and suppress the individual."[3] Thus becomes available "all the statesmanship there is among all the people."[4]

[1] *House Bill*, 1913, no. 365, sec. 4. See also *Oregonian*, June 17, 1913, p. 8, col. 2, June 20, 1913, p. 10, col. 2. *Cf.* Ohio *Laws*, 1914, p. 119, sec. 1.
[2] *Oregonian*, June 28, 1906, p. 8, col. 2.
[3] J. Bourne, *Initiative, Referendum and Recall*, *Atlantic Monthly*, vol. 109, pp. 122, 125–6 (1909). [4] J. Bourne, *Oregonian*, May 16, 1907, p. 8, col. 6.

But the great practical difficulties of the situation militate against this exaltation of the individual. "Here is the initiative . . . under which every citizen is given a glorious opportunity to make his own law. But does he? He does, if he will prepare his proposed law, circulate petitions, undertake a campaign of education, and spend his time and money in getting favorable consideration for his measure."[1] As a matter of fact it is very probable that no measures have been brought before the people by any individual without some sort of an organization behind him. But the individual may so dominate the organization as to be practically identified with it. This is the case of W. S. U'Ren, "the father of the Oregon System," especially in his connection with the People's Power League, through which much legislation of the greatest importance has been submitted to the people. "Now Mr. U'Ren proposes to draft a law regulating the use of money in political campaigns. Will it be enacted? Of course it will. In Oregon the state government is divided into four departments — the executive, judicial, legislative and Mr. U'Ren — and it is still an open question which exerts the most power. One fact must be considered in making comparisons: That the legislature does not dare to repeal the acts of Mr. U'Ren, the executive has no power to veto them, and thus far the judiciary has upheld all his laws and constitutional amendments. On the contrary, Mr. U'Ren has boldly clipped the wings of the executive and legislative departments, and when he gets time will doubtless put some shackles on the supreme court. To date, the indications are that Mr. U'Ren outweighs any one, and perhaps all three, of the other departments."[2] Especially during the earlier years of direct legislation many voted for "U'Ren measures" on general principle — "all U'Ren measures looked alike to them." But with the failure of some of the more radical proposals with which he

---

[1] *Oregonian*, June 12, 1910, sec. 3, p. 6, col. 2.

[2] *Ibid.*, July 17, 1906, p. 8, col. 4. See also especially *ibid.*, Jan. 30, 1908, p. 8, col. 2.

has been identified in more recent elections, the "eclipse of the law-giver" is proclaimed by his opponents, and it is declared that "the day of personal lawgiving in Oregon is passed."[1] No other individual in the state has attained any such prominence in the operation of direct legislation.

3. Associations.

Probably every measure that has been submitted to the people has had some form of organization behind it, although in some cases the organization has been rather intangible or ineffective. Most such organizations have been constituted temporarily for the purpose of securing the initiation or reference of a particular measure. The organizations have generally assumed the form of a small committee, self-constituted, or representing a larger committee or "mass meeting" of parties interested. But many permanent organizations have also been active in this direction. Business organizations — the Brewers and Wholesale Liquor Dealers' Association, the Travelers' Protective Association, the Employers' Association, commercial clubs, have looked after certain interests. A railway company, casualty insurance companies, and other corporations are known to have been, or are strongly suspected of having been, the real authors of some measures. The Anti-Saloon League, the Oregon Woman's Suffrage Association, the Oregon State Federation of Labor, the Portland Central Labor Council, and the State Grange have concerned themselves with measures of wider interest. But by far the most important organized influence in direct legislation has been the People's Power League, under the guidance of W. S. U'Ren. Most of the reform legislation enacted by the people has been submitted by this organization. The Socialist Party of Oregon initiated a measure in 1914.

4. Radicals and Conservatives.

The adoption of the system of direct legislation was intended by its chief supporter to furnish "a safe and practical method

[1] *Oregonian,* Jan. 21, 1913, p. 6, col. 2. See also *ibid.,* Nov. 5, 1914, p. 10, col. 2.

The Authors of Proposed Legislation

for reformers and agitators" to get a decision directly from the people.[1] More conservative persons feared that the system would fall into the hands of "demagogues" and "faddists." "The danger in the present innovation lies in the fact that the most radical fanatic may and will assume leadership and carry his schemes to success without any of those responsibilities that attach to and sober representative minds in a representative form of government. The occupation of public agitator will be fostered and exploited by the vicious demagogues and its practice will become necessary on the part of the substantial citizens of the county."[2] And some years of experience with the system assured conservatives that their fears had been well founded. "There are numerous political fad factions in Oregon which at every election, try to force their notions on the people by the initiative and referendum. Each of these factions is a minority. . . . They all boost the initiative and referendum because it gives them their only access to legislation. They have found themselves pestiferous annoyances to the people of the state, disturbers of the political peace and breeders of political strife."[3] And measures proposing approaches to the single-tax, liquor prohibition, woman's suffrage, control of corrupt practices at elections, elimination of free railway passes, the direct primary, proportional representation, the recall, an easier method of a amending the constitution, the people's gazette and inspectors of government, the abolition of the state senate, etc., have all alike been given in evidence of the tendency toward "freak" legislation under the system.

However unconvincing most of this evidence may generally appear, it is certainly true that conservatives are at a disadvantage in direct legislation. "The dice are loaded against them. The various radical groups, the socialists, the single-taxers, the

---

[1] W. S. U'Ren, *Operation of the Initiative and Referendum in Oregon*, Arena, vol. 32, pp. 128, 131 (1904).

[2] G. H. Burnett, *Recent Legislation, Proceedings of the Oregon Bar Association*, 1904–6, pp. 17, 25 (1904).

[3] *Oregonian*, Sept. 17, 1909, p. 10, col. 3.

woman suffragists, and the rest will sign each other's petitions and get their different propositions before the people. When the campaign opens the radicals are already organized. They know what they want, and they will coöperate energetically to secure it. But the conservatives are handicapped. It is always harder to organize the negative than the affirmative. And if the conservatives defeat distinctive changes in the fundamental law at one election, they cannot rest upon their arms. They must be continually upon guard, for at the very next election the same battle may have to be fought over again." [1]

[1] F. Foxcroft, *Initiative-Referendum in the United States, Contemporary Review*, vol. 99, pp. 11, 18 (1911).

CHAPTER III

THE MOTIVES IN LEGISLATION

It had been hoped that the system of direct legislation would escape the harmful influence of selfish special and local interests to which the general welfare has, to a greater or less extent, always been sacrificed in legislative assemblies. But from practical experience it is found that attempts to accomplish the promotion of selfish ends have been made to a considerable extent in direct legislation.

From a consideration of all the measures which have so far appeared on the ballot it appears that in the great majority of cases the proposal or opposition of measures has been made with a view, whether or not mistaken, to promote the general interests of the state. The interests of laborers and employers, hardly less wide, have caused several measures to be submitted to the people.

Special, narrow interests have operated in a number of cases. The first attempts to use the referendum were made, apparently, by railway interests against a state railway project, and by other special interests against a corporation regulation bill. The liquor interests have been responsible for at least two measures on the ballot. The owners of a toll road filed a bill providing for the purchase of the road by the state. One referendum resulted from a conflict between a sheriff and a county court. Apparently some special interests referred the public utilities act of 1912. Disappointed candidates for appointment are suspected to have been behind the county attorney referendum, and casualty companies and "ambulance-chasing" lawyers are likewise charged with holding up the workmen's compensation act. The abortive attempt to refer the dental act of 1913 perhaps came from "advertising" dentists. "Painless Parker's" dental bill of 1914 was submitted solely for the purpose of making eligible to practice a dentist who could not otherwise qualify. The bill of the same year for the abolition of the office of corporation commissioner by consolidation of the corporation and insurance departments came from a company disgruntled by the commissioner's refusal to permit the company to issue some bonds. The bill of the same year for the consolidation of the state land board and the desert land board was likewise, in part at least, an attack upon an officer who was obnoxious to the real author of the bill.

Local interests have been the cause of submitting many measures to the voters. The majority of these have been new-county or county-boundary bills, eight at a single election, submitted to the people of the state at a time when there was yet no provision for determining the question by the localities affected. The three normal schools, whose appropriations had been cut off by the legislature, were provided for in three bills submitted by people of their respective localities.[1] The conflicting interests of the upper and lower Columbia river fishermen appeared in their two conflicting bills. The Rogue river fishing bill favored interests of the upper river against the cannerymen of the lower river. The freight-rate bill of 1912 was initiated by the interested localities. Local interests have combined with others in case of some of the university appropriation referenda.

Pernicious log-rolling and blackmailing among localities have appeared to some extent in direct legislation.

A comparatively innocent illustration of this log-rolling is the initiative bill of 1912 for the division of counties and consolidation of cities. "The bill was originated in Cottage Grove, which is interested in county division. The provisions for consolida-

---

[1] The two localities which were defeated at the election succeeded in inducing the legislative assembly to resubmit the question again to the people at a later election.

tion of cities are in the interests of Seaside and St. Johns. The three cities have pooled their interests and will endeavor to secure the help of other cities and counties interested in the provisions of the bill." [1]

The evil possibilities of the system are most evident in case of referenda against the university appropriations. The referendum of 1912 is of special interest in this connection. "The origin of the movement to refer the measure in question is not altogether creditable to its promoters. The state university is located at the city of Eugene, in Lane county. Certain citizens of the southern portion of the county, including the city of Cottage Grove, were desirous of being incorporated into a new county, with Cottage Grove as its county seat. This was strenuously opposed by the citizens of the northern part of the county, and particularly by those of Eugene, and the measure was defeated. As a matter of retaliation, or, perhaps, to convince the citizens of Eugene that their city and its inhabitants would be better off without Cottage Grove in the same county, this movement was inaugurated." [2] After a fruitless attempt to "effect a deal with the Eugene people" the referendum petitions were filed. At the following session of the legislature the Cottage Grove interests threatened to hold up the university appropriations again, if their opponents did not support a general county division bill favored by Cottage Grove. Such support was given. Local newspapers tell the rest of the story. "A much different feeling prevails here now than did two years ago when Cottage Grove itself started the referendum on the appropriations. Since then Eugene and Cottage Grove have been brought closer together by the efforts put forth in behalf of this city in the recent legislature by the Lane county delegation. Although there has been talk of going after some of the other appropriations, so far the only remarks made publicly concerning the university appropriations have been favorable

[1] *Oregon Journal*, July 5, 1912, p. 6, col. 2.
[2] *State* v. *Olcott, Oregon Reports*, vol. 62, pp. 277, 284 (1912).

ones. . . . The majority seems to hope that such occasions as those of two years ago will not again be deemed expedient."[1] "Every precinct in Cottage Grove voted in favor of the university appropriations, giving evidence of a friendly feeling that will not soon be forgotten in Eugene."[2]

In 1909 a movement to refer the agricultural college appropriation was started by residents of Ashland, the seat of a normal school, to coerce the members of the legislative assembly from Benton county, the seat of the college, to support an appropriation for the normal school, but the movement was later dropped. Other such attempts have been made or threatened.

The motive of personal spite has operated in direct legislation, but probably only to a very limited extent.

Of course all these abuses of direct legislation have met with vigorous protest. "No one has a right to use the referendum for revenge. No one has a right to use the referendum against one bill in order to coerce members of the legislature into supporting another bill. Every measure should stand upon its own merits. . . . Trading has always been one of the greatest evils of legislation and it seems that we are to have it even under the initiative and referendum."[3] Moreover, this is very dangerous business. "Militancy must meet with militancy, and fire with fire."[4] The backers of the referendum of the portage railway bill were threatened with retaliatory legislation, and the circulation of the referendum petitions ceased. "Opponents of the portage road bill may yet regret the day when they and their superserviceable tools inaugurated the referendum movement against it. It is a poor rule that does not work both ways, and the initiative is sometimes an even more powerful weapon than the referendum."[5] The casualty insurance companies, suspected of part of the responsibility of referring the workmen's

[1] Cottage Grove *Sentinel*, reprinted in Eugene *Guard*, Apr. 11, 1913, p. 4, col. 2.
[2] Eugene *Register*, Nov. 8, 1913, p. 4, col. 2.
[3] *Oregonian*, March 15, 1909, p. 6, col. 2.
[4] Eugene *Guard*, March 31, 1913, p. 4, col. 1.
[5] *Oregon Journal*, May 15, 1903, p. 4, col. 1.

compensation act, were threatened with annihilation, and there are other such cases. "The initiative and referendum was not intended as an instrument to further the private interests of any person or set of persons, and he who tries so to use it, is juggling with a two-edged sword."[1]

It is safer for special and local interests to adopt the opposite policy and come to each other's aid in obtaining their respective ends by the method of log-rolling long practiced in legislative assemblies. So recently we find the supporters of a state institution in one locality becoming zealous advocates of the interests of a state institution in another locality. A state institution goes to great lengths to secure the favorable vote of the labor interests, and the labor interests demand and receive substantial return. A resident in a locality where a state institution is established is urged to withdraw her candidacy for the presidency of a woman's club for fear she may arouse the jealousy of rival candidates and their supporters from other localities and thus endanger legislation pending for that institution. And other such things take place. "Yet we have been told that the Oregon System would put an end to the ancient and dishonorable practice of legislative log-rolling."[2]

But the ultimate failure of most of these movements which have been actuated by selfish special or local interests discourage such abuses of the system of popular government.[3]

[1] C. D. Babcock, quoted in *Oregon Journal*, May 12, 1913, p. 1, col. 7.

[2] *Oregonian*, Nov. 19, 1913, p. 10, col. 4. "It would seem that [in direct legislation] the method frequently adopted by members of the legislature of securing votes for the passage of a bill by promise of reciprocal support of other measures could not be pursued." *State* v. *Richardson, Oregon Reports*, vol. 48, pp. 309, 319 (1906).

[3] *Below*, pp. 113–5.

CHAPTER IV

THE PREPARATION OF MEASURES

THE methods of preparing initiative measures of course vary with the authorship of the measures. But it seems that usually the principles of the measure are determined only after consideration by a number, and often a large number of men, and that the measure is put into final form by practical lawyers, or under their advice. The study and care given to the preparation of measures are different in different cases. Some of them have been prepared within a very limited period. Others are the result of the work of many months.

The procedure of the People's Power League in this regard is thus described by one of its members. "The method of the League is simple, straightforward and open. Some member makes a suggestion which may be considered worth attention by some others. On the lists of members are hundreds who may be asked to give their ideas upon this suggestion. If pretty generally favorable the legal form is gotten up and publicity given. Finally a committee confers, perhaps several times. The proposed measure may be dropped entirely. It may be shelved for a few years. If the sentiment back of it is strong enough to secure the requisite means it is printed and put out for initiative signatures. Any suggestions made by friends or enemies are carefully considered. Advice is asked of constitutional lawyers, journalists, teachers, thinkers, leaders in and out of the League. This was the case with the direct primary law that has done so much to bring about a revolution in political procedure throughout the nation. It was the result of the ablest thought in the United States compiled and presented by the People's Power League and its secretary. So with the recall, proportional representation, corrupt practices act, application of direct primary to election of delegates to national conventions, and other measures." [1]

The history of the "blue-sky" bill is thus described by the man chiefly responsible for its preparation. "I believe it was V. Vincent Jones who suggested that a meeting of the representatives of the commercial bodies of Portland and state officers be held for the purpose of taking some definite steps to better conditions and safeguard the small investor. This meeting was called and held at the office of the Chamber of Commerce in Portland, and was attended by representatives of the Chamber of Commerce, Commercial Club and Realty Board of Portland, and by Governor West, Secretary Olcott and the writer. The matter was discussed at some length and a plan agreed upon for safeguarding the people as far as possible until adequate legislation could be secured. It was the sense of the meeting that a bill similar to the Kansas blue sky law should be prepared and submitted to the voters at the November election, and at the request of the Portland commercial bodies the secretary of state agreed to undertake the task of framing the bill. The writer considers it an honor to have been connected, in a humble way, in the preparation of this bill, the first draft of which was completed in May, 1912, and immediately submitted to the board of trustees of the Portland Chamber of Commerce, through its secretary, Mr. E. C. Giltner. The fact that the bill was being prepared had been reported in the daily press and many of the most prominent lawyers and business men in Portland took occasion to call at the office of Mr. R. W. Montague, a member of the board of trustees of the Chamber of Commerce, and a well-known Portland lawyer, who labored zealously to perfect the measure, or at the office of Mr. Giltner, to examine the bill and suggest possible improvements. The bill formed the principal topic of discussion at a meeting of the Realty Board, where it

[1] A. D. Cridge, *Oregon Journal*, June 20, 1912, p. 8, col. 4.

was extensively reviewed by ex-Senator Fulton, who approved the measure in the main, but suggested certain changes, most of which were made before the bill was finally completed. The bill also was considered at a meeting of the Rotary Club and I believe was discussed by other organizations in Portland. Before the last revision had been made the entire bill was rewritten four or five times and some parts of it eight or ten times, and not less than six or seven meetings of the representatives of the commercial bodies and of the state department had been held." [1]

But it is certain that such careful methods are not always used. Of course *referendum* measures involve little difficulty in preparation.

The initiative has been criticized as a method of law-making because the measures, proposed not by "the people" or their representatives, but by individuals or groups acting upon their own responsibility, are, necessarily, not subject to any amendment after submission, however desirable amendment may be, but must be simply accepted or rejected as they are by the people. "There is and always will be one very serious difficulty in the enactment of laws by the initiative — that the measure cannot be amended after it has once been framed and submitted. It is indeed a wise man or body of men who can draft a bill without serious defects. Discussion almost invariably discloses an error which the authors of the bill did not see. But once a proposed law has been published and put in circulation for initiative signatures, it is too late to amend, and the measure must stand or fall, the good with the bad." [2]

But, fortunately, in comparison with practices often prevailing in legislative assemblies, this vice sometimes becomes a real virtue. "Instead of being a cause for criticism, this is one of the strongest reasons for commendation, for we have learned that one of the most common methods by which vicious legis-

---

[1] C. D. Babcock, *Oregon Journal*, Oct. 27, 1912, p. 8, col. 1.

[2] *Oregonian*, Jan. 19, 1906, p. 8, col. 4. See also *ibid.*, May 7, 1910, p. 10, col. 2; June 12, 1910, sec. 3, p. 6, col. 2.

lation is secured is to introduce a harmless or a beneficial bill and let it secure a favorable report from a legislative committee, but with a slight amendment inserted therein which entirely changes its character or effect in some important particular and thereby serves some selfish interest. When it is known that a bill must be enacted or rejected exactly as drawn, the framers of the measure will spend weeks and months studying the subject and writing the bill in order to have it free from unsatisfactory features." [1]

In practice something like amendment of proposed legislation at the instance of the people is at times attained. This is true especially in the case of measures submitted by the People's Power League. It has been the policy of the League to distribute copies of tentative drafts of measures widely over the state in order to sound public opinion upon them, and it has, in accordance with criticism received, essentially modified or even dropped measures proposed. The State Grange has pursued a similar course with some measures. Of the road bill prepared by the "harmony committee" in 1912 it was said: "The six measures will be published in the Portland papers Sunday. Copies will be sent to all papers in the state. In this manner it is expected that the voters will study them carefully, and if any organized or widespread objection is raised to any feature of the several bills, effort will be made to eliminate the objectionable part or rectify it so they will stand a better chance of being passed." [2] But in the vast majority of cases the general public hears nothing of the measures until the circulation of petitions begins.

Because of the use of misleading ballot titles by some parties filing petitions,[3] a law of 1907 requires that the ballot titles shall be prepared by the attorney-general, but appeal from his action may be taken to the circuit court.[4]

[1] J. Bourne, *Initiative, Referendum and Recall, Atlantic Monthly*, vol. 109, pp. 122, 128 (1909). [2] *Oregonian*, Mar. 22, 1912, p. 14, col. 2.

[3] *Ibid.*, Jan. 21, 1907, p. 9, col. 1; W. S. U'Ren, *ibid.*, June 2, 1907, p. 38, col. 1; G. A. Thacher, *Interesting Election in Oregon, Independent*, vol. 69, pp. 1434, 1437–8 (1910). [4] *Laws*, 1907, ch. 226, sec. 5; *Laws*, 1913, ch. 36; *below* pp. 52–3.

"The possibilities of the adoption of crude and conflicting laws . . . might be guarded against . . . by some provision for a revision and editing of the propositions filed for submission to the people."[1] Accordingly proposals for the establishment of some kind of a commission for this purpose have been made in Oregon.[2] But such an *authoritative* commission could practically nullify the power of the people to initiate laws,[3] and the provision at best would but further complicate an already overcomplicated government.

This is a very different proposition from that of establishing some *advisory* office or commission for the aid of individuals or associations in the drafting of bills. The state library, already furnishing efficient aid by way of information to individuals and associations in connection with direct legislation, might well be further developed to meet this need.

In view of both advantages and disadvantages which are inherent in the formulation of measures by the legislative assembly on the one hand and by individuals or groups on the other, it has been proposed to adopt the plan, already in use elsewhere, of requiring all initiative measures to be submitted to the assembly, which shall either enact the measure into law, or amend it and let the people choose between the original and the amended measure.[4]

[1] F. Foxcroft, *Initiative-Referendum in the United States, Contemporary Review*, vol. 99, pp. 11, 17 (1911).

[2] *House Bills*, 1911, nos. 38, 112, 236; *Oregonian*, Dec. 4, 1914, p. 8, col. 2.

[3] See especially reports in *Oregonian*, Jan. 16, 1911, p. 4, col. 1; Jan. 25, 1911, p. 6, col. 1; *Oregon Journal*, Jan. 25, 1911, p. 1, col. 1.   [4] *Below*, pp. 164–5.

CHAPTER V

THE SUBSTANCE AND FORM OF MEASURES

I

The Measures Submitted [1]

1. By far the largest class of measures submitted to the people have related to the machinery of government.

(1) Initiative constitutional amendments granting the suffrage to women appeared at four succeeding elections, and later an amendment limiting the suffrage to citizens of the United States was submitted by the legislature.

(2) A large number of initiative measures intended to increase "the people's power" have been submitted. These include the direct primary bill, the bill instructing members of the legislative assembly to vote for the people's choice for United States senator, and the presidential primary bill; the constitutional amendments for changing the method applying to constitutional amendments submitted by the legislative assembly and requiring calls for constitutional conventions to be submitted to the people, "home rule" city charters, the recall of officers, and the extension of the initiative and referendum to the localities, authorizing legislation for proportional representation and preferential voting, establishing proportional representation in the house of representatives, abolishing the state senate, two amendments for the entire reorganization of the legislative department of the state,[2] and another for the reorganization of the judicial department, the bill creating "people's inspectors of government" and an "official gazette," and the

[1] See *below*, pp. 241–53.   [2] *Below*, pp. 254–66.

corrupt practices bill. The initiative amendment for "majority rule" in the adoption of initiative measures, the initiative amendment, mentioned below, requiring a two-thirds vote for the amendment of a certain article of the constitution, and the initiative pre-primary convention bill, were considered attacks upon "the people's power." And this was true also of three measures submitted by the legislative assembly — a constitutional amendment providing for "majority" rule in the adoption of constitutional amendments, another providing for separate districts for senators and representatives (directed against proportional representation), and the act calling for a constitutional convention.

Two other initiative bills aimed to extend the system of "home rule" — one providing methods for creating new towns, counties, and municipal districts, and changing county boundaries, and a later bill providing for the consolidation of cities and the organization of new counties. The non-partisan judiciary bill was another reform measure.

(3) A third class of measures relates to the creation or regulation of public offices or institutions or functions, in most cases involving the expenditure of public money.

The legislative assembly submitted constitutional amendments providing for the increase of the compensation of the members of the assembly — twice, for the reorganization of the judicial system and addition to the number of justices of the supreme court, for the creation of the office of lieutenant governor — twice, and for authorizing the organization of railroad districts and the operation of railroads by the state and localities, an act for the establishment of an insane asylum, two millage-tax acts for the support of normal schools, and some constitutional amendments not involving expenditure of money — for the manner of location of state institutions, and for the change of date of general elections. The two amendments submitted by the assembly permitting the consolidation of cities with counties, and permitting the consolidation of adjoining cities favored

The Substance and Form of Measures   33

the reduction of the number of offices. A constitutional amendment, proposed by the legislative assembly, increased the maximum limit of state indebtedness for irrigation and water-power operation and the development of untilled lands.

An initiative amendment provided for a department of industry and public works, mentioned below. Initiative bills have proposed the creation and maintenance of other new offices — a commission on employers' liability, mentioned below, a state highway department, a state hotel inspector, "people's inspectors" and "official gazette," mentioned above, a corporation department, mentioned below, a state road board, with provision for road bonds, and a tax-code commission. The eight initiative county-division bills (two other initiative county bills involved only changes of boundaries) of course involved the multiplication of offices, and this was also involved in the general measures, mentioned above, providing for the creation of new counties and districts. But one of the latter contained a provision for the consolidation of cities, and thus favored the reduction of the number of offices. The two companion initiative measures — the public docks and water-front amendment, and the municipal wharves and docks bill, — while permitting the lease of the beds of navigable waters for private docks, vested the ownership of the submerged land in the state, and authorized the ownership and operation of wharves and docks by the municipalities. The proposal for the state's purchase of a toll road was contained in an initiative bill. Another initiative bill provided for a millage tax for the university and the agricultural college and for the consolidation of the government of the two institutions. Two others authorized the issue of county road bonds. One constitutional amendment submitted by initiative petition increased the maximum limit of county indebtedness for roads, and another granted "home rule" to counties in the matter of indebtedness for roads.

The regulation of the office (especially the compensation) of the state printer was the purpose of the initiation of one constitutional amendment and two bills. One initiative bill provided for the reduction of the number of state offices by the consolidation of the desert land board and the state land board. The elimination of offices involved in another initiative bill for the consolidation of the corporation and insurance departments was offset by its creation of the office of state fire marshal. Two constitutional amendments submitted by initiative petition limited state and county indebtedness for roads. The initiative bill providing for the increase of the term of certain county offices should also be included with economy legislation.

Referendum petitions placed on the ballot the act for additional districts attorneys and, mentioned below, the workmen's compensation act (creating an industrial commission and industrial fund), one general appropriation act, an armory appropriation, five university appropriations, and an act requiring of a county the appropriation for an increase of the salary of the circuit judge.

(4) Methods of taxation have been the subject of many measures. The legislative assembly has submitted seven "tax-reform" constitutional amendments (substantially the same measures were resubmitted in some cases) — repealing the constitutional requirement of equal and uniform taxation, amending this requirement, authorizing the levy of state and local taxes on separate classes of property, and another amendment excepting laws regulating taxation or exemption from "emergency" legislation and repealing the provisions of the initiative "constitutional home-rule" amendment, mentioned below. Other measures dealing with the administration of taxation have been submitted by initiative petition. These include two corporation-tax bills, two modified "single-tax" constitutional amendments, a constitutional amendment providing for the abolition of the poll tax, requiring all laws regulating taxation or exemption from taxation throughout the state to be referred to the people, exempting from constitutional restrictions all measures approved by the people declaring what shall be sub-

ject to taxation or exemption and how it shall be taxed or exempted, and authorizing each county to regulate taxation and exemption subject to the general laws of the state (the "county home-rule" amendment), a constitutional amendment permitting the taxation of incomes, another providing for a graduated "extra tax" on land, another ("anti-single-tax") retaining the "equal and uniform" taxation requirement of the constitution, permitting certain exemptions from taxation, and forbidding the amendment or repeal of this amendment except by a two-thirds vote of all electors voting on the issue; and bills providing, respectively, for the exemption of household goods from taxation, for the exemption of money and credits from taxation, for the exemption from taxation of goods and improvements on land held by any one person to the extent of fifteen hundred dollars valuation, for revising the inheritance tax laws, and mentioned above, for a tax-code commission.

2. Protective functions of the state have been the concern of a number of measures.

(1) Six measures related to the administration of the criminal law. Of these, two were initiative bills — one prohibiting the employment of state and local prisoners by private persons and authorizing their employment by the state and counties, and the other abolishing capital punishment and regulating the pardoning power. Two were constitutional amendments initiated by petition — one providing for indictment by grand jury, and the other abolishing capital punishment. The others were acts referred by petition — one providing for the custody of persons in county jails by the sheriff, authorizing the county court to direct the work of the prisoners, and regulating the salaries of guards and the prices of prisoners' meals in one county, and the other providing for the sterilization of habitual criminals and other degenerates.

(2) Seven initiative measures were concerned with the liquor traffic — three bills and one constitutional amendment dealing with "local option" (one of them also providing for local regula-

tion of pool rooms, etc.), and two amendments and one bill providing for state-wide prohibition of the liquor traffic.

(3) One initiative bill regulated the licensing of dentists (by lowering the standards).

(4) Provisions affecting corporations and other "interests" were contained in five initiative bills. The two corporation-tax bills above mentioned are included here. One bill prohibited the issue of free passes and discrimination by railroads and other public-service corporations, another, the "blue-sky" bill, which provided for the corporation department mentioned above, regulated corporations dealing with corporate securities, and another regulated freight rates. The legislative assembly submitted a constitutional amendment providing for double liability of bank stockholders. Two acts of the assembly regulating corporations were referred by petition — one requiring railroads and other common carriers to grant free passes to certain public officials, and the other providing for the control of public-service corporations. Three initiative bills affected the fishing interests connected with the Columbia and Rogue rivers.

3. Some aspects of social legislation were covered by a third class of measures. Most of these had to do with the interests of labor. Three initiative bills and two initiative amendments favored the labor interests — the employers' liability bill, bills for an eight-hour day on public works, for an eight-hour day and ventilation of working rooms for female workers, and amendments, one for a universal eight-hour day, and the other for a department of industry and public works (mentioned above) for the benefit of the unemployed. Three initiative bills were hostile to the labor interests: the bill providing for a commission for the investigation of the subject of employers' liability (mentioned above) — a substitute for the employers' liability bill; another prohibiting boycotting or picketing workshops, etc., and another prohibiting in the larger towns the use of streets, etc., for public meetings or discussions without the consent of the mayor. The workmen's compensation act, mentioned above,

was referred by petition. Social legislation was also of course the aim of some of the taxation measures mentioned above.

4. Ten measures dealing strictly with local interests were the eight county-division measures and the two county-boundary measures, initiated by petition.

Under present conditions the measures initiated by petition and those referred by petition are no index whatever to public opinion in this direction, but that, so far as indicated, is indicated rather by the vote at the election.[1]

2

Suitable and Unsuitable Subjects

There has been much discussion in Oregon as to the subjects proper for direct legislation. In the first place attempt at distinction has been made between propositions which are "elemental," "along fundamental lines," or "political" in character on the one hand, and propositions which are "non-elemental," "not along fundamental lines," "administrative," or "technical" in character on the other. "It is evident that in cases where the question is one of general policy or principle, on which he [the voter] can express himself by a yes or no vote, the best judgment and will of the majority of the people may be secured. In cases, however, where the measure consists of many intricate and involved provisions, the fact that there can be no opportunity of amendment, or any guarantee that the measure will be read, or fully comprehended in all its bearings points to a danger in this mode of securing legislation."[2] "The mass of men will not study a law which is of abstract interest, or of great length and legal technicality, . . . and therefore it seems to me the people will not vote intelligently on any but clear-cut, briefly stated questions, such as approach the character of fundamental

[1] *Below*, pp. 105–25.
[2] C. H. Carey, *New Responsibilities of Citizenship, Proceedings of the Oregon Bar Association*, 1908–10, pp. 18, 39 (1909).

constitutional provisions."[1] And it has been suggested that, in view of the difficulty in the way of the proper preparation of measures of the latter class as well as the difficulty in the way of their proper consideration by the voters, such measures should either not be allowed to be submitted under the initiative at all, or only after demand and refusal by the legislature;[2] that the initiative should be used to secure a vote only on the *general policy* advocated and not on a *formal bill* submitted.[3]

An extreme illustration of technical legislation is the initiative freight-rate law of 1912, covering a subject for the consideration of which not even legislatures are adapted, much less the people. "When the Medford Traffic Bureau proposes to resort to the initiative to fix railroad rates it is suggesting the use of an implement for a purpose for which it is unwieldy, wholly unadapted, and certain to prove unsatisfactory. The initiative is properly the means of correcting abuses or providing betterments that are understood and recognized by the ordinary voter and denied them by the legislature. . . . Railroad rate-making calls for the exercise of an abstruse and complicated science. The exercise of the initiative should call only for ordi-

[1] C. E. S. Wood, quoted by L. Pease, *Initiative and Referendum — "Oregon's Big Stick,"* Pacific Monthly, vol. 17, pp. 563, 575 (1907).

[2] *E.g. Oregonian,* Jan. 19, 1906, p. 8, col. 4; Oct. 3, 1912, p. 10, col. 1; Eugene *Register,* May 26, 1912, p. 1, col. 1. *Below,* pp. 164–5. "The powers defined herein as the 'initiative' and 'referendum' shall never be used to pass a law authorizing any classification of property for the purpose of levying different rates of taxation thereon or of authorizing the levy of any single tax on land or land values or land sites at a higher rate or by a different rule than is or may be applied to improvements thereon or to personal property." Ohio *Constitution,* art. 2, sec. 1 (1912).

[3] "Let the vote of the people be a command to make a law, not the law itself. For instance, instead of submitting to the vote of the people a number of voluminous and conflicting laws on the subject of good roads, let the subject be submitted in this way:

"No. 1. Shall the state aid in the construction of highways?

"No. 2. Shall the counties be authorized to issue bonds for the construction of highways?

"If both these propositions were adopted by the people, then the next legislature must carry them into effect by proper legislation and the details would be worked

nary or general, not unusual or specialized, intelligence. The adoption of a table of maximum distance class rates would not be accomplished without appeals to prejudice against corporations, without the influence of rivalry between communities or without the expression of opinions by the mass of arbiters on an issue of which they had no thorough understanding. It was so when in other days the legislature attempted ratemaking and because it was so quasi-judicial and semi-legislative powers were delegated to a railroad commission after insistent demands by the people. . . . If Medford and other interior cities have a railroad rate grievance there is a properly constituted and thoroughly equipped body to which it may be presented and that body is the railroad commission, not the public. If the railroad commission is prejudiced, neglectful or incompetent the thing to do is to change the commission. To ask the people to decide distributive rate controversies is preposterous."[1] Soon after its approval at the election the law was declared unconstitutional by a federal court.[2] "The outcome should be a lesson. There is no use to try to make a railroad commission out of the electorate. The people cannot qualify as a mass to pass upon a system of railroad rates; and it is both foolish and inexcusable to bother them with such measures."[3]

out after open discussion and consideration. Such legislation would be subject to the referendum and to subsequent amendment in the usual way. The great trouble with the present law is that it requires the voter to consider a thousand details which he knows nothing about and which he does not consider, as a matter of fact, and could not alter if he did. It would be quite as reasonable for a community to turn out en masse and try to build a town hall. The majority might be in favor of the building of a town hall, but very few would know how to build it. What the community should do is first to determine that they want a town hall and then employ mechanics to do the work. Let the people order the kind of laws they want and require the legislature to fill the order. Our present system produces confusion, promotes litigation and unsettles business." A. S. Hammond, *Oregonian*, Jan. 13, 1913, p. 6, col. 6. But past experiences with constitutional requirements for legislation along lines specified in general terms is conclusive evidence that such a plan is not at all sufficient. However, see *below*, pp. 157–8.

[1] *Oregonian*, Sept. 2, 1911, p. 8, col. 1.
[2] *Southern Pacific Co.* v. *Railroad Commission of Oregon, Federal Reporter*, vol. 208, p. 926 (1913). [3] *Oregon Journal*, Sept. 30, 1913, p. 8, col. 1.

It is generally admitted that matters of local interest are not suitable subjects for submission to the voters of the state. This has been discussed particularly in connection with the numerous measures for county divisions. "The *Register* knows nothing of the merits of this particular plan for division, nor does it especially care to. It is a local matter purely and simply, and is of interest only to the territory concerned, within and without the new boundaries. The rest of the people of the state do not care whether a new county is formed or not, and should not be asked to make a decision." [1]

In case of the referendum, if the previous action of the legislative assembly is to be considered worthy of any respect at all, the difficulties in dealing with unsuitable subjects are not so great, but it has been suggested that the referendum might be restricted "to particular classes of acts, to be carefully defined," [2] and especially it has been urged that appropriation bills are not proper subjects for review by the people.

Doubtless measures, and especially initiative measures, that are not "elemental" in character should not be submitted to the people except in case of great urgency, but all schemes for a classification of measures by law in this connection are utterly impracticable, and the "protest" of the voters must remain the only check against the submission of improper subjects for direct legislation.

There are no authoritative tests for the determination of the distinctions between suitable and unsuitable subjects for direct legislation above discussed, and of course in the application of the theoretical distinctions to a classification of the measures actually submitted to the voters there must be a difference of opinion. However, it would seem that probably something less than half of the measures submitted would generally be considered clearly "elemental" in character,[3] including especially such

---

[1] Eugene *Register*, Oct. 12, 1912, p. 4, col. 1. See also *Oregonian*, Aug. 1, 1910, p. 6, col. 2.   [2] *Oregonian*, July 21, 1909, p. 8, col. 2.

[3] Much lower estimates have been made by some observers.

measures as the various prohibition measures, the suffrage amendments, the anti-pass bill, the majority-vote amendments, the flat-salary bill, the non-partisan judiciary bill, etc.[1] A number of other measures, including the direct primary bill, the corrupt-practices bill, the employer's liability bill, the workmen's compensation act, etc., contain an "elemental" principle readily understood, but at the same time contain a mass of "administrative" or even "technical" details. The direct primary bill, of forty-six sections, covered forty-eight pages of the voters' pamphlet; the corrupt-practices bill, of fifty-three sections, covered nineteen pages; the workmen's compensation act, of thirty-four sections, covered over thirteen pages. Moreover some of these measures were in part highly technical. The numerous measures dealing with the subject of taxation form another class, in which fundamental policy is involved in at least some cases, and especially in case of the approaches to the "single-tax," although in most cases the measures should probably be classified, in whole or in part, as administrative. One was highly technical. Another group of measures, including the county-prisoners' bill, the several fishery bills, the judiciary amendments (to a considerable extent), the freight-rate bill, the "blue-sky" bill, etc., are more clearly "administrative," and in some cases very technical. Of the numerous appropriations bills some should be considered as purely administrative, but others were submitted chiefly or partly in order to determine questions of general policy. Most of the measures of a local character have been new-county bills.

Over two fifths of all of the measures submitted have called for constitutional amendment. So far there has been little inclination to offer ordinary legislation in the form of constitutional provisions.[2]

[1] But some measures, of which the home-rule charter amendment is a good example, on the face very elementary in character, have been found later to involve far-reaching complications. *Cf.* F. V. Holman, *Some Instances of Unsatisfactory Results under Initiative Amendments of the Oregon Constitution* (1910).

[2] *Below*, pp. 180–1.

3
Deception in Measures

There has been much complaint about the presence of "jokers" in initiative measures, but often the alleged "joker" has been simply some part of a measure obnoxious to the hostile critic. However, measures have not always been what they seemed. The instance usually cited in illustration is that of a taxation amendment of 1910.[1] This amendment begins, "No poll or head tax shall be levied or collected in Oregon," and then provides that "no bill regulating taxation or exemption throughout the state shall become a law until approved by the people of the state," that "none of the restrictions of the constitution shall apply to measures approved by the people declaring what shall be subject to taxation or exemption or how it shall be taxed or exempted"; and that "the people of the several counties are hereby empowered and authorized to regulate taxation and exemptions within their several counties, subject to any general laws which may be hereafter enacted." The purpose of the three last provisions was to "pave the way" for the single-tax, allowing the individual counties to adopt such tax and preventing the legislature from changing the "home-rule" system. The poll-tax provision was clearly "bait" to catch votes for the other provisions of the measure. But the much-repeated assertion that this provision was wholly deceptive on account of the fact that the poll tax had been abolished several years before is untrue. The state one-dollar poll tax had been abolished, but the three-dollar county road poll tax was still in force, although practically obsolete in some parts of the state.

In other cases voters have unintentionally aided in enacting legislative provisions which they have not favored, but this has been due not so much to the presence of "jokers" in the measures as to the form in which amendments have been drawn,

---

[1] *Constitution*, art. 9, sec. 1a (1910); amended in 1912.

The Substance and Form of Measures 43

to deceptive or inadequate ballot titles, or, probably by far the most often, to the inadvertence of the voters.[1]

It has been broadly asserted that authors of measures "put an attractve label on a bill which contains little that is good and a great deal which is radical and bad; and the people, deceived by the label, swallow the bill as a mass on the faith of the label."[2] But, although "catchy" titles may have been used, attempts at actual deception have probably been very few. Much complaint was made against the liquor interests' "amendment to the local option law giving anti-prohibitionists and prohibitionists equal privileges," which, it was considered, would practically abolish local option; the bill initiated by the owners of a toll road "to abolish tolls on the Mount Hood and Barlow road, and providing for its ownership by the state," in fact providing for the purchase of the road by the state, and the "taxpayers' suffrage amendment," which in fact gave the suffrage to women whether taxpayers or not. It was to eliminate misleading titles that the power to formulate the ballot titles of measures was taken from the authors and given to the attorney-general.[3]

The constitutional requirement that "every act shall embrace but one subject and matters properly considered therewith, which subject shall be expressed in the title,"[4] was intended, in part, to obviate the legislative practice of "inserting in an act clauses involving matter which the title is not calculated or adequate to give or convey any intimation." It was intended that the legislature should thus be fairly apprised of the purpose of a measure by an inspection of the title and not be "surprised or misled by the subject which the title purported to express."[5]

---

[1] *Below*, pp. 51–3, 107–13.

[2] W. Minor, *Closing Address, Proceedings of the Oregon Bar Association*, 1908–10, pp. 166, 175. [3] *Above*, p. 29; *below*, pp. 52–3. [4] *Constitution*, art. 4, sec. 20 (1859).

[5] *Clemmensen* v. *Petersen, Oregon Reports*, vol. 35, pp. 47, 48 (1899). See also *State* v. *Shaw, ibid.*, vol. 22, pp. 287, 288 (1892); *Bailey* v. *Benton Co., ibid.*, vol. 61, pp. 390, 394 (1912). "When two or more amendments shall be submitted . . . to the voters of the state, at the same election, they shall be so submitted that each amend-

This requirement does not apply to direct legislation.[1] But, although often its purpose is not achieved in the action of the legislative assembly, the extension of the provision to direct legislation would at least aid in preventing the use of misleading titles in direct legislation.

4

The Combination of Subjects in Measures

The constitutional provision just noticed [2] was intended, further, to discourage log-rolling in the legislative assembly — to prevent the practice of "combining subjects representing diverse interests, in order to unite the members of the legislature who favored either, in support of all." [3] "Thus, it was designed by the framers of the constitution that in every case the proposed measure should stand upon its own merits." [4]

The restriction has been rather ineffective in properly controlling the legislative assembly but even an *ideal* legal standard is wholly wanting for direct legislation.[5] At any rate it has hap-

ment shall be voted on separately." *Constitution*, art. 17, sec. 2 (1906). *Cf. Constitution*, art. 17, sec. 2 (1859).

[1] *Palmer* v. *Benson, Oregon Reports*, vol. 50, pp. 277, 279 (1907); *State* v. *Langworthy, ibid.*, vol. 55, pp. 303, 309 (1910). *Contra*, *State* v. *Richardson, ibid.*, vol. 48, pp. 309, 318 (1906). [2] *Above*, p. 43.

[3] *State* v. *Shaw, Oregon Reports*, vol. 22, pp. 287, 288 (1892).

[4] *Clemmensen* v. *Petersen, ibid.*, vol. 35, pp. 47, 48 (1899). See also *Simpson* v. *Bailey, ibid.*, vol. 3, pp. 515, 517 (1869); *State* v. *Richardson, ibid.*, vol. 48, pp. 309, 318 (1906); *Palmer* v. *Benson, ibid.*, vol. 50, pp. 277, 279 (1907); *Bailey* v. *Benton Co., ibid.*, vol. 61, pp. 390, 394 (1912).

[5] *Palmer* v. *Benson, Oregon Reports*, vol. 50, pp. 277, 279 (1907); *State* v. *Langworthy, ibid.*, vol. 55, pp. 303, 309 (1910). *Contra*, *State* v. *Richardson, ibid.*, vol. 48, pp. 309, 318 (1906). *Cf.* W. P. Malburn, *Can Two Propositions be Submitted to One Vote? American Law Review*, vol. 47, pp. 392–431 (1913).

"When a law comprised very various provisions relating to matters essentially different, it was called *lex satura*, and the *Lex Cæcilia Didia* [B.C. 98] forbade the proposing of a *lex satura*, on the ground that the people might be compelled either to vote for something which they did not approve, or to reject something which they did approve, if it was proposed in this manner." Yonge, note to *Cicero's Orations*, Yonge's trans., vol. 3, p. 21. *Cf.* Finley and Sanderson, *American Executive*, pp. 64–5 (1908).

The Substance and Form of Measures 45

pened that sometimes measures of direct legislation do *not* stand on their own merits, that several and even very many propositions may be combined into one measure in order to secure as many supporters as possible.

But this abuse has actually occurred in only a few cases. The combination of the poll tax, county "home-rule" taxation, and other propositions has already been described.[1] The amendment by which this was repealed was just as comprehensive. The bill of 1910 providing methods for the organization of new towns, counties, and municipal districts and for changing the boundaries of existing counties, and the bill of 1912 providing methods for the consolidation of contiguous incorporated towns, legalizing consolidations before attempted, and providing a method for the organization of new counties, may be criticized as "initiative log-rolling." The latter was drawn by representatives of towns desiring consolidation and of a district desiring the organization of a new county. But most complaint has been directed against the initiative "near-constitutions" of 1910 and 1912, which aimed to reorganize radically the whole legislative system. Even the lengthy ballot titles of these measures are not fully adequate to indicate "the wilderness of provisions" included.[2] One of these has been estimated to contain "thirty-two distinct subjects."[3] But it is somewhat consoling to re-

[1] *Above*, p. 42. [2] *Below*, pp. 254–66.
[3] C. H. Carey, *Oregon Journal*, Nov. 20, 1913, p. 16, col. 2.

The real scope of an initiative bill of 1912 providing for the abolition of capital punishment was much greater than would appear from an inspection of the measure; for the governor had reprieved until after election all convicts sentenced to be hanged and made their execution depend on the fate of the bill. Thus at the same time the voters acted on a general provision of law, they were made to feel a responsibility for the execution of certain convicts. "In this way the people of the state will act as a jury. There will be plenty of time for discussion of the proposition before next November, and all who vote for it will go into the polling booths with their eyes opened to the fact that they are either voting to aid in hanging these men or to save their necks." Governor West, quoted in *Oregonian*, Jan. 4, 1912, p. 7, col. 1. "These miserable wretches will be used as a bogey to frighten the people into voting down capital punishment." Eugene *Register*, Jan. 1, 1912, p. 12, col. 2. Similar circumstances involved the amendment for the abolition of capital punishment submitted in 1914.

member that the people of other states are occasionally called upon to consider the merits of the revision of an entire constitution.

Particularly on account of this "initiative log-rolling" it has been proposed to require the subject-matter of initiative measures to be "single in character," limited to "a single proposition in concrete form."[1] Although the practicability of such suggestions has been doubted,[2] it would seem that some such restriction would at least be as effective as in case of ordinary legislation, and that the provisions now applying to only one kind of legislation might well be extended to include both.[3]

In this connection it may be observed that sometimes, instead of a combination of subjects that are not properly related into one initiative measure, there has been a separation of subjects that are properly related into two measures, with the hope of securing the enactment of one even if the other should be defeated. The two gross-earnings tax bills of 1906 and the two convict bills of 1912 are illustrations of such separation.[4]

The people are protected to some extent against combinations of unrelated provisions by the legislative assembly, which might make the invoking of the referendum impossible or unwise, by the constitutional amendment which permits the attack of one or more items of a measure without involving the others,[5] after the manner provided in some states for the governor's veto of separate items. This amendment was enacted after the referendum of the general appropriation act of 1905, which was invoked chiefly on account of the presence of items for normal schools, but necessarily involved the other state institutions provided for in the same act.[6]

---

[1] C. H. Carey, *Proceedings of the Oregon Bar Association*, 1908–10, pp. 18, 41 (1908); *Oregon Journal*, Nov. 29, 1908, p. 2, col. 1; *ibid.*, Nov. 20, 1913, p. 16, col. 2.

[2] *Cf. Oregon Journal*, Nov. 22, 1908, sec. 5, p. 6, col. 2.

[3] *Cf. Oregonian*, July 26, 1913, p. 6, col. 1.

[4] Where two or more provisions are related and offered as separate measures, the failure of one may largely or wholly nullify the effect of another which has passed.

[5] *Constitution*, art. 4, sec. 1a (1906).   [6] *Cf. Oregonian*, Sept. 10, 1905, p. 24, col. 1.

5
Conflicting Measures

If two or more conflicting laws or conflicting constitutional amendments are approved at the same election, the measure receiving the greatest number of votes is "paramount in all particulars as to which there is a conflict."[1]

Since there is no method of insuring coördination of the various separate movements for direct legislation — except those inaugurated by the legislative assembly — at a given election there is of course a possibility of great confusion as a result of the appearance of two or more conflicting measures at the same time.

In 1906 several sets of rival measures appeared, but rivalry was eliminated before the measures were filed. In 1908 two opposing bills for the control of fishing in the Columbia river were initiated. In 1910 one measure providing for single-

---

[1] *Laws*, 1907, ch. 226, sec. 7; *Lord's Oregon Laws*, sec. 3477. "In other words, where two bills on the same subject are adopted it is necessary to combine them into one act, retaining the parts of both that do not conflict and eliminating the conflicting provisions from the one receiving the lesser affirmative vote." *Oregonian* Nov. 26, 1912, p. 10, col. 1. Note a discussion on the question held in the absence of statutory provision. *Ibid.*, Jan. 24, 1906, p. 8, col. 1; Jan. 29, 1906, p. 1, col. 1; Jan. 31, 1906, p. 6, col. 1; Feb. 3, 1906, p. 14, col. 1; Feb. 5, 1906, p. 6, col. 2. No provision is made regarding a conflict between a constitutional amendment and a statute approved at the same election, but probably, upon principle, the constitutional amendment would prevail. *Cf. Oregonian*, Nov. 26, 1912, p. 12, col. 1; *Oregon Journal*, June 8, 1913, p. 2, col. 3. But see *Oregonian*, Nov. 30, 1912, p. 8, col. 2; Sept. 9, 1913, p. 6, col. 1; opinion of attorney-general, *ibid.*, Dec. 10, 1912, p. 7, col. 4. A constitutional amendment submitted in 1912 "amends and repeals all constitutional amendments or acts in conflict herewith, including any acts or provisions relating thereto submitted to the people concurrently with this amendment." *Referendum Pamphlet*, 1912, no. 360, p. 206.

Statutes and constitutional amendments are put on exactly the same footing by amendments proposed by the People's Power League. "If conflicting measures submitted to the people shall be approved by a majority of the votes severally cast for and against the same, the one receiving the highest number of affirmative votes shall thereby become law as to all conflicting provisions." *Referendum Pamphlet*, 1910, no. 360, sec. 1, p. 187; *Referendum Pamphlet*, 1912, no. 362, sec. 1a, p. 210. City charter amendments and ordinances are already on the same footing in this respect. *Laws*, 1907, ch. 226, sec. 12; *Lord's Oregon Laws*, sec. 3482.

district elections and another including provision for proportional representation in the legislative assembly had places in the ballot, and a provision for a commission on employers' liability had place with an employers' liability bill. In 1912 there was a conflict between the "single-tax" proposal and the proposal for exemption of household goods from taxation,[1] and another, apparently, between this household exemption bill and a taxation amendment,[2] another conflict between three sets of road measures, one of them a constitutional amendment, two "majority rule" amendments appeared, the proposal of the office of lieutenant-governor conflicted with a provision in another measure for an election in case of a vacancy in the office of governor, and the university and agricultural college millage-tax bill was really a substitute for the university appropriations referred at the same election. At the election of 1914 the two amendments abrogating the rule of "equal and uniform" taxation were in direct conflict with another amendment which retained this rule, and the latter amendment contained a tax exemption provision which conflicted with the fifteen-hundred-dollar exemption amendment. Moreover, the tax-code commission bill submitted at this election was really the rival of all the tax administration bills submitted.[3]

---

[1] "It is conceivable that a man who favors single tax would as second choice vote for the bill exempting household effects from taxation. Had both household exemption and single tax carried, the former by the higher affirmative vote, we should have attained a ridiculous situation. The single-tax measure would have exempted all household effects, other personal property and improvements from taxation. The specific household exemption bill would have conflicted with the other in probably but one particular. It affirmatively declared that any building used jointly for public worship and for business purposes should be taxed. The single-tax measure would, without conflict, have exempted all other buildings. If the household exemption bill had received the greater affirmative vote and both had carried, the only building of any kind that would be taxed would be the church used for other purposes than public worship. What could be more senseless?" *Oregonian*, Nov. 26, 1912, p. 10, col. 1. See also *ibid.*, Oct. 1, 1911, p. 7, col. 3; *Oregon Journal*, June 6, 1913, p. 2, col. 3. [2] *Below*, p. 116.

[3] A conflict, in *form*, between measures appeared in the case where the same numbers of article and section of the constitution were appropriated for two initiated amendments adopted at the election of 1914. This doubtless has no legal significance. *Cf. Oregonian*, Nov. 30, 1914, p. 9, col. 3.

The Substance and Form of Measures

Such complications put difficulties in the way of intelligent voting by confusion of the voters and may even induce them to refrain from voting. Or, where no such confusion arises, measures which are really favored by a majority of the voters may be defeated by the minority. "Two bills are offered for the purpose at the same election. Either of them if standing alone might well receive the support of almost the entire four-fifths. Yet the voters are divided according to their individual ideas as to the better method and vote against the one they favor the less. This adverse vote, with that of the one-fifth who are opposed to the project itself, defeats both measures. We thus have the spectacle of legislation blocked by a small minority of adverse sentiment."[1] Or, further, sinister interests are thus invited to put measures on the ballot solely for the purpose of defeating legislation obnoxious to them. "Persons not in sympathy with legislation the majority desire may propose alternative measures for the concealed purpose of defeating the will of the people. . . . By invoking the referendum and later submitting an alternative measure of the same purport opponents can defeat almost any act the legislature may devise. If aware in time of plans to submit legislation by initiative, they can defeat these measures as well."[2] It has been charged that the defeat of proposed legislation by this method was attempted in case of the employers' liability bill through the initiation, by employers, of another bill providing for a commission for the investigation of the subject of employers' liability. That the apprehension of evil effects from the presence of conflicting measures at the election has some foundation has become evident in the actual operation of the system.[3]

This "vulnerable point" in the system might be protected in some degree by a method of preferential voting on conflicting measures.[4]

---

[1] Quoted in *Oregonian*, Nov. 26, 1912, p. 10, col. 1.
[2] *Oregonian*, Nov. 12, 1912, p. 8. col. 3.   [3] *Below*, pp. 115–7.
[4] *Cf. Oregonian*, July 26, 1913, p. 6, col. 1. "When conflicting measures are submitted to the people the ballots shall be so printed that a voter can express separately

6

The Form of Measures

In direct legislation the matter of form is even more important than in action by the legislative assembly.

There has been much criticism of crudely drawn initiative measures.[1] But, although there has been at times good ground for such complaint, on the whole the measures submitted through the initiative compare well in form with the legislation enacted by the assembly.

"It is not unreasonable to assume that any organization that wishes to get a measure referred to the people under the initiative will take rather more pains to have it well drawn and as clear and simple as possible than a member of the legislature would do in proposing a bill to that body, to say nothing of the chance of having his bill mutilated in the committees of two houses and emasculated by amendments on the floor. I am aware that the latter form of procedure is supposed to make for prudence and care, but I doubt if any careful student of legislation by congressional or state bodies will seriously maintain that practice confirms the theory."[2]

And indeed practice has *not* confirmed the theory in Oregon. "The quality of the bills passed is a matter upon which it is impossible to adduce within reasonable limits any evidence other

---

by making one cross (X) for each, two preferences, first, as between either measure or neither, and, secondly, as between one and the other. If the majority of those voting on the first issue is for neither, both fail, but in that case the votes on the second issue shall nevertheless be carefully counted and made public. If a majority voting on the first issue is for either, then the measure securing a majority of the votes on the second issue shall be law." Washington *Constitution*, art. 2, sec. 1a (1912). *Cf.* Ohio *Constitution*, art. 2, sec. 1g (1912).

[1] *E.g.* F. V. Holman, *Some Instances of Unsatisfactory Results under Initiative Amendments of the Oregon Constitution* (1910). The absence of enacting clauses in case of *two* initiative bills has been the text for much criticism in this connection.

[2] G. A. Thacher, *Initiative and Referendum in Oregon, Independent*, vol. 64, pp. 1191, 1194 (1908). See also J. Bourne, *Initiative, Referendum and Recall, Atlantic Monthly*, vol. 109, pp. 122, 129 (1909).

than individual judgment. This shall be my apology for offering my personal opinion, based upon an examination of all the general laws of Oregon in force in 1910, in pursuance of the duty of compiling the official publication of the statutes, made under public authority in that year, that in all that pertains to the technique of draftsmanship, legislation passed under the initiative is markedly superior to the average of the statutes passed by the legislature. This superiority is not inherent, of course, but results naturally from the fact that these laws have mostly been drafted by a rather large committee of persons having a lively interest in the matter in hand and some practical knowledge of it, besides what knowledge they may have of the general requirements of legislation; and that the framers were aware that their measure once launched, must go as it is, for better or worse. The technical part of a legislator's work — the mere framing of a law in such a way that it may possibly accomplish what it is intended to do — is done with such incredible badness in at least one American state that anything which promises improvement in it ought to be hailed with glad acclaim." [1]

Experience has emphasized, in one particular at least, the importance of the mechanical side of drafting legislative measures to be submitted to the people. It is often impossible to determine from the face of a proposed measure the extent of change of the existing constitutional or statutory provisions contemplated. "Article VII of the constitution of the state of Oregon shall be and the same hereby is amended to read as follows," introduced the reorganization of the judicial system of the state. "Section 1a of article IX of the constitution of the state of Oregon, shall be, and hereby is, amended to read as follows: No poll or head tax shall be levied or collected in Oregon. The legislative assembly shall not declare an emergency in any

---

[1] R. W. Montague, *Oregon System at Work*, National Municipal Review, vol. 3, pp. 256, 266 (1914). See also J. N. Teal, *Practical Workings of the Initiative and Referendum in Oregon*, Proceedings of the Cincinnati Conference for Good City Government, 1909, pp. 309, 318.

act regulating taxation or exemption," does not itself indicate the fact that it is proposed to repeal the requirements for the submission of legislative tax laws to the people, remove tax measures approved by the people from exemption from constitutional restrictions, and repeal "county home rule" in taxation. Of course, it would often be impossible to indicate by any mechanical means all the implications of proposed measures in regard to existing law, even if they should be known to the authors; but when a measure purports to amend specific constitutional or statutory provisions, those provisions should be indicated with the changes proposed, in order that the voter may by comparison see for himself the extent of the changes proposed.[1]

Difficulty in the way of the identification of measures on the ballot due to the inadequate system of ballot titles employed has

---

[1] *Cf.* M. C. George, *Oregon Journal*, Dec. 5, 1912, p. 8, col. 5; E. W. Allen, Eugene *Register*, Mar. 27, 1914, p. 4, col. 3. "If any measure shall be submitted proposing an amendment of the constitution or an amendment of any law, the existing section or sections of the constitution or the law and the section or sections as proposed to be amended shall be printed in parallel columns in such petition and in the pamphlet . . . to the end that the voter may readily compare the proposed changes." *House Bill*, 1909, no. 1, sec. 2, *Cf.* California *Laws*, 1913, ch. 630.

Section 11. Section 2428 of the statutes is amended to read:

113.11. *Every term in any county is a special term for every other county in the same circuit, unless the presiding judge files with the clerk of the court at least twelve days before the term an order directing otherwise as to any such other county.* Whenever *At* any term of the circuit court in any county shall have been declared *which is* by law to be a special term for the whole judicial circuit or for any other designated *county or counties,* all business may be done at such term arising in any *such other* county *or counties* in such circuit or in the counties so designated respectively which might be done at a general term *in the county where the business arose,* except the trial of issues of fact by a jury in cases other than those arising in actions of quo warranto and mandamus, and excepting also the trial of issues of fact in actions made local by law and arising in some county other than the one in which such special term shall be *is* held. All orders, judgments, findings, proofs, testimony and other proceedings had or made at any such *special* term, being authenticated by the clerk of such court, shall be filed and entered of record in the office of the clerk of the circuit court in the county where the action *or proceeding* shall be pending; or the proceeding arose; and no entries need be made in the office of the clerk of the circuit court of any other county. Wisconsin *Senate Substitute Amendment,* no. 2, to *Senate Bill,* 1913, no. 103.

been a more serious matter. The possibility of drafting intentionally misleading titles has been reduced, as above indicated, by a requirement that the attorney-general shall prepare the titles.[1] The law of 1907 provides that the ballot title shall not contain over one hundred words; and that "in making such ballot title the attorney-general shall, to the best of his ability give a true and impartial statement of the purpose of the measure, and in such language that the ballot title shall not be intentionally an argument, or likely to create prejudice, either for or against the measure."[2] But the clumsy ballot titles which have resulted from describing or attempting[3] to describe all the subjects, sometimes very numerous,[4] included in a measure, have at times actually resulted in making very difficult the identification of measures by the voters.[5] To remedy this difficulty, an act of 1913 provides that, in addition to the "general title" heretofore required, the attorney-general shall prepare a "distinctive short title in not exceeding ten words by which the measure is commonly referred to or spoken of by the public or press."[6] The innovation has been very satisfactory.[7]

[1] *Above*, p. 29. [2] *Laws*, 1907, ch. 226, sec. 5; *Laws*, 1913, ch. 36.

[3] "This year's election indicates that the attorney-general should be a professional psychologist and an advertising expert as well as a lawyer in order to be impartial." G. A. Thacher, *Interesting Election in Oregon, Independent*, vol. 69, pp. 1434, 1437–8 (1910).   [4] *E.g. below*, pp. 254–66.

[5] *Cf. Oregon Journal*, Dec. 5, 1912, p. 8, col. 1; Dec. 17, 1912, p. 8, col. 3; *Pacific Grange Bulletin*, vol. 5, p. 42 (1912).   [6] *Laws*, 1913, ch. 36.

[7] Initiated by W. S. U'Ren, Oregon City, Oregon, G. M. Orton, 82½ Front Street, Portland, Oregon, W. H. Daly, City Hall, Portland, Oregon, H. D. Wagnon, Worcester Block, Portland, Oregon, A. D. Cridge, 954 E. 22d Street, Portland, Oregon, Fred Peterson, Klamath Falls, Oregon, E. J. Stack, 162 Second Street, Portland, Oregon, C. Schuebel, Oregon City Oregon. — $1500 TAX EXEMPTION AMENDMENT. — Its purpose is to exempt from assessment and taxation, dwelling houses, household furniture, live stock, machinery, orchard trees, vines, bushes, shrubs, nursery stock, merchandise, buildings and other improvements on, in and under lands made by clearing, ditching and draining, but not to exempt the land; it is intended to exempt up to $1500, all kinds of personal property and land improvements of all kinds, but the land itself shall be assessed.   Vote YES or NO
326   Yes
327   No
A ballot title of 1914.

CHAPTER VI

THE MAKING OF PETITIONS

I

The Percentage of Signatures Required

UNDER the constitutional provision now in force an initiative measure may be proposed by a petition signed by a number of "legal voters" equal to eight per cent of the votes cast for justice of the supreme court at the election next preceding the filing of the petition, and a referendum may similarly be called by a petition containing five per cent of this number.[1] No distinction in this regard is made between statutes and constitutional amendments. The actual number of signatures required of course automatically increases roughly in proportion to the increase of the number of the qualified voters of the state. The number of signatures required for measures submitted at the election of 1904 was 4386 for referendum petitions, and 7018 for initiative petitions. These numbers have increased until at the election of 1914, 6312 signatures were required for referendum petitions, and 10,099 for initiative petitions.

On account of the ease of securing signatures under the present provisions and the consequent over-burdening of the ballot with initiative and referendum measures, there has been some agitation for the increase of the percentages at present required.[2] However, the successful operation of the system of direct legislation in Oregon has been attributed in part to the low percentages

---
[1] *Constitution*, art. 4, sec. 1 (1902). Sometimes petitions are circulated *against* the proposed submission of measures to the voters.
[2] *E.g. Senate Concurrent Resolution*, 1911, no. 13.

heretofore required. "To go beyond this is to make it almost impossible to submit any measure that is desired in the interests of the common people, or those who have little money or none at all besides what they earn by day's wages."[1] But most of the criticism of the present low percentages is based upon the abuse of direct legislation by narrow selfish interests to the detriment of the public welfare. Raising the percentages would simply result in increasing the amount of fraud already prevalent in the circulation of petitions.[2] However, it is probable that the increase of actual numbers required in the future by the extension of suffrage to women will render petition making really more difficult. "It might be inferred from casual consideration that when the voting population is doubled the ease of obtaining signatures is increased in the same proportion. This might be true if the added voters were men and if all direct legislation and all recalls were founded on widespread public demand. But hard cash is the motive power that turns the petition machinery of these newly-adopted principles of government in Oregon. . . . The petition circulator is paid by the name. He gets the names in the barrooms, cigar stores, on the street corners and at the noon hour near the large factories. He operates where men congregate. Where do women congregate? At any place where a paid petition circulator can approach them? Doubling the voting population by giving votes to women will not double the number of loafers in the saloons, increase the crowds in the cigar stores or augment the pedestrians on the street. A male solicitor would not have much success in stopping women on the street. A female solicitor might meet with a small measure, though we doubt it. About the only additions to the solicitor's prey will be in the factories, where women are employed. But in return for this small help he must get double the number of names."[3]

[1] W. S. U'Ren, quoted in *Equity*, vol. 14, pp. 18–19 (1913). *Cf. Equity*, vol. 13, pp. 65–6 (1911).   [2] *Below*, pp. 65–8.
[3] *Oregonian*, Oct. 14, 1911, p. 10, col. 1. See also *ibid.*, Oct. 14, 1912, p. 6, col. 2.

It should be mentioned in this connection that sometimes a large surplus of signatures is obtained, partly as a safeguard against failure of a measure from the presence of irregular signatures, and partly from prestige real or supposed, given a movement backed by many petitioners.

But the number of signatures does not, even in the absence of fraud, under present conditions, give any true indication of public opinion in regard to the measures submitted. The fact that "the procuring of the necessary signatures to a petition is, in effect, the introduction of a bill before a legislative body composed of the whole people,"[1] is unfortunately often not realized by persons whose signatures to petitions are solicited. There is much evidence for the proposition that "anybody will sign any kind of a petition." Persons approached with petitions very seldom have time to read the measure, sometimes of great length, and the circulators are anxious to have the business over as soon as possible. Any information as to the nature of the measure thus usually comes, if it comes at all, from the interested circulator.[2] Often with little or no knowledge whatever about the measure, persons sign names to accommodate the circulator or to get rid of his importunity.[3] Often, again, they sign "to give the people a chance" to decide upon the measure. "It

---

[1] J. Bourne, *Oregon Journal*, Jan. 25, 1914, sec. 2, p. 3, col. 1.

[2] Testimony in court regarding the circulation of petitions:

"Levi J. Robinson . . . said he did not know he had signed the referendum, and did not intend to do so. However, he identified his signature as genuine. He said the petition had been presented to him by Matthews, whom he knew, and he was told it was for a municipal paving plant. He was busy, and did not read it." *Oregon Journal*, Oct. 6, 1911, p. 19, col. 1.

[3] Testimony in court regarding the circulation of petitions:

"O. C. Potts was an example of the doubtful witness. He said he had signed some petitions, he could not be sure what ones. After examining his name on the petition for some time, he said he did not believe he had written it . . . Dayton Trussell . . . said he did not remember signing, but would have done so if the petition had been presented. He did not believe his name on the petition to be genuine." *Ibid.*, Oct. 6, 1911, p. 19, col. 1. "Lots of men said they would sign the petition just so Harbeck could get the five cents, but nearly all said they would not vote for the excise board." Circulator, quoted in *Oregonian*, Apr. 26, 1909, p. 13, col. 1.

The Making of Petitions

is asked [by the promoters of the "harmony" road bills] that signers of petitions remember one thing especially, namely, that by signing the petitions they do not cast a vote in favor of the bills, but merely thus indicate that they are willing for the bills to go to the people for acceptance or rejection."[1] Thus the number of petitioners is seen to have little proper significance.[2]

But recently there has been some healthy reaction against all this indiscriminate signing of petitions, and it has become somewhat more difficult than formerly to secure signatures to petitions. The proper purpose of the petition as an indication of public opinion is now better appreciated. "In refusing to sign the petitions that are presented to them, the people are choosing the most effective method of discouraging those who are responsible for over-loading the ballot. . . . In the past too little stress has been placed on the fact that the voter is called upon to exercise just as exact and careful judgment when he signs a petition as when he votes on the measure at the general election. Signing a petition is in effect a vote in favor of the measure for which it is being circulated, and a refusal to sign the petition is an effective vote against the proposed law. People can vote against a proposed measure just as effectively by refusing to sign the petition as by voting 'No' at the election, and in addition can save expense and cumbrance of the ballot. It is generally admitted that the initiative and referendum are being abused. The most effective means of checking the abuse

---

[1] *Oregon Journal*, June 28, 1912, p. 23, col. 6.

"It is not necessary, legally or otherwise, that I favor or even understand the merits of the measure that I ask to be submitted. Frankly I confess that I do not know everything and for that reason I am anxious to learn. . . . Is not the day of election and not the filling of the petition the trial of the merit of the measure and the legitimate test of the law to be enacted or rejected?" C. W. Barzee, *Oregonian*, Jan. 3, 1914, p. 6, col. 5.

[2] Similar difficulties have occurred in case of the direct primary law. "As the system has developed it has proven to be extremely farcical. It has provided temporary jobs for men who have circulated the petitions and has given them a pretty graft. It has simply degenerated into a system whereby a man buys his way to secure a place on the ballot." W. S. U'Ren, quoted in *Oregonian*, May 7, 1912, p. 6, col. 3.

is by giving just as careful consideration to petitions as to the measures on the ballot."[1] "The voter who refuses to sign a referendum petition often does more benefit for the state than when he casts his vote."[2]

Possibly a provision requiring that petitioners in affixing their signatures should at the same time pledge themselves to vote for the measure at the election might aid in increasing the sense of responsibility for signature.[3]

2

The Geographical Distribution of Signatures

Under the provisions of the law now obtaining there are no restrictions upon the proportion of signatures which may be secured in any one locality. Since it is easier to solicit signatures where the population is densest, most signatures are secured in Portland and Multnomah county and the country immediately surrounding, containing over a third of the population of the state. Petitions are thus not geographically representative, although the whole state bears the ballot's burden for which one section of the state is largely responsible. Not only for this reason, but also, and especially because securing signatures in the more densely populated districts is considered too easy, and the temptations to fraudulent practice are greater there than elsewhere, the requirement of some distribution of

---

[1] Eugene *Register*, June 7, 1912, p. 4, col. 1.

[2] *Oregonian*, Apr. 22, 1913, p. 8, col. 4. See also *Oregon Journal*, June 6, 1912, p. 8, col. 1. For the election of 1914 the circulation of forty-three bills was undertaken, but only twenty-nine of them were finally submitted to a vote.

[3] "There shall also plainly appear on all initiative and referendum petitions . . . these words, 'I hereby declare that before signing this petition, I have carefully read all of the above described . . . or the whole thereof has been read to me in an intelligible manner, that I believe I fairly understand the same, and my attention was called to this declaration by the person presenting this petition to me before I signed it.'" And the circulators are penalized for failure to call such attention. *House Bill*, 1911, no. 9, sec. 6. See *Oregon Journal*, Dec. 7, 1910, p. 5, col. 1; Jan. 18, 1911, p. 6, col. 5.

signatures over the state has been advocated. It has been suggested that petitions should represent "several counties," one fifth of the counties, even two thirds of the counties, or that each county should be represented on the petition in proportion to its population.[1] Such suggestions accord with the principle of the provision in the direct primary law, which requires that the necessary number of signers of petitions for candidates for state offices shall include voters residing in each of at least seven out of the thirty-five counties of the state.[2] The extension of the provision from direct nomination to direct legislation would seem to be a not unreasonable requirement.[3]

3

The Payment of Circulators

Petitions for some measures have been circulated wholly by volunteers interested in the good of the cause involved. But such cases have been comparatively few. "It is difficult to find citizens who are so devoted to their principles as to be willing to circulate such petitions without compensation."[4]

At times attempt has been made to procure the required number of signatures for very meritorious measures without the aid of paid circulators, but, finally, in most cases, the promoters of the measures have been compelled to resort to the usual method. Necessity for reliance upon paid circulators has been largely reduced when the promoters of measures have had strong organizations back of them. But paid circulators were found

---

[1] C. N. McArthur, *Need of a Constitutional Convention, Proceedings of the Oregon Bar Association*, 1908–10, pp. 148, 158; S. A. Kozer, quoted in Eugene *Register*, July 1, 1913, p. 4, col. 1; C. J. Hurd, *ibid.*, Dec. 6, 1913, p. 4, col. 5; Eugene *Guard*, Dec. 8, 1913, p. 4, col. 1; Dec. 11, 1913, p. 4, col. 1; J. M. Shelley, *ibid.*, Dec. 13, 1913, p. 4, col. 2; *Oregonian*, Dec. 20, 1913, p. 8, col. 2. *Cf.* Montana *Constitution*, art. 5, sec. 1 (1906); Ohio *Constitution*, art. 2, sec. 1g (1912).

[2] *Laws*, 1905, ch. 1, sec. 14; Lord's *Oregon Laws*, sec. 3362.

[3] For the contrary view, see *Equity*, vol. 13, p. 66 (1911).

[4] *State* v. *Olcott, Oregon Reports*, vol. 62, pp. 277, 284 (1912).

necessary even in the case of the direct primary bill, the corrupt-practices bill, the presidential primary bill, and the constitutional amendments for the recall, home-rule city charters, and local initiative and referendum, all very popular and all promoted by the strongly organized People's Power League. The State Grange, in spite of its strong organization, could not secure enough signatures for the gross-earnings corporation-tax bills without payment for the circulation of petitions, and the same is true of the State Federation of Labor in case of the employers' liability bill. Yet these measures were approved at the polls by large majorities.[1] So the "industry"[2] of "petition peddling" has been developed to meet these conditions. For signatures to petitions for a single measure circulators, probably in most cases, receive five cents a name, but especially when they circulate petitions for two or more measures at the same time, they receive less — three and a half cents, three cents and less. Toward the end of the season for securing signatures the "referendum market" is at times very active, and the price of signatures goes up to ten cents or more.

On account of the loose practice prevailing in the signing of petitions,[3] the "professional circulator" is largely responsible for placing on the ballot measures in which he has only a pecuniary interest, the petition is deprived of true representative character, and law-making becomes a mercenary matter.[4] "Any one or any interest willing to pay the price can hold up any legislative bill, however meritorious and however much needed or desired by the public."[5] "The critical weakness in the present system is that it gives the interests that can com-

[1] See especially W. S. U'Ren, quoted in *Oregon Journal*, Nov. 2, 1913, p. 2, col. 3; F. M. Gill, *Pacific Grange Bulletin*, vol. 6, p. 74, col. 4 (1914).

[2] "A contract was made with Mr. Parkinson for 3000 names at 3½ cents each, or 7 cents for the two names, to be paid for as fast as delivered." J. Spray, Cottage Grove *Leader*, reprinted in Eugene *Register*, Nov. 3, 1911, p. 1, col. 1.

[3] *Above*, pp. 54–8.

[4] See especially *Oregonian*, Feb. 7, 1908, p. 8, col. 2; Apr. 26, 1909, p. 13, col. 1; *Pacific Outlook*, reprinted in *Oregonian*, Mar. 3, 1908, p. 8, col. 6.

[5] *Oregonian*, Oct. 10, 1911, p. 8, col. 2.

mand money a practical monopoly of the business of petition making. The question now is not so much the existence of a general demand for the legislation that is contemplated as whether there is money enough at hand to pay for the circulation of the petitions. Any person with sufficient money knows that he can get any kind of legislation on the ballot."[1] "Paid circulation tends to shirking of responsibility and creation of hired instrumentalities for the propagation of ideas. . . . Payment for circulation of petitions tends to develop selfishness rather than interest in the general welfare. The effect cannot be otherwise than corrupting when the citizen circulates for pay a petition for a measure in which he does not believe."[2] Further, it has been urged, inequality of opportunity in direct legislation is fostered by the method of employing hired circulators. "If the common people, the small tax payers, want a law for protection against unjust legislation they must squeeze out the money here and there. They must first beg and solicit funds to pay the petition-shover to beg and solicit names. But the corporation, the 'vested interest' or 'big business,' when it takes a hand in law-making, dips into a well-filled cash box and never misses the money."[3] However, the extensive practice of fraudulent methods by hired circulators in the past[4] has probably had much more to do than any other consideration with the growing popular disgust with "petition-hawking." "So long as there is money reward for securing signatures, there

[1] Eugene *Register*, Dec. 31, 1913, p. 4, col. 1.
[2] J. Bourne, *Oregon Journal*, Nov. 9, 1913, sec. 2, p. 8, col. 5.
[3] *Oregonian*, Dec. 18, 1913, p. 8, col. 1. See also *Oregon Journal*, Apr. 19, 1911, p. 8, col. 1; J. Bourne, *Oregon Journal*, Nov. 9, 1913, sec. 2, p. 8, col. 5.

"Special interests will not in our belief, be able under any circumstances, to initiate legislation detrimental to public interests because of this restriction against the payment of petition circulators. In any of the states where money can be freely used for these purposes, a great portion of the time and energies of the public-spirited organizations is necessarily devoted to killing off legislation submitted by special interests through the use of finances always at their command for the liberal payment of petition circulators and publicity gained by the power of money upon the public press." *Report of Legislative Committee of Washington Grange, Pacific Grange Bulletin*, vol. 6, p. 102, col. 2 (1914). [4] *Below*, pp. 65–8.

will be men who will perpetrate frauds on the initiative and referendum."[1]

For several years there has been an agitation for a law to make the giving or receiving of payment for the circulation of petitions a penal offense, and thus to put petition-making wholly in the hands of unpaid volunteers.[2] "If a measure is not of sufficient importance and public interest to enlist the voluntary service of the people in circulating petitions, it should never go before the people under the initiative or referendum. Under the present practice, the man or group of men who have money to spend, and who are willing to spend it, can secure submission of any measure to a vote of the people, even though it be against public interest. . . . If the practice of hiring men to circulate petitions were abolished by stringent criminal laws, there would be no resort to direct legislation unless the real interests of the people demanded such a course."[3]

But in view of the difficulties of enforcing such a prohibition, it seems that the prohibition would result in hampering those acting in good faith without preventing the unscrupulous from acting in violation of the law.[4] Great business interests, acting through their armies of employees, could probably easily evade the provision.[5] Further, without any evasion of the law it is

---

[1] *Oregon Journal*, Oct. 5, 1911, p. 8, col. 2.

[2] *Senate Bill*, 1909, no. 81; *House Bill*, 1913, no. 103; A. T. Buxton, reported in *Oregonian*, May 15, 1908, p. 6, col. 5; J. Bourne, *Oregon Journal*, Oct. 28, 1913, p. 3, col. 4; *Oregonian*, June 17, 1913, p. 8, col. 2; report in *Oregonian*, Dec. 26, 1913, p. 5, col. 2. *Cf.* South Dakota *Laws*, 1913, ch. 202; Washington *Laws*, 1913, ch. 138, sec. 32; Ohio *Laws*, 1914, p. 119.

[3] *Oregonian*, Mar. 27, 1908, p. 8, col. 4. See also especially A. T. Buxton, quoted in *Oregonian*, Mar. 24, 1908, p. 6, col. 1; *Oregon Journal*, Apr. 19, 1911, p. 8, col. 1; debate in senate, *Oregon Journal*, Feb. 3, 1909, p. 4, col. 5; J. Bourne, *Oregon Journal*, Oct. 28, 1913, p. 3, col. 4.

[4] Debate in senate, *Oregon Journal*, Feb. 3, 1909, p. 4, col. 5; Eugene *Register*, Dec. 6, 1913, p. 4, col. 1; *Oregonian*, Dec. 31, 1913, p. 4, col. 1; Jan. 8, 1914, p. 8, col. 1.

[5] A. D. Cridge, *Oregon Journal*, Nov. 11, 1913, p. 8, col. 4.

The members of a county court are reported to have succeeded in having an act of the legislature referred to the voters thus. "Every employee at the mercy of the

The Making of Petitions 63

considered that such a provision would operate to discriminate against the poorer classes. "Workingmen have not the time or opportunity to lay down their daily task and give all their time to petition circulating, even though it be favorable to their class. They can, however, by stinting themselves, give of their wages to compensate a paid circulator."[1] There is a great deal of opinion to the effect that the provision would practically destroy the legitimate use of the initiative and referendum,[2] especially in view of the fact that heretofore many measures, clearly favored by the people, could not have been placed on the ballot without the aid of paid circulators.[3]

But it has been urged that such payment has been necessary in the past largely because payment has been allowable. "While paid circulation of petitions is the universal custom, there will be few volunteers, for most people will either decline to work without pay while others are paid, or will hesitate to put themselves in the class of paid workers. When all those who circulate petitions do so because they sincerely believe in the end to be accomplished, it will be an honor to be enlisted in the ranks of the workers."[4]

county commissioners was required to secure signatures to the referendum petition. . . . One aged bridge-tender who refused to circulate a petition was promptly discharged . . . and others who were somewhat slow in filling their lists were threatened." *Oregonian*, Sept. 4, 1907, p. 8, col. 2. "The most active of these county employees since received increases in salary." *Ibid.*, June 23, 1907, p. 13, col. 2. "Now there is nothing compulsory about this kind of work . . The petitions are lying there in the office. An employee drops in to report or receive instructions. He sees them there and is casually told what the blanks are for. It is his privilege to take no further interest in the matter. It is none of his business. But then a nice job is such a comfortable thing . . . and, well, it's not always best to take any chances." *Ibid.*, Mar. 15, 1907, p. 10, col. 3. See *below*, p. 212, note 2.

[1] C. W. Barzee, *Oregonian*, Jan. 3, 1914, p. 6, col. 5.

[2] *E.g.* debate in senate, *Oregon Journal*, Feb. 3, 1909, p. 4, col. 5; A. D. Cridge, *Oregon Journal*, Nov. 11, 1913, p. 8, col. 4; W. S. U'Ren, *Oregon Journal*, Nov. 22, 1913, p. 4, col. 5.

[3] W. S. U'Ren, quoted in *Oregon Journal*, Nov. 2, 1913, p. 2, col. 3; F. M. Gill, *Pacific Grange Bulletin*, vol. 6, p. 74, col. 4 (1914); J. King, *Concerning the Cost of Petitions*, Equity, vol. 14, p. 18 (1912); J. King, *Safeguarding Petitions*, Equity, vol. 16, pp. 80–5 (1914). [4] J. Bourne, *Oregon Journal*, Nov. 9, 1913, sec. 2, p. 8, col. 5.

Of course the actual abolition of valuable consideration in petition making might not altogether eliminate motives for fraudulent petition making, for frauds may be perpetrated in behalf of a *cause*.[1]

Opponents of the plan to do away with the payment of circulators consider that danger of fraud can be eliminated by the proper enforcement of the criminal law, especially in view of the recent provision which requires the circulator to swear that he is personally acquainted with every person who signs the petition.[2]

On the whole it would seem that as long as the circulation of petitions is permitted — substitutes have been proposed [3] — it would be unwise to prohibit the payment of the circulators.

4

The Methods of Circulators

Individual circulators may have charge of petitions for only one measure or for several measures. The tendency of "professional" circulation is toward the latter plan. Such combinations result from the support of more than one measure by the same parties, or from the independent employment of the same agents by the supporters of different measures; or the supporters of different measures unite and employ joint agents to circulate the petitions for the several measures together.

Signatures are solicited on the streets, from house to house, in stores and private offices, in saloons and other questionable places, in railroad stations, on trains, in public offices,[4] at

[1] *Cf. Oregonian,* Jan. 2, 1914, p. 10, col. 1.

[2] W. S. U'Ren, quoted in *Oregon Journal,* Nov. 2, 1913, p. 2, col. 3.

[3] *Below,* pp. 74–7.

[4] "Although a number of complaints have been made concerning petitioners who hang around at the very doors of the registration office in the court house, nothing has been done yet, while the petitioners are springing up like mushrooms. In the past week, each day, there has been another petitioner added to the little crowd collecting names, until now there are about a dozen through which women must pass before getting out of the court house. As a person comes out of the registration

church,[1] and other places where men do congregate. Often provision for signing petitions at designated places is made, and the supporters of the measure solicit signatures by advertisement in the newspapers or otherwise.

The fraudulent practices of hired circulators have recently caused more discussion in Oregon than any other matter concerning direct legislation, and have been the cause of most of the present agitation for changes in the initiative and referendum laws. How extensive such fraudulent practices have generally become it is impossible to say. There has been nothing like a thorough investigation of the petitions except in a few cases, but the fraud disclosed by such investigations creates a suspicion that very much more fraud remains undisclosed. Although in some cases circulators may have been imposed upon by forgers of signatures, apparently in most cases the circulators themselves have alone been guilty of fraud.

The fraudulent methods practiced in case of the referendum of the university appropriations of 1912 have been the most notorious. A statement of the fraud in that case, which is to

office he or she is grabbed by the arm, a pencil is placed into his or her hand and before the victim knows what has happened a new name has been added to the petitions. Many women have complained to the registration clerks, some claiming that they had been insulted by those in charge of petitions. Complaint was made a few weeks ago about these same collectors using tables that had been left in the hall. When officials heard of this the tables were removed and the petitioners took up their station on the outside of the building. One by one the collectors went back into the building. From some place two tables appeared and now the name gatherers have the use of them. When the registration is slack the collectors make the rounds of the building seeking names. One of the most brazen of the name agents seized the opportunity a few days ago, walked into the registration office and asked each of the clerks in the office to affix their signatures to a petition. He got no names, however." *Oregon Journal*, Mar. 25, 1913, p. 11, col. 5. "By an order passed by the county commissioners yesterday in the future no petitions may be circulated in the corridors of the court house." *Oregonian*, Jan. 28, 1914, p. 1, col. 2.

[1] "The best place to catch people for a petition of that kind [an initiative excise ordinance] is at churches on Sunday. I went up town one Sunday and stopped people going to and from church. Most of the men had their wives with them and almost had to sign when they saw what kind of a petition it was. I could fill a whole book with names on Sunday in that way." A. G. Ross, quoted in *Oregonian*, Apr. 26, 1909, p. 13, col. 1.

F

say the least, not overdrawn, appears in the decision of the circuit court. "It is charged in the complaint that some twenty-five different persons who circulated different parts of this petition, as the agents of H. J. Parkison, conspired and confederated together to corruptly make a spurious and false petition by the writing of fictitious names and addresses therein, and by forging the names of legal voters of this state; and that in pursuance thereof, the said conspirators did write into said petition large numbers of spurious names and forged the names of many legal voters of the state thereon; and by reason thereof all of the names in that part of the petition, verified by these several circulators, are spurious and void, and their affidavits false. The part of the petition thus challenged, includes about ten thousand names out of a total of thirteen thousand six hundred fifteen. Quite [a] proportion of these alleged fraudulent names go to make that part of the petition which is void as to its form. These charges of fraud and conspiracy made in the complaint are denied by the answer, and the plaintiff has the burden of proof as to that issue.

"As the taking of the testimony on this issue progressed at the trial, plaintiff made such a forcible and conclusive case of the alleged fraud to such a degree that defendant, by his counsel, voluntarily admitted in open court that names to the number of at least 3722 on this petition were and are fraudulent and void. . . . The public interest . . . demands that the full extent of the fraud, shown by the plaintiff's case, be considered and exposed to public view, to the end that the danger to public institutions may be appreciated and some corrective remedy applied by the legislative branch of the state government. Plaintiff's evidence, viewed in its entirety, challenges by testimony more or less persuasive, the integrity of over 6000 names on the petition other than those admitted by the defendant's counsel to be void. . . .

"Plaintiff has made its prima facie cause of fraud against the following parts of the petition . . . the whole aggregating some 6110 names, which do not include 3722 names admitted to be fraudulent. There is no reason why defendant's counsel should have stopped in their admissions when they came to the work of Walter B. Thurber, for many pages of his part of the petition appear to be almost entirely made up of fraudulent and fictitious names. Section 61 is in part verified by Harry Goldman, whose other work in this petition amounting to 1100 names is admitted to be void for fraud. The work of C. L. Woolwein, who verified the remainder of that section, is scarcely an improvement on his associate. Sections 16, 59, and 112 by E. Wallace ought to be cast out if for no other reason than that it is admitted that his true name is E. J. Rahles, but there is shown to be fictitious and forged names therein, put therein by the said Rahles alias Wallace. Sections 31 and 105 verified by Charles Matthews are mostly forgeries upon the face of the petition without the aid of extrinsic or other evidence. The strongest evidence of the alleged fraud is the petition itself. The identity of the handwriting in the face of the petition with that in the affidavits convicts this circulator not only of fraud, but of falsifying his own oath upon the witness stand. . . . The defendant's expert witnesses gave testimony tending to show that many names in Matthews' petitions were written by one and the same hand. Besides many cases of specific proof of forged names in this part of the petition are shown, none of which has in any way been refuted by the defense. Many names have been judged to be bad or forgeries by the defendant's expert witnesses. The same comments may be made as to the work of F. M. Raymond, who, it appears, fled the state as soon as the investigation of this petition began. The report made by the defendant's expert witnesses and put in evidence shows that they examined 6753 names, and found only 2902 of that number registered, while 3525 of those not found registered reported as having no evidence in the appearance of the writing itself sufficient to say that they were fraudulent. 131 other names were catalogued as suspected of being fraudulent, and 195 were listed as fraudulent and void. Of these registered names, 1783 appear upon that part of the petition attacked by plaintiff's proof, and deducting

68   Initiative, Referendum, and Recall in Oregon

that number from the total of 9788 disqualified by plaintiff's evidence and by the defendant's admissions, leaves 8003 names as the total number affected by plaintiff's case, and not overcome by the defendant. Deducting this number from the total number on the petition, leaves but 5612 names which may be said to represent the valid part of the petition upon this view of the case. This does not take into account more than 200 names which on a careful computation ought to be deducted for duplication and for lack of proper verification by omitting a name from the affidavit or the failure of the circulator to sign the same." [1]

Investigation of charges of such fraudulent practices is very expensive, and generally there have not been interests sufficiently affected by the proposed legislation to provide the necessary funds for the purpose.[2]

In addition to their forgery of signatures, circulators of petitions have sometimes been guilty of misrepresenting the nature of the measures included in the petitions.

In the case of at least one measure circulators of petitions have been bought off by opponents of the proposed legislation,[3] and in another case a promise was made, with apparent power to make good the promise, to see that a referendum was dropped upon the payment of a stipulated sum.[4]

---

[1] *Friendly* v. *Olcott*, circuit court of Marion county, Eugene *Register*, Dec. 22, 1911, p. 3. See also especially *Oregonian*, Oct. 6, 1911, p. 16, col. 1; Oct. 10, 1911, p. 8, col. 2; *Oregon Journal*, Nov. 4, 1911, p. 16, col. 2. The supreme court was more conservative in its estimate of the amount of fraud. *State* v. *Olcott*, Oregon *Reports*, vol. 62, pp. 277, 284 (1912).

[2] *Cf. Oregonian*, July 9, 1913, p. 8, col. 1. A county clerk of long experience testified in court that "he did not remember ever having checked a petition where all the names were good. In liquor license petitions, he said, usually about half are bad, and in nominating petitions about twenty per cent are bad." *Oregon Journal*, Nov. 21, 1911, p. 10, col. 1.

[3] In this case of a local initiative ordinance, after the author of the measure discovered the sale of petitions, he expressly authorized trusted circulators to sell some petitions, and used the proceeds to circulate new petitions.

[4] "His interest in the act at a later date culminated in his magnanimous offer to see that the referendum (which had been started) was dropped. He was willing to accomplish this if $1500 could be raised for the purpose. Since this couldn't be done he promised to undertake the matter for various other sums ranging from $1000

The Making of Petitions

Of course these outrageous abuses have met with general reprobation. They operate to discredit the whole system of direct government. "The offense is not merely the forgery of names. It is a far higher moral crime. It is a deliberate assault on the sacred instrumentalities of the popular legislation."[1] "It can be said without fear of successful contradiction, that if the way is left open for perpetration of fraud in making up petitions the people of Oregon will repudiate the initiative and referendum."[2]

But it is very difficult to control these abuses.

In the absence of final determination of the question by the courts, until recently the authority of the secretary of the state in dealing with irregularities in petitions filed in his office has been uncertain.[3] But it is now decided that it is his duty in the first instance, subject to a review by the courts, to determine by inspection of the petitions whether or not signatures are genuine and regularly authenticated.[4] The regularity of a petition may be attacked in spite of *apparent* regularity,[5] but proof of irregularity is very difficult.

Of course, in the first instance, the burden of proof is against the existence of fraud in a petition.[6] However, "as the circulator of a petition is the agent of the signer, and his oath is the only

---

to $400. Inasmuch as the $400 was not forthcoming at 4 o'clock on the last day for filing the referendum petitions they were duly filed." A. H. Eaton, *Eugene Register*, Nov. 4, 1913. p. 4, col. 4.   [1] *Oregon Journal*, July 9, 1913, p. 8, col. 2.

[2] *Eugene Register*, Oct. 15, 1911, p. 12, col. 1.

[3] "As the courts have never passed on the authority this office has in these matters, no standard has been set and we have to proceed according to our best judgment. We have been lenient in all matters where a mistake might be merely a clerical error, such as the transcribing of the names on the back of the sheets of the petition, but we have been careful as to verification of the seal and the affidavits." Secretary of state, quoted in *Oregon Journal*, June 13, 1913, p. 21, col. 4.

[4] *State* v. *Olcott, Oregon Reports*, vol. 67, p. 214 (1913). *Contra, State* v. *Olcott, ibid.*, vol. 62, pp. 277, 279 (1912); circuit court of Marion county, *Oregon Journal*, Sept. 2, 1913, p. 1, col. 1; *Oregonian*, Sept. 3, 1913, p. 10, col. 2. It has been proposed to make the secretary's decision final in case of the *acceptance* of petitions. Reported in *Oregon Journal*, Jan. 14, 1913, p. 14, col. 5.

[5] *State* v. *Olcott, Oregon Reports*, vol. 62, pp. 277, 278 (1912).

[6] *Woodward* v. *Barbur, ibid.*, vol. 59, pp. 70, 76 (1911).

evidence of the genuineness of the signature, it follows as a matter of course that, when he is shown to have acted fraudulently, the value of his verification is destroyed, and the petition must fall, unless the genuine signatures are affirmatively shown. But, in the absence of evidence of intentional fraud or guilty knowledge on the part of the circulator, it would be an unjust rule to deprive the honest signer of his right to have his signature counted, merely because some disqualified person signed, or because some person without the knowledge of the circulator affixed a fictitious name, or gave a fictitious address." [1]

The great difficulty, at times amounting to practical impossibility, of disproving the genuineness of each fraudulent signature in such a great mass of signatures is clearly apparent. "Under our present laws, as interpreted by the courts, there is no protection against fraud and forgery or crookedness of any sort. All that is necessary is to practice fraud upon a scale so large that detecting and proving it will be a task so large and so expensive as to deter any one from attempting it." [2]

Under the original law the initiative and referendum petitions were checked up by the county clerks, who compared the signatures with the registration books, and certified as to the genuineness of the signatures to the secretary of state.[3] But the clerks objected to this burden of work,[4] and under the act of 1907 initiative and referendum petitions are verified by affidavit of the circulators.[5] Under the existing law comparison with the registration books is thus made a matter of great difficulty.

But many signers of petitions have not registered, and hence comparisons are in such cases impossible. This has caused an agitation for a change in the law to require registration as a qualification for signing petitions. "None but registered voters should be permitted to sign initiative and referendum petitions.

---

[1] *State* v. *Olcott, Oregon Reports*, vol. 62, pp. 277, 286 (1912). See also *State* v. *Olcott, ibid.*, vol. 67, p. 214 (1913).   [2] Eugene *Register*, Oct. 23, 1913, p. 4, col. 1.
[3] *Laws*, 1903, p. 244, sec. 3.   [4] *Oregonian*, Jan. 21, 1907, p. 9, col. 1.
[5] *Laws*, 1907, ch. 226, sec. 3; *Laws*, 1913, ch. 359, sec. 2.

The Making of Petitions 71

Each petition should have a precinct heading and signatures should be taken accordingly. This would enable county clerks to quickly check the signatures and when necessary certify the list to the secretary of state. As the matter now stands it is physically impossible for the secretary of state to check the signatures on the petitions filed in his office." [1]

Illegibility of signatures does not invalidate them,[2] and this leaves a way open for fraud.[3] Further, it is uncertain as to how definitely the signers' residence must be indicated in the petitions.[4] Because of complaint by circulators of petitions that some persons had signed fictitious names,[5] a provision of law was enacted requiring a clause to be inserted in every petition warning signers that forgeries of signatures, etc., on petitions are felonies,[6] but this provision has been held to be directory only.[7]

As the earlier statutory provisions [8] were interpreted, although it was required that every sheet for petitioners' signatures must be attached to "a full and complete copy of the title and text" of the measure proposed by *initiative* petition, no such requirement applied to *referendum* petitions, in case of which any

---

[1] Governor West's *Message*, 1913, p. 21. See also circuit court of Marion county, *Oregon Journal*, Sept. 2, 1913, p. 1, col. 1; *Oregon Journal*, Jan. 16, 1915, p. 1, col. 3; *Referendum Pamphlet*, 1912, no. 362, sec. 1b, pp. 210, 221–2; *Senate Joint Resolutions*, 1915, nos. 6, 7; California *Laws*, 1913, ch. 138. In view of the fact that under constitutional provision petitions may be signed by "legal voters," the qualification of registration cannot be imposed without a constitutional amendment. *Woodward* v. *Barbur, Oregon Reports*, vol. 59, p. 75 (1911); *State* v. *Olcott, ibid.*, vol. 67, p. 214 (1913); *State* v. *Dalles City, Pacific Reporter* (Oregon), vol. 143, pp. 1127, 1136 (1914). *Senate Joint Resolutions*, 1915, nos. 6, 7, provided for such constitutional amendment. *Senate Joint Resolution*, 1915, no. 8, made similar provision in regard to the recall. [2] *State* v. *Olcott, Oregon Reports*, vol. 67, p. 214 (1913).

[3] *Cf.* Eugene *Register*, Oct. 23, 1913, p. 4, col. 1.

[4] *Report of Attorney General*, 1906–8, p. 124. Absence of the street address of the signer will not invalidate the petition. *State* v. *Olcott, Oregon Reports*, vol. 67, p. 214 (1913).   [5] W. S. U'Ren, *Oregonian*, June 2, 1907, p. 38, col. 1.

[6] *Laws*, 1907, ch. 226, sec. 2; *Lord's Oregon Laws*, sec. 3471.

[7] *Stevens* v. *Benson, Oregon Reports*, vol. 50, pp. 269, 275 (1907); *Report of Attorney General*, 1906–8, p. 124.

[8] *Laws*, 1903, p. 244, sec. 2; *Laws*, 1907, ch. 226, sec. 2.

number of sheets might be attached to one copy of the measure.[1] It is obvious that such a condition opened the way to gross fraud. "Sheets of names can be transferred from one petition to another. Signers can be readily deceived. When the voter signs a referendum petition, he will have no assurance that his name will be used for the purpose for which he gives it."[2] Recently the statute has been amended to put referendum petitions on the same footing with initiative petitions in this respect.[3]

Another recent act of the legislature is intended to aid in the elimination of fraud in petitions. The law had previously required that the circulator should make an oath that the signer signed the petition in his presence and that he believed the signer had stated his name, post-office address, and residence correctly, and was a legal voter.[4] The act of 1913, in addition to this provision, requires that the circulator shall make affidavit to the effect that he is "personally acquainted" with all those who sign the petition.[5] A strict construction and enforcement of this new law doubtless "would operate as a check upon the present promiscuous securing of signatures to initiative and referendum petitions and accomplish much in eradicating from the circulation of them the fraud which has been in evidence for the last few years."[6] But it was predicted that enforcement would be difficult. "The men to whom petition circulating offers attractive remuneration are not as a rule men of wide acquaintance. If they were actually to solicit only the signatures of men whom they personally knew, petition circulating would be an arduous and ill-paid occupation. Yet it is not to be confidently expected that there will be any change of method of

[1] *Palmer* v. *Benson, Oregon Reports*, vol. 50, p. 277; *State* v. *Olcott, ibid.*, vol. 62, pp. 277, 282 (1912).

[2] Eugene *Register*, July 25, 1912, p. 4, col. 1. See also *Report of Attorney General*, 1906–8, p. 139; *Friendly* v. *Olcott*, circuit court of Marion county, Eugene *Register*. Dec. 22, 1911, p. 1, col. 1; Eakin, C. J., dissenting, *State* v. *Olcott, Oregon Reports*, vol. 62, pp. 277, 288 (1912). [3] *Laws*, 1913, ch. 359, sec. 1.

[4] *Laws*, 1907, ch. 226, sec. 3. [5] *Laws*, 1913, ch. 359, sec. 2.

[6] Eugene *Register*, July 15, 1913, p. 3, col. 1. See also W. S. U'Ren, quoted in *Oregon Journal*, Nov. 2, 1913, p. 2, col. 5.

The Making of Petitions 73

paid circulators under the operations of the new law. They will continue to approach loafers in the park blocks and saloons and other places where indifferent and uninformed voters congregate. The new verification is identical with that which has heretofore been required of circulators of nominating petitions and it is a matter of common knowledge that nominating petitions have been filled wherever the circulators could find strangers willing to sign."[1] And, to a considerable extent at least, this is the actual experience under the new law. Indeed a strict enforcement of the law might unduly impede honest petition-making.[2]

At present the criminal law does not make punishable the greatest misrepresentations of the circulators.[3] Neither is the soliciting or giving of money to suppress petitions covered by the criminal law.[4] It is apparent that the corrupt-practices act should be extended to cover all the operations connected with direct legislation.

At this time there are absolutely no legal qualifications prescribed for circulators of petitions, except of course that they must be able to understand the significance of the affidavit required of them. In order to reduce the number of irresponsible persons engaging in this occupation, it has been urged that the circulator should at least be a registered voter and able to supply "some written testimony as to his good moral character."[5] "If one is a registered voter and can produce recommendations from three freeholders he ordinarily can be trusted."[6] A bill which failed to pass the last legislative assembly provided that no person might solicit more than two hundred names without first securing a license from the governor.[7] Another proposition

---

[1] *Oregonian*, Dec. 15, 1913, p. 6, col. 1.

[2] This danger does not seem to have been apprehended by defenders of the system of direct legislation. *Cf.* W. S. U'Ren, quoted in *Oregon Journal*, Nov. 2, 1913, p. 2, col. 5.   [3] *Cf. Oregonian*, June 6, 1913, p. 10, col. 1.

[4] *Ibid.*, July 9, 1913, p. 8, col. 1. But the corrupt-practices act covers improper inducement to vote for or to refrain from voting for measures submitted. *Laws*, 1909, ch. 3, sec. 31; *Lord's Oregon Laws*, sec. 3515.

[5] *Oregonian*, Dec. 15, 1913, p. 6, col. 1.   [6] *Ibid.*, Dec. 18, 1913, p. 8, col. 1.

[7] *House Bill*, 1913, no. 365.

goes farther, and would make the circulator of petitions a public officer.[1]

But the only proper solution of the difficulty — which would reach other difficulties in the system as well — would seem to be abolition of the circulation of petitions altogether, and the substitution of something else in its place.

5

Substitutes for Circulation

For several years it has been urged that as a substitute for the circulation of petitions, petitions should be left in charge of the registration officers[2] of the county and signed only in the presence of the officer.[3] "Prohibiting the circulation of initiative and referendum petitions and requiring that they be left with some constituted authority where petitioners may go and voluntarily affix their signatures is desirable for several reasons. One is that it offers a feasible means of checking the fraud and

[1] "The governor shall appoint and authorize persons to circulate initiative and referendum petitions in like manner and subject to like conditions of character and fitness as may be required by the governor for the appointment of notaries public, and any person so authorized and appointed to circulate initiative and referendum petitions shall also give a sufficient bond to the people of Oregon, in the sum of five hundred dollars, conditional for the faithful performance of his duties and compliance with the laws of Oregon, in soliciting and verifying signatures of such petitions . . . and every such appointment shall be for the period of two years from the date of the appointment." *House Bill*, 1913, no. 365, sec. 2. See also J. D. Wheelan, *Oregon Journal*, Nov. 6, 1913, p. 9, col. 4.

[2] It has also been suggested that signatures should be made before the election judges at the primary election. H. Denglinger, *Oregon Journal*, Feb. 5, 1913, p. 8, col. 4. "If the proper period were established between the date of the primary and the date of the general election the posting of petitions in the election booths on primary days would be the ideal plan. They would then be subject to official supervision, accessible only to registered voters and be conveniently available for perusal and consideration by every one entitled to sign." *Oregonian*, Jan. 2, 1914, p. 10, col. 2.

[3] *E.g.*, P. Hume's resolution, *Oregonian*, June 16, 1909, p. 10, col. 1; W. G. D. Mercer, Eugene *Register*, Dec. 14, 1913, p. 11, col. 1; *Oregonian*, Mar. 13, 1915, p. 8, col. 1. See *House Joint Resolution*, 1915, no. 2; *Senate Bill*, 1915, no. 59; Washington *Laws*, 1915, ch. 54, sec. 7.

The Making of Petitions

forgery that is becoming an annual scandal and that threatens to bring popular government into disfavor. Another is that petitions could thus be made to express genuine opinion. Everyone knows that under the present system petitions do not express real opinion. They are signed for a variety of reasons, among which are desire to be rid of the solicitor or to help him earn a day's wages, and the natural tendency to do that which is requested providing it costs nothing. Petitions signed voluntarily by persons who would take the trouble to go to the registration clerk and affix their names would be a real call from the people for initiating or referring any measure. The professional tinkerer would be left out in the cold, for he would have to have a legitimate proposition before he could hope for a hearing." [1]

But, on the other hand, there is apprehension that such a provision would render petition-making so difficult that it would practically nullify the initiative and referendum.[2] However, this objection might be overcome by a reduction of the percentages of signatures now required.[3] A provision which would result in securing "representative" signatures would be preferable to the present plan, even if the *number* of signatures required should be very materially reduced.

Less reduction would be necessary perhaps, if, as has been widely urged recently,[4] petitions were allowed to be placed in charge of responsible persons at places of business and other convenient places designated as depositories, as well as with the registration officers.[5] With the percentages now required, in

---

[1] Eugene *Register*, Dec. 18, 1913, p. 4, col. 1.

[2] *E.g.*, A. D. Cridge, *Oregon Journal*, Dec. 4, 1912, p. 8, col. 5; W. S. U'Ren, quoted in *Oregon Journal*, Nov. 2, 1913, p. 2, col. 3; *Oregon Journal*, Jan. 22, 1915, p. 6, col. 1.

[3] Reduction from eight to six per cent for initiative petitions, and from five to three per cent for referendum petitions, has been suggested. G. Parrish, reported in *Oregon Journal*, Jan. 1, 1915, p. 2, col. 3.   [4] *Oregonian*, Dec. 15, 1913, p. 6, col. 1.

[5] Voting for measures at the *primary* election has been offered as a substitute for the signature of petitions. "Have all proposed laws listed, in the first place, on the primary ballots, where they could be voted on the same as candidates, only those measures which should receive the legal proportion of primary votes to be allowed on

case of many really popular measures the method of placing petitions in designated places and advertising for signatures has met with disappointing results.[1]

"Attention to a proposal can be attracted by a dozen different methods and opportunities for voluntary subscribing thereto can be arranged in a dozen different ways" — the platform, press, billboard, hand bill, circular, public address, personal solicitation, etc.[2]

Any necessity for making registration a prerequisite to signing a petition[3] vanishes with the provision for signature at official depositories, for such signature amounts practically to registration.[4]

It has been proposed that the verdict of a jury to the effect that the enactment of a measure by the legislative assembly

the ballots of the general election. . . . This proposal would in no way interfere with any one presenting any bill he chose, but it would certainly insure against any bill going on the general ballot for which there was not a sincere demand by a legal percentage of voters." H. Denglinger, *Oregon Journal*, Feb. 5, 1913, p. 8, col. 4. (See also J. L. Schuyleman, quoted in *Oregon Journal*, Dec. 14, 1913, p. 15, col 4; F. E. Olson, *Oregonian*, Jan. 11, 1914, p. 17, col. 3.) Of course this is a practical equivalent to the signature of petitions in the presence of the election officers. The plan is objectionable in that it would increase the load of the already overloaded primary ballot.

A modification of this plan provides for placing measures on the primary ballot upon the payment of a two-hundred-dollar filing fee. This is even more objectionable, for it would not only lengthen the primary ballot, but would doubtless very greatly add to the number of initiative and referendum measures submitted to the voters. "The trouble with the Crawford plan is that it puts the proposal of initiative measures upon a strictly cash basis — and a cash basis at that which is smaller than the present cost of circulating petitions. It gives the people no opportunity to prevent the overloading of the ballot with useless measures. There are already too many on the ballot at every election, and this measure would probably result in increasing the number many times." Eugene *Register*, Apr. 16, 1914, p. 4, col. 1. *Cf. Oregon Journal*, Apr. 2, 1914, p. 8, col. 2. An act of 1915 permits the payment of a filing fee as an alternative to the circulation of a petition in direct primary elections. *Laws*, 1915, ch. 124.   [1] *Above*, pp. 59–60.

[2] *Cf. Oregonian*, Dec. 15, 1913, p. 6, col. 1; Jan. 2, 1914, p. 10, col. 1; *House Joint Resolution*, 1915, no. 2. "Elimination or modification of the form of verification would be necessary, but with the signing wholly voluntary verification need not be hedged about with many safeguards." *Oregonian*, Dec. 15, 1913, p. 6, col. 1.

[3] *Above*, pp. 70–1.

[4] Letter in Eugene *Register*, Dec. 14, 1913, p. 11; Eugene *Register*, Dec. 18, 1913, p. 4, col. 1.

was induced by any form of "undue influence" should operate as a referendum petition.[1]

[1] This alternative to referendum petitions was contained in a proposed initiative constitutional amendment, but was eliminated before the amendment was submitted to the people in 1910. "Any ten citizen freeholders shall have right to unite in bringing an action in the circuit court at the seat of government against any measure within ten days after it is passed by the legislative assembly, alleging that the same was passed by bargaining, trading, logrolling or other forms of undue influence. Summons and a copy of the complaint shall be served upon the attorney-general and the presiding officers of both houses as other process is served. The attorney-general shall defend the action, but senators and representatives may employ assistant counsel. The case shall be advanced on the docket if necessary and tried within twenty days after the close of the session. The verdict of the jury shall be on preponderance of evidence. If the jury finds from the evidence that they believe the bill was passed by any undue influence, that verdict shall be filed with the secretary of state; and as to such measure the verdict shall have the same effect as a petition for the referendum; said bill shall be referred to the people by the secretary of state for approval or rejection at the next regular election. Senators, representatives, officers, and other persons may be subpœnaed and compelled to testify after the close of the session, but they shall not be prosecuted criminally or civilly for any action to which they shall testify." W. S. U'Ren and others, *Senate Document*, no. 603, 61st Congress, 2d session, p. 157, sec. 37 (1910). Reprinted in Beard and Shultz, *Documents on the Initiative, Referendum and Recall*, pp. 373–4 (1912). Apparently the proposition was not generally well received.

CHAPTER VII

THE MULTIPLICITY OF MEASURES

I

The Number of Measures

When the system of direct legislation was established it was believed that the people would not often use their reserve power.[1] Direct legislation was to be "the medicine of the constitution, cautiously administered when occasion might require; not its daily bread."[2] But the "hope that there would be so much consideration and self-restraint on all sides that the new methods would not be pushed to the extreme, but would be used only on rare occasions for remedial purposes," was, it was declared, even before the ballot had reached its present length, "a fallacious hope."[3]

Since the system of direct legislation was established there have been six general elections and one special election at which measures have been submitted to the people. The provision for another special election, in 1903, was conditional upon the referring of a certain act of the assembly by petition, and the referendum was not invoked. At the special election held in 1913 only measures referred by petition could be submitted. At the election of 1904 three measures were submitted, one a proposal for a constitutional amendment referred by the assembly, and two initiative bills. In 1906 eleven measures were submitted, including five initiative measures for the amendment of the constitution, five initiative bills, and one act referred

---
[1] *Oregonian*, June 30, 1902, p. 8, col. 3.
[2] Reported in *Oregonian*, Feb. 18, 1908, p. 8, col. 1.
[3] *Oregonian*, July 6, 1909, p. 8, col. 1.

The Multiplicity of Measures

by petition. In 1908 the number of propositions increased to nineteen, of which four were constitutional amendments referred by the assembly, six constitutional amendments initiated by petition, five were bills so initiated, and four were acts referred by petition. In 1910 the number increased to thirty-two. Four of these were constitutional amendments referred by the assembly, two were acts referred by the assembly (neither of these could be enacted finally by the legislature), seven were constitutional amendments initiated by petition, eighteen were bills so initiated, and the other was an act referred by petition. There were thirty-seven[1] measures in 1912. Of these six were constitutional amendments proposed by the assembly and eight by petition, twenty bills proposed by petition, and three acts referred by petition. At the special election of 1913,—at which only measures referred by petition could be submitted — five acts were referred by petition. At the election of 1914 — at which measures referred by petition could not be submitted — there were twenty-nine measures on the ballot,—ten proposed by the legislative assembly, including eight constitutional amendments and two acts and nineteen measures initiated by petition, including eleven constitutional amendments and eight bills. The two elections of 1913 and 1914 may for some purposes be considered complementary parts of *one* election, at which thirty-four measures were submitted.[2]

Thus it appears that the people have voted on sixty constitutional amendments and seventy-six statutes, a total of one hundred and thirty-six measures, of which twenty-seven were referred by the legislative assembly, and the one hundred and nine others initiated (ninety-five) or referred (fourteen) by petition. The submission of equivalents, or substantial equivalents, of

---

[1] Thirty-eight measures appear in the voters' pamphlet, but one of them, a law referred by petition, was kept off the ballot by action of the court.

[2] Three constitutional amendments and no statutes were submitted by the legislative assembly of 1915 to the regular election to be held next year. Provision was made for a special election in 1915 in case any acts of the session should be referred by petition, but no referendum petitions were filed.

measures rejected by the voters at previous elections is an established practice. Perhaps a dozen measures on the ballot of 1914 may be said to have been before the voters previously in one form or another.

But the amount of legislation attempted is not fully indicated by the mere number of measures submitted, since many of them have been extremely complicated.[1] And it must be remembered that except in case a special election (even at the special state election of 1913 local elections were held in some parts of the state) to consider the measures is called, at the same election numerous candidates for office, both state and local, must be considered; that local measures may also appear on the same ballot; and that other local measures and candidates for local offices may be voted for at an election held soon after. "The sample ballot for the state election of 1912 is a dark yellow broadside, thirty-four inches long and eighteen inches wide, and it therefore contains six hundred and twelve square inches or about four and one-half square feet. It is nearly as large as two ordinary newspaper pages, and contains the names of one hundred and seventy-six candidates for office and the titles of forty separate measures submitted under the initiative and referendum. On November 2, three days before the general election, the Portland public will at a special election pass on the new city charter and the various charter amendments. There are two proposed charters and twenty charter amendments. The ballot is no such barn-door affair as the state ballot, but it does fairly well in size and variety. Here, then, is a total of sixty-two measures the electorate must study under the referendum, and 176 candidates whose merits it must consider. The grand total for the inspection and determination of the intelligent voter is therefore 238 separate and distinct items. Yet there are people who think the tendency of the times is toward the short ballot and simplification of issues."[2]

[1] *Cf. Oregonian*, Aug. 18, 1912, sec. 3, p. 4, col. 1.
[2] *Oregonian*, Oct. 25, 1912, p. 12, col. 2.

2

The Burden on the Voters

The friends of direct legislation early sounded warning against overworking the system. "There are so many things to cover in an election, so many features to consider, and the ballot can be made so complicated, that the average voter becomes confused, with the outcome that the very best result is not secured. The real friends of the initiative law will be slow to invoke its aid, and when they do it will be to remedy a manifest evil that it is ordinarily difficult if not impossible to reach."[1] But "the burden of the ballot" has grown from year to year until it is undeniable that abuse of the power of the people is becoming an issue.[2]

This burden greatly overtaxes the capacity of the voters, to a certain extent thereby defeats the purpose of the system of direct legislation, and even, it has been feared, endangers the existence of that system.

It is no reflection upon the intelligence of the voters to say that it is absolutely impossible for them adequately to consider such masses of legislative proposals. "The excess of such questions on a single ballot constitutes a weakness of the system of the initiative and referendum as worked out in the far western state. There may be a score of important measures calling for the vote of the people at one time or another, as the people may become well informed enough to decide upon them; but it is absurd to put many of them up to the people at a single election. . . . Scattering the attention of the voters among several questions of much importance must tend to weaken the popular judgment."[3]

Moreover, these excesses may defeat the purpose of direct legislation. They certainly tend to discourage the voter, and may lead him "to vote negatively in all measures, those that ought to pass included."[4]

---

[1] *Oregon Journal*, Jan. 31, 1906, p. 4, col. 2. [2] *Oregonian*, July 5, 1912, p. 10, col. 1.
[3] *Springfield* (Mass.) *Republican*, reprinted in *Oregonian*, July 23, 1912, p. 8, col. 5.
[4] *Oregon Journal*, June 6, 1912, p. 8, col. 1.

Finally, it is feared by friends of the system that its overuse will bring reaction and endanger its existence. "To the present numerous enemies, open and secret, of the initiative, there may be added many present friends who will become disgusted with the miscellaneous and futile flood of measures offered. Speaking as a proved defender of the system, *The Journal* looks upon the growing number of ballot measures as a matter of more or less gravity. It fully realizes that a time might come when its enemies could muster greater numerical strength than could its friends and the system be either scuttled or abandoned."[1]

Of course the same excesses may be found in the legislative assembly, and this is some comfort to the friends of direct legislation.[2]

3

The Causes and the Remedies

Many measures have appeared on the ballot because under the terms of the constitution the approval of the voters is required in such cases. This is true of all the measures, except two acts, referred to the people by the legislative assembly. And the adverse action of the people at a previous election upon similar proposals made the final enactment of these two measures by the assembly impracticable. The initiative was the only method under the provision of law then in force, for the determination of the numerous county-division proposals which were submitted to the voters.

Many other measures have come before the people on account of the "sins of omission" or the "sins of commission" of the legislative assembly.[3]

A feeling that, at least in some matters of legislation, the people are, under any circumstances, better qualified than the assembly has doubtless caused some use of direct legislation. "I

---

[1] *Oregon Journal*, June 6, 1912, p. 8, col. 1. [2] *Cf. ibid.*, Mar. 8, 1908, p. 8, col. 3.
[3] *Below*, pp. 159–63.

The Multiplicity of Measures 83

have decided that the cause of good roads will be advanced rather than checked if highway bills are given to the initiative rather than to the legislature. . . . I am of the firm opinion that the laws for roads should be put up to the people. It is a matter of greatest importance, and one affecting the interests of every man, woman and child in the state. Therefore, I believe the people should be given the best opportunity to express their desires in so important a matter. Undoubtedly the initiative furnishes the best opportunity." [1]

Part of the ballot's burden has been due to the desire to demonstrate that the system of direct legislation is all that has been claimed for it by its supporters. "We should do something with the power as soon as possible, and should continue doing. When a farm machinery agent has a good machine, he always wants you to see it work in the field. We believe our new machine is a good one for making laws. Let us offer the field tests. . . . Where we have direct legislation we should show that it really is in practice all that in theory it promises to be. Perhaps no measure that is offered to the people will win the first time, but that is not the point — the important thing to do is to show that the people can and will use it." [2] "It was but natural that everybody should desire to see the system tried out." [3]

Doubtless some of the overuse of the system has been due to "overstrained logic." [4] "There is always temptation to ride a good horse to death." [5]

Perhaps the "newness" of the initiative and referendum may still explain some of their use. "It is the bent of the race to always overuse a new thing. . . . When the right of referendum and initiative was given the people it was but natural that they would be tempted to overuse the new power. The newness

[1] Governor West, quoted in *Oregon Journal*, Sept. 29, 1911, p. 1, col. 5. *Below,* pp. 159–63.   [2] W. S. U'Ren, *Direct Legislation Record*, vol. 7, p. 60 (1901).
[3] *Oregon Journal*, July 6, 1914, p. 6, col. 1.
[4] *Oregonian*, Aug. 30, 1909, p. 6, col. 1.
[5] *Oregon Journal*, Apr. 5, 1909, p. 8, col. 2.

will presently wear off and then the resort to either will not be undertaken except in cases of great provocation or unusual necessity."[1]

Haste to secure the enactment of law is another motive for substituting direct legislation for action by the legislature, especially in the case of constitutional amendments. For several months can thus be saved in case of statutes, and two years in case of constitutional amendments.

As above explained,[2] the extreme ease of securing signatures to petitions heretofore has been a condition most favorable to the lengthening of the ballot. If this condition were remedied, it would seem that the causes which operate to bring legislative measures before the people would not generally result in the submission of an unreasonable number of measures at the elections.

But in the absence of reform in this direction, it has been seriously proposed to place arbitrary limitations upon the number of measures, particularly initiative measures, allowed at any election, and upon the resubmission of measures once defeated. It has been suggested that only three or five bills shall be allowed on the ballot, and only one, two or three constitutional amendments, or that no more than a dozen measures all together shall be allowed, and that measures offered shall take precedence according to excess number of signatures or according to the order of filing.[3]

But these proposals have met with little favor. It is clear that under provisions for precedence of measures in order of filing the legislature or special interests might so load the ballot as largely or completely to destroy the practical value of the system of direct legislation.[4] Precedence in accordance with the excess number of signatures would of course be absurd.

The reappearance of especially the woman's suffrage amend-

[1] *Oregon Journal*, Apr. 5, 1909, p. 8, col. 2.   [2] Pp. 54–8.
[3] H. Heaton, *Oregon Journal*, May 26, 1908, p. 8, col. 6; C. H. Carey, *New Responsibilities of Citizenship*, Proceedings of the Oregon Bar Association, 1908–10, pp. 18, 32–3. C. H. Chapman and others, *Introductory Letter*, 1909, p. 13; S. A. Lowell, *Oregon Journal*, Nov. 19, 1912, p. 6, col. 1.
[4] *Cf. Oregonian*, Jan. 7, 1913, p. 8, col. 2; *Oregon Journal*, Jan. 8, 1913, p. 8, col. 1.

The Multiplicity of Measures 85

ment and the "single-tax" propositions at succeeding elections has been the cause of a plan to prohibit the resubmission of proposals once defeated at an election for a given period — six years, eight years, ten years.[1] The prohibition of the resubmission of the *same measure* would of course easily be defeated by redrafting the measure.[2] But it has also been suggested that the *substance* of the defeated measure shall not be incorporated into another during the specified period.[3] But of course any such limitation would be an unbearable obstacle to the expression of change in public opinion.[4]

A requirement that initiative measures should first be submitted to the legislative assembly[5] might, through the acceptance of the measures by the assembly, decrease to some extent the number of measures submitted to the people. Further, some reduction of the present amount of constitutional restriction upon action by the assembly, practicable on account of the alternative check now supplied by the referendum,[6] would tend to the same result.

"The only apparent relief for the present portentous situation, and the only way out of a serious dilemma, which everyone recognizes and all are anxious to avoid, is to vote down all miscellaneous legislation for which there is not an ascertainable demand from the people and for which there is a method open besides the initiative and referendum."[7]

---

[1] *House Joint Resolution*, 1909, no. 4; *Senate Bill*, 1913, no. 32; debate in house of representatives, *Oregonian*, Feb. 16, 1909, p. 7, col. 3; debate in senate, *Oregon Journal*, Jan. 22, 1913, p. 5, col. 5; C. H. Carey, *Oregon Journal*, Nov. 20, 1913, p. 16, col. 2; *Oregonian*, Jan. 12, 1913, sec. 3, p. 6, col. 3.

[2] Debate in senate, *Oregon Journal*, Jan. 22, 1913, p. 5, col. 5; *East Oregonian*, quoted in *Oregonian*, Jan. 12, 1913, p. 6, col. 3.

[3] *House Joint Resolution*, 1909, no. 4; *Oregonian*, Jan. 12, 1913, sec. 3, p. 6, col. 3. "Any measure rejected by the people, through the provisions of the initiative and referendum, cannot be again proposed by the initiative within three years thereafter by less than twenty-five per centum of the legal voters." Oklahoma *Constitution*, art. 5, sec. 6 (1907). "The same measure, either in form or in essential substance, shall not be submitted to the people by initiative petition (either affirmatively or negatively) oftener than once in three years." Nebraska *Constitution*, art. 3, sec. 10 (1912).   [4] *Cf. Oregon Journal*, Jan. 17, 1913, p. 8, col. 2.   [5] *Below*, pp. 164-5.

[6] *Below*, pp. 171-2.   [7] *Oregonian*, Aug. 8, sec. 1912, sec. 3, p. 4, col. 1.

CHAPTER VIII

CAMPAIGN ORGANIZATION

THE campaign in favor of initiative and referendum movements naturally comes for the most part from the parties — associations or individuals (usually backed by associations [1]) — who originated the respective movements. But aid in their campaign comes from other associations or individuals interested. In some cases, support, including substantial financial contributions, has come from "foreign" sources. This is notably true in the case of the "people's power" measures, and the "single-tax" measures.[2]

The opposition of movements to initiate or refer measures is, in general, not nearly as well organized as the promotion, and in some cases there is no organized opposition at all. At every election there is apprehension that some measures will pass "by default," and this may have actually occurred at times. Organized opposition is on the same general lines as that of the promotion of movements. Permanent associations — the People's Power League, the State Grange, the State Federation of Labor, business organizations, commercial clubs, alumni associations, etc., have led active campaigns of opposition. The Oregon State Association Opposed to the Extension of Suffrage to Women was organized permanently to combat the woman's suffrage movement. Temporary organizations, like the People's Higher Education League, for the university interests, and the Greater Home Rule Association, in opposition to the prohibition movement, are sometimes formed. Occasionally a few individuals, or a lone individual, presents opposition arguments in the voters' pamphlet.

[1] *Above*, pp. 16–18.   [2] *Below*, pp. 89–90.

CHAPTER IX

FINANCE

THE cost of promoting initiative and referendum measures includes legal services in drafting measures, printing measures, the making, verification, and filing of petitions, the publication of arguments in the voters' pamphlet, expenses for letters, circulars, office management, speakers, etc. It is the same for opposition except that there is no cost for petitions. The items, of course, vary with the different measures and the different promoters.

It is often impossible to obtain accurate information in regard to expenditures in the promotion or opposition of measures. The corrupt practices act of 1908 requires that persons spending more than fifty dollars to aid in the approval or defeat of a measure before the people shall, after the election, file with the secretary of state an itemized statement of receipts and expenditures for every sum paid in excess of five dollars.[1] But, although there has recently been improvement in complying with the law, in many cases no statements whatever have been filed, and in other cases statements are not at all reliable.[2]

However, from official and other sources, it appears that expenditures generally vary from a few hundred dollars to many thousands of dollars. The direct primary law of 1904 cost its

[1] *Laws*, 1909, ch. 3, sec. 12; *Lord's Oregon Laws*, sec. 3497.

[2] As an aid in securing complete returns, it has been suggested that persons proposing to spend money on measures before the voters should be required to file a statement of such intention *before* the election, just as candidates for office are required to file a declaration of intention. Reported in *Oregonian*, Dec. 4, 1912, p. 18, col. 3. See *House Bill*, 1913, no. 365; *above*, pp. 15–16.

88 Initiative, Referendum, and Recall in Oregon

promoters $1710.52.[1] The State Federation of Labor and the Portland Labor Council spent together $1070.33 on the employers' liability bill of 1910. The woman suffrage amendment of 1912 cost its friends and opponents together $15,775.85. The heaviest expenditures have been incurred in promoting and opposing "prohibition" and the "single tax."

In regard to such expenditures, one of much experience in this connection writes thus: "If petitions are secured by voluntary solicitors the cost is not much, if any, below that of paid solicitors. The clerical work, postage, etc., is greater in cost and if traveling expense, to secure by personal solicitation and lectures these voluntary circulators, is necessary — as it usually is — the expenses may be very great. It does not take much in the printing line to run up a $100 printing bill, and $50 postage will not cover very much correspondence and mailing of circulars. By starting in early an initiative petition may be secured through paid circulators for about $350 to $500 plus some printing, and legal services in drawing up the bill. But it is more likely to total $700 to $1000 if all services are paid for. . . . A great many people never stop to think that to stamp, mail, and print a circular and enclose it with a personal letter takes about 5 cents each, or more if allowance is made for clerical work. Blank petitions cost for postage alone by the time they are returned filled with names over 10 cents each, and many more must be printed than sufficient to just cover the legal number of names required by law. Meetings and traveling expenses eat

[1]
Postage	$ 284.35
Legal services	111.20
Telephone and telegraph	45.76
Traveling expenses	31.65
Printing	358.25
Envelopes	57.00
Canvassers	483.36
Folders from Michigan League	8.05
Mailing folders and circulars, etc.	106.75
Office and miscellaneous	35.15
Total	$1710.52

Oregonian, July 9, 1904, p. 6, col. 1.

up money very rapidly if indulged in. The sacrifice of time made by volunteers is very great and cannot be estimated."[1]

In addition to the expenditures incurred by the promoters and opponents of measures, there are large expenditures incurred by the state under the system of direct legislation. In 1914 the cost of the voters' pamphlet[2] alone to the state was $12,873.40 — a considerable reduction from previous expenditure. Moreover, direct legislation has materially increased the size of the ballot and the labor of canvassing the election returns, and has thus added materially to the cost of elections.

"It is believed in official circles that, once the law is put to the test and the people have an opportunity to realize the enormous expense attached, it will be no easy matter to invoke the initiative and referendum upon any measures except those of extraordinary importance or which are construed to be vicious or detrimental to the interests of the commonwealth."[3] But, in fact, such considerations have so far apparently had very little effect.

The parties directly concerned with the measures advance funds for the campaign, and subscriptions are solicited from all kinds of sources. Public-welfare organizations tax themselves for various causes. The Fels Fund Commission, a "foreign" organization, has contributed many thousands of dollars to the campaign for progressive and radical movements, with special interest in the "single-tax" propositions. This has aroused bitter opposition in some directions, and a cry for "home rule in Oregon" has been raised. "There is in Oregon a coterie of paid employes of an eastern organization. The object and purpose of that organization is to impose somewhere in the United States untried experiments in government and untested theories in economics. Oregon with its wide open initiative is a fertile field for its operations. Therefore, it has dumped its wealth into Oregon. It has provided its employes with a war chest, collected in this and foreign countries, with which to pay for literature,

---

[1] A. D. Cridge, *Oregon Journal*, Jan. 20, 1914, p. 6, col. 4.
[2] *Below*, pp. 93–4.   [3] *Oregonian*, Apr. 15, 1907, p. 5, col. 1.

speakers, and petition shovers. It has compelled property owners of Oregon to contribute to a fund to defend against invasion of their property rights."[1] "There is need of a law which will prevent foreign organizations and residents of other states from employing attorneys or lawgivers to draft initiative measures, paying the stipends of petition hawkers, hiring press agents, spending vast sums for literature in behalf of their own and against other specific measures and in contributing to the success or defeat of state or local candidates for office. Efforts in behalf of economic theories or principles when directed from without should cease at a certain point and that point should be when a measure or the representative of a political policy is before the people and there through the effort of Oregon citizens. There is no better reason for permitting organizations or persons that have no citizenship interests in Oregon to force consideration of measures or aid in the election or defeat of measures or candidates than there is for permitting them to sign the petitions or participate in the balloting."[2]

This view was the cause of an attempt made in the legislative assembly of 1913 to enact a law making it a crime to receive any money from without the state for assistance in the adoption or defeat of any measure submitted by the initiative.[3]

Under the corrupt practices act[4] the amount of money to be spent by candidates for office is limited, but no limitations are placed upon the expenditure for initiative or referendum measures. In order "to put the poor man on an equality with the rich man" in this regard, it was claimed,[5] an attempt was made in the legislative assembly of 1913 to place strict limitation upon the amount of expenditure in case of any initiative measure,[6] but the proposition was not accepted.

---

[1] *Oregonian*, July 5, 1912, p. 10, col. 1.   [2] *Ibid.*, Dec. 5, 1912, p. 10, col. 1.

[3] *Senate Bill*, 1913, no. 125. There was no intention of limiting contributions to campaigns prior to the actual filing of measures. *Cf. Oregonian*, Jan. 26, 1913, sec. 3, p. 6, col. 3.   [4] *Laws*, 1909, ch. 3, sec. 8; *Lord's Oregon Laws*, sec. 3494.

[5] E. E. Blanchard, quoted in *Oregon Journal*, Jan. 17, 1913, p. 20, col. 2.

[6] *House Bill*, 1913, no. 103.

CHAPTER X

THE EDUCATION OF THE VOTE

I

The Study of Measures

THE grave responsibility which the people have imposed upon themselves by the adoption of the system of direct legislation is continually emphasized by the press and on the platform. "The people of Oregon are to determine for themselves great problems deeply concerning their welfare. A single mistake will be serious; several mistakes will be unfortunate; a series of mistakes — and there is opportunity for them — will be disastrous. It behooves the voter to begin now the most careful and thorough consideration of the initiative and referendum measures, that his action in November may be informed, deliberate, judicious and safe."[1] "He must first learn the fact that he is one of a large legislative body empowered to enact laws and amend the constitution, then to be as painstaking and as honest as he expects and demands a member of the state legislature should be."[2] But with the steadily increasing burden of the ballot the proper consideration by the great mass of the voters of all the measures submitted, many of them extremely complex, has become an absolute impossibility,[3] and thus any serious study of the measures is more or less discouraged. Although probably great numbers of voters give all the consideration to the questions before them which could be reasonably

[1] *Oregonian*, May 11, 1912, p. 10, col. 1.
[2] Woodburn *Independent*, reprinted in *Oregonian*, Jan. 25, 1908, p. 8, col. 5.
[3] *Above*, pp. 78–82.

expected, it is certain that very many others give little or no attention to them. Some voters shift the responsibility of decision upon others whose opinions or whose standing they respect.[1] Others must vote wholly or partly at random.

That any trouble at all on the part of the voters to inform themselves upon the issues of the election is necessary has even been denied upon the ground that the manner in which one decides the question as to how he should vote upon a measure depends wholly upon his temperament and not at all "upon the degree of his intelligence or of his information relating to it," as is shown by the fact that the most intelligent and best informed persons may be found on opposite sides of the same question.[2] There is another heretical doctrine to the effect that the proper consideration of all the measures by the voters presents no serious difficulty. "Each is printed in full three months before election in the state pamphlet, and is either self-explanatory, or is accompanied by arguments pro and con. In addition, the advocates and opponents of the measures indulge in state-wide campaigns in the press and on the stump. It doesn't take very much time or very much brains to go over the measures and arrive at a decision."[3] At any rate, it is maintained, the difficulties here are at least less than in the intelligent choice of public officers.[4]

---

[1] "In all our work we have found the great value of well-known names attached to our measures as officers or members of committees. Though not all of our friends were able to give much time, their names worked for them. You see, the average voter is too indolent, too busy, or too distrustful of his own judgment to study or decide for himself upon the details of a law on a great public question. People always ask of a proposition to enact a principle they approve, 'Who is back of it?' If they find it endorsed by men whose reputation would forbid them to allow the use of their names with any unpractical, improper, or sinister law to apply the principle, they promptly conclude that it is right and worthy of support." W. S. U'Ren, quoted by L. Pease, *Initiative and Referendum — Oregon's "Big Stick,"* Pacific Monthly, vol. 17, pp. 563, 574–5 (1907). See *below*, pp. 98–9.

[2] T. T. Greer, *Oregonian*, Jan. 6, 1914, p. 6, col. 6.

[3] *Medford Mail Tribune*, reprinted in Eugene *Guard*, Oct. 15, 1912, p. 4, col. 5.

[4] "As a matter of fact it is much easier and requires much less knowledge and acumen to determine whether a proposed measure is what one wants to vote for

2

The Means of Information

At first the state did not undertake, for the benefit of the voters, the publication of information on the measures submitted, but provision was made for distribution to the voters, through the secretary of state and the county clerks, at public expense, of pamphlet arguments offered by parties interested in measures and of copies of the measures to the voters.[1]

The law of 1907 provides for an official state publication generally known as "the voters' pamphlet." Not later than the ninetieth day before a general election and not later than thirty days before a special election at which any measures are to be submitted to the voters, the secretary of state is required to send to each registered voter a copy of the pamphlet, printed under his direction, containing the title and text of each measure, with the number and form in which the ballot title will be printed and the arguments which may have been filed regarding the measures. Only the person filing an initiative petition is allowed space in the pamphlet for arguments favoring the measure, but any one may insert arguments opposing it, and any one may insert arguments either for or against any referendum measure. The cost of paper and printing for the arguments — for the election of 1914 thirty-four dollars and thirteen cents for each page of the pamphlet — is borne by the persons presenting the arguments.[2]

---

than to make an equally well advised decision about a candidate. It is easier to tell whether the general purpose and intent of a measure is acceptable or not, and a month or two of hostile criticism — the only true test — is pretty likely to disclose any serious defects in detail. On the other hand, the public is notoriously subject to be deceived as to the genuineness of a man's professions. What a man really represents is known only to him and his Maker, and his future conduct in detail under new and untried conditions is past finding out." R. W. Montague, *Oregon System at Work, National Municipal Review*, vol. 3, pp. 256, 267 (1914).

[1] *Laws*, 1903, p. 244, sec. 8.

[2] *Laws*, 1907, ch. 226, sec. 8; *Laws*, 1913, ch. 359, sec. 4. It has been proposed that two pages for affirmative and two for negative arguments should be provided at

There is at present no limitation upon the amount of space in the pamphlet given to arguments other than this expense to the persons presenting them. With the steady increase of the number of measures submitted the size of the pamphlet has increased, until at the election of 1912 it contained two hundred and fifty-two pages. The reduction of the size of the pamphlet of 1914 to one hundred and ten pages was due largely to the disposal of the statutes of the assembly of 1913 referred by petition at the special election held for the purpose that year, and some condensation of form and the use of smaller type. It may possibly become necessary to limit the amount of matter of arguments for any one person or any one measure.[1] So far the pamphlet has contained affirmative arguments for nearly two-thirds of the measures submitted, and negative arguments for only a little over two-fifths of the measures.[2] It is seldom that more than one argument on a side is filed. At the session of the legislative assembly in 1913, it was proposed to make the attorney general a sort of *advocatus diaboli* against measures lacking negative arguments.[3]

The pamphlet arguments vary in length, but most of them are short and to the point. They have great variety of merit. The arguments are partisan statements, and could not reasonably be expected to be otherwise. However, some downright misstatements of fact in the pamphlets constitute an abuse which it seems impossible to correct.[4]

the expense of the state. *House Bill*, 1913, no. 365. It is customary for the secretary of state to furnish proofs of affirmative arguments upon request of parties desiring them, and he will furnish certified copies of the arguments, as public records at the legal rate; but there is no express provision of law relating to the matter. *Cf. Oregonian*, July 15, 1912, p. 6, col. 2; July 18, 1912, p. 2, col. 4.

[1] *Cf.* G. H. Haynes, *Education of Voters, Political Science Quarterly*, vol. 22, pp. 484, 495–7 (1907).

[2] In some cases arguments have been filed too late for publication, under terms of the law.

[3] "If no argument shall be offered against a measure, the attorney general shall prepare a statement of not more than two pages setting forth the reasons why said measure should be rejected by the people." *House Bill*, 1913, no. 365, sec. 7.

[4] Official censorship has been suggested. Eugene *Register*, Nov. 15, 1912, p. 4,

The Education of the Vote

The pamphlet is the only means available to the great majority of voters for getting a first-hand knowledge of the measure submitted, and is the only source of information on the measures which may be expected to reach all the voters, or rather all the registered voters of the state.[1]

The extent to which the voters in general make use of the pamphlet is very uncertain. The size of the document as well as other difficulties certainly discourage many voters and keep them from reading it at all. Probably not one person in hundreds reads the whole of the pamphlet or any considerable part of it even in a cursory manner, much less makes a thorough study of much of its contents. But the pamphlet is used a great deal for reference to supplement other sources of information, and has probably had most of its usefulness in this direction. Moreover, the arguments in the pamphlet are published in condensed form by newspapers, and thus reach many voters.

The only other official sources of information on measures are the "sample ballots" and the ballots voted at the election. Probably very many voters *read* nothing else in regard to the measures except the ballot title.[2] Voters have been known in some cases — probably very few — to spend from one to two hours in the voting booths. And, although the mere identification of the numerous measures, under the method of writing ballot titles employed until recently, has, in the absence of proper de-

---

col. 1. Penalty and forfeiture of bonds is another suggestion. Klamath Falls *Northwestern*, reprinted in Eugene *Register*, Nov. 28, 1912, p. 4, col. 1.

"If in the opinion of the secretary of state any argument for or against any measure offered for filing contains any obscene, vulgar, profane, scandalous, libelous, defamatory or treasonable matter or any language tending to provoke crime or a breach of the peace, or any language or matter the circulation of which is prohibited by any act of congress, the secretary of state shall refuse to file such argument: *Provided*, That the person submitting such argument for filing may appeal to a board of censors consisting of the governor, the attorney general and the superintendent of public instruction, and the decision of a majority of such board shall be final." Washington *Laws*, 1913, ch. 138, sec. 26.

[1] It has been proposed to eliminate all those voters who have not registered from voting on measures, "of which they can have but scanty information." Reported in *Oregonian*, Oct. 19, 1912, p. 6, col. 2. [2] *Below*, pp. 208–9.

vices used by the voter, required a great deal of time, it is probable that in these cases the voter has spent most of his time "studying" the measures as described by their titles.[1]

By far the most influential source of information for the voters is the public press. Some of the newspapers published at Portland have an especially great influence, but the local press as well plays a great part in determining the results of the election. Even the state papers disclaim any attempt thoroughly to discuss *all* of the measures submitted, and many measures receive but little attention from the press. But questions of large policy in which the public is most deeply interested are discussed at length in probably all the papers. At times papers expressly decline to give any opinion whatever on subjects which they consider unsuited for decision by the people.[2]

The discussion of the questions by the press begins with the circulation of the petitions, and ends only with the election. Editorials, some of great length, and briefer comments upon measures are abundant. Cartoons relating to measures appear frequently. Just before the election it is customary for both state and local papers to give a column or so to a very brief statement of the nature of each measure, in ballot order, and at the same time to recommend approval or rejection. A still briefer "vest-pocket" edition also sometimes appears.[3] There is undoubtedly a great deal of reliance upon the press by the voters. Many of them clip out the brief lists of recommendations, and

[1] *Above*, pp. 51–3.

[2] "As a matter of duty to its readers, *The Oregonian*, prior to every election in which measures are to be submitted, details members of its staff to study the legislative issues. Not only is information obtained from public records, but frequently competent legal opinion is sought as to the effect of proposed laws or amendments." *Oregonian*, Dec. 8, 1913, p. 6, col. 2. But the editor, as well as the average voter, has difficulties. "The editor has been again wading through the Oregon political pamphlet in an attempt to form an intelligent judgment on the thirty-eight proposed . . . bills. He finds it absolutely impossible to do so. It is our shame that not one per cent of the voters at the polls in Oregon in November will be able to cast an intelligent ballot." Ashland *Tidings*, reprinted in *Oregonian*, Oct. 3, 1912, p. 10, col. 2.   [3] *Below*, pp. 275–9.

take them to the polls. Some make no secret of the fact that they vote the list exactly as recommended. In addition to the discussions which authoritatively express the policy of the newspapers, the papers contain a great deal of discussion upon measures in the form of letters to the editor, special articles, and debates. Some measures are thus discussed in the papers from almost every conceivable point of view.

For years the state library has collected information upon measures submitted, and this information has been made available to both individuals and associations.

It has been proposed that some sort of an official advisory commission should be established whose duty it should be to study the measures submitted and make recommendations upon them for distribution to the voters.[1]

Associations of all descriptions have an important part in the education of the vote in direct legislation. Permanently organized bodies, like the bar associations, granges, labor unions, commercial clubs, good-government clubs, literary associations, church organizations, etc., etc., study and discuss the measures, and sometimes publish recommendations to the voters.[2] A huge mass of "resolutions" on the merits of questions come from innumerable associations. In probably most of these cases, however, the "resolution" has been written by outside parties interested in the particular measure, and the passing of the resolution is probably generally a mere perfunctory act. Temporary organizations are sometimes formed for the special purpose of preparing for the election. Neighborhood gatherings for the discussion of measures are customary, both in town and country, and "mass meetings" are held for the same purpose.

There is a great deal of discussion of questions before the voters in ordinary conversation. The persons particularly interested in the measures proposed carry on a campaign of education by means of pamphlets, circular letters, individual letters, hand

[1] D. J. Beasly, *Oregonian*, Feb. 2, 1913, p. 6, col. 5. *Above*, p. 30.
[2] *Below*, pp. 266–74, 280–8.

H

bills, advertisements in the newspapers, etc.[1] Written argument is supplemented to a considerable extent by public addresses and debates and addresses before all sorts of organizations. There has been some house to house canvassing in behalf of certain measures.

These various influences have been estimated to be of such importance as to have developed a system of "representative government" in direct legislation. "The truth is that the initiative and referendum have developed in Oregon into a representative system of lawmaking. Probably fewer than one-tenth of the voters make a systematic study of proposed legislation. The hard work in that respect is done by the committees of the Grange and other farmers' organizations, by labor federation committees, by leaders in tax organizations and other leagues. The ordinary voter pins his faith to the judgment of some society, of which there are many, when it comes to matters of ordinary legislation. The press performs an important function. Each newspaper gives its advice and each has a large clientele that accepts its decisions. On questions like prohibition, capital punishment or woman's suffrage the voter thinks for himself, but on the piffling laws with which theorists, schemers and some honest but misguided enthusiasts burden the ballot somebody else does the voters' thinking for them. Oregon has two legislatures of a representative type. One is the duly elected, responsible assembly that meets for forty days in each biennium. The other is a non-elective volunteer body of public advisers each integral part of which works independently and has a constituency of uncertain and varying proportions. The chief

[1] The corrupt practices act requires that all paid advertisements in newspapers shall be marked as such, and that all circulars, etc., shall bear the names of author and printer. *Laws*, 1909, ch. 3, secs. 33, 35; *Lord's Oregon Laws*, secs. 3517, 3519.

"The management of the recent ["graduated-single-tax"] campaign has unquestionably overestimated the value of indiscriminate distribution of literature. Experience has taught us that literature is of little or no value unless preceded by some kind of a personal overture. Thousands of dollars have been literally thrown away in the distribution of reading matter that was never taken out of its wrapper." Letter in *Oregonian*, Dec. 8, 1912, sec. 2, p. 6, col. 1.

difference in their operations is that the one does its own voting and the other tells the people how to vote. The present and many preceding generations in America have grown up under a representative form of government. It is a difficult thing to abandon. Oregon has not done so except on fundamental questions. The multitudinous laws and amendments on the Oregon ballot which give uneasiness elsewhere where direct legislation is in prospect are in fact approved or rejected by a roundabout representative system. A great many in Oregon do not yet realize this fact, but they will in time." [1]

The legislative assembly of course has greater opportunities for the proper consideration of legislation than the voters can generally have, but these opportunities under conditions that have prevailed in the past have not, unfortunately, been used to their full extent, and hence there is widespread opinion that the advantage is rather with the people. "I have heard more than one member of the legislature declare, as the press and tumult of the session began to distract him, that he believed the initiative method with its prolonged and searching discussions during the campaign before the voters was a better way to make laws than he was attempting to practice." [2]

3

The Results of Education

The actual amount of knowledge of the issues involved which is gained by the voters from the various available sources of information is of course problematical. Some views of the matter are very pessimistic. "After all the discussions of the initiative and referendum propositions it is doubtful whether one voter in ten has distinct ideas about most of them. Legislation after

[1] *Oregonian*, May 6, 1914, p. 10, col. 3. *Cf. above*, p. 92, note 1.
[2] R. W. Montague, *Oregon System at Work*, *National Municipal Review*, vol. 3, pp. 256, 266 (1914). See also J. Bourne, *Initiative, Referendum and Recall*, *Atlantic Monthly*, vol. 109, pp. 122, 127 (1909).

this manner is a leap in the dark." [1] Other views are more cheerful. But whatever may be the difference of opinion as to the amount of knowledge obtained by the voters, there is general agreement in the view that the educational effect of the campaign is of very great value. "It takes time to educate a people into fitness for self-government. We are not completely fit, no doubt, but the very use of this privilege and power will make the people more fit, constantly and even rapidly." [2] "It keeps the average citizen in touch with current legislation. It brings home to the average citizen the duty and responsibility of helping make laws. It awakens every citizen's mind to a realization of factorship in state concerns. Nobody knows how much benefit has already come to the men of Oregon by the reflection and study incident to initiative law making. Nobody knows how many average minds are now grappling with current problems who never did so in the old days, because all our law making and all our public thinking was done for us by proxy. Nobody knows the full extent of the informative influence exercised on tens of thousands of voters by perusal and study of the measures in the state pamphlet and in the reflection incident to determining whether to vote for or against the various measures." [3]

[1] *Oregonian*, June 1, 1908, p. 8, col. 4. "Since receiving the book of laws to be voted upon this fall, I have been trying to post myself upon the miscellaneous measures therein in order to vote intelligently upon the same. I frankly admit that I feel incompetent to perform the duty properly. I have talked to others — some who have intelligence above the average — and they have admitted their incompetency also, principally because it is out of their line of business." S. V. Rehart, *Oregonian*, Sept. 30, 1912, p. 8, col. 6.   [2] *Oregon Journal*, Feb. 29, 1908, p. 6, col. 2.
[3] *Ibid.*, Aug. 30, 1912, p. 8, col. 1.

CHAPTER XI

THE VOTE IN DIRECT LEGISLATION

I

The Interest in Elections

"THAT voting in an election is a patriotic duty that no man should neglect has long been urged upon the electorate. But there is even stronger reason why the people should vote on direct legislation. Election to office is a contest between two or more candidates. The voter who stays away from the polls divides his vote equally among the several candidates. Oregon state and county elections have developed largely into a popularity test between personalities. The office will be filled and the business of the government carried on in spite of widespread dereliction in the exercise of the franchise. An initiative measure or one subjected to the referendum, on the other hand, is an issue in itself. We either adopt it or reject it. We either accept its virtues or its evils or we deprive ourselves wholly of them. Failure of many to vote leaves the control of government affairs, in sometimes unsuspected instances, to a compact group or class that is actually in the minority. Indifference of the majority, or its failure to discern the significance of a proposed law, may wreak disaster upon the majority or give the minority special advantages or privileges to which it is not entitled." [1]

But that the voters are not as much interested in the enactment of direct legislation as they are in the choice of officers clearly appears from the fact that when officers and measures

[1] *Oregonian*, Sept. 10, 1912, p. 8, col. 1.

are voted upon at the same election — which has been the case at every election under the new system except the special election of 1913 — on the average only seventy-three per cent of the total vote cast at the election is received by a measure, in contrast to the average of eighty-eight per cent received by an officer. Further, at the special election of 1913, when no officers were elected,[1] the total vote cast on the measures was only seventy-one per cent of the total vote cast at the election the year before, although since then the extension of the suffrage to women had increased the electorate probably over forty per cent. "It has been suggested that this, at worst, results only in a kind of natural selection of the intelligent and interested — an oligarchy of the thoughtful, which some believe to be the goal of politics."[2]

There is much variation of interest shown in the particular measures appearing on the ballot. The greatest variation appears in the election of 1910, when the highest number of votes cast on a measure was eighty-eight per cent of the total votes cast at the election, and the lowest sixty-one per cent.

The chief interest of the voters, so far as this is indicated by the percentages of votes cast on the various measures, is in matters of general state policy — liquor legislation, woman's suffrage, the "single-tax," etc.; and their least concern is generally with matters of a special local nature, as county divisions, with technical questions, as the details of tax administration, and with complex subjects, as the reorganization of the legislative department. Progressive and even radical measures at times receive low percentages of the votes cast when the measures are much involved, and this has happened even where single issues have been submitted in such cases.[3]

---

[1] Except local officers in some places.

[2] R. W. Montague, *Oregon System at Work*, *National Municipal Review*, vol. 3, pp. 256, 268 (1914).

[3] Why the constitutional amendment for the local initiative and referendum received the least number of votes cast on measures at the election of 1906 does not appear.

Although promoters of initiative and referendum movements sometimes are anxious that their measures should be filed in time to get "good places" on the ballot, there is no evidence that the place on the ballot has anything to do with the consideration of a measure by the voters.

2

Minority versus *Majority*

From a study of the votes for the measures which have been approved at the several elections, it appears that of the fifty-one measures which received a majority of the votes cast on the particular measure, only nineteen, or a little under two-fifths of these measures, received a majority of the votes cast at the election. The majority is generally reduced as the number of measures on the ballot increases.

For years there has been complaint, especially in regard to the initiative, that the provision which permits the passage of measures submitted to the people by the majority of the votes cast on the particular measure instead of the majority of all the votes cast at the election, and thus puts into effect legislation approved by only a minority of the voters, substitutes minority rule for majority rule as a principle of government.[1] Accordingly, in 1912, proposals for constitutional amendments were submitted to the people, which provided, one for the approval of all constitutional amendments, the other for the approval of all initiative measures, by the majority of all the votes cast at the election.[2]

---

[1] *E.g., Oregonian*, Feb. 18, 1908, p. 8, col. 1; *Referendum Pamphlet*, 1912, pp. 85–6.
[2] *Referendum Pamphlet*, 1912, nos. 310, 322, pp. 31, 83. Earlier proposals: A. T. Buxton, *Oregonian*, May 15, 1908, p. 6, col. 3; *Oregon Journal*, Nov. 22, 1908, sec. 5, p. 6, col. 2; proposed Grange resolution, *Oregonian*, May 13, 1909, p. 6, col. 3; *House Joint Resolution*, 1911, no. 11. "Any measure referred to the people by the initiative shall take effect and be in force when it shall have been approved by a majority of the votes cast in such election. Any measure referred to the people by the referendum shall take effect and be in force when it shall have been approved

In favor of the amendments, it was urged that under the present system the indifferent voters are virtually counted in favor of the measure; that in the presence of any real popular demand for legislation there would be no difficulty in securing the majority of all the votes cast at the election; and appeal was made to the precedent established in case of the legislative assembly, where the votes of a majority of all members of each house are required for the enactment of legislation.[1]

But the proposals were fiercely attacked as attempts toward the destruction of popular government.[2] Such a regulation, it was urged, in substance makes every vote *not* cast on any measure a vote against it, and allows the fate of that measure to be decided by the negligence and indifference of the non-voters, instead of by the intelligent vote of electors who have taken sufficient interest in the measure to vote upon it.[3] Moreover, "indifferent voters would be encouraged to be more indifferent. Realizing that no-vote would be counted as a vote against a pending bill, the indifferent voter would take no trouble to examine it. Knowing that his vote would be counted against it, he would not give a whoop whether the bill was good or bad."[4] Further, it was declared that many really popular measures would have failed in the past under such majority requirements,

---

by a majority of the votes cast thereon and not otherwise." Oklahoma *Constitution*, art. 5, sec. 3 (1907). "All such measures shall become the law or a part of the constitution when approved by a majority of the votes cast thereon, provided, the votes cast in favor of said initiative measure or part of said constitution shall constitute thirty-five per cent of the total vote cast at said election, and not otherwise." Nebraska *Constitution*, art. 3, sec. 10 (1912). One-third. Washington *Constitution*, art. 21, sec. 1d (1912). At the election of 1914 the voters of Oregon defeated an attempt to prevent any "single-tax" legislation in the future, through a constitutional amendment which contained a provision that the section amended should not be amended or repealed except by a two-thirds vote of the electors voting upon the issue. *Referendum Pamphlet*, 1914, no. 356, p. 97.

[1] Majority Rule League, *Referendum Pamphlet*, 1912, pp. 85–6.

[2] *E.g., Oregon Journal*, Oct. 21, 1912, p. 8, col. 2.

[3] Taxpayers' League, *Oregonian*, Nov. 3, 1912, p. 15, col. 3; *Oregon Journal*, Oct. 3, 1912, p. 8, col. 2; Oct. 21, 1912, p. 8, col. 2.

[4] *Oregon Journal*, Oct. 3, 1912, p. 8, col. 2.

and the experience of Oklahoma was also cited to show the difficulties in the way of legislation under a similar provision.[1] It is certainly true that some of the measures which would have failed under the proposed majority requirements, as the local initiative and referendum amendment, the corrupt practices bill, the employers' liability bill, the presidential primary bill, and perhaps others, are now, at least, favored by most of the voters.

3

The Amount of Legislation Enacted

At the first election under the new system in 1904, all three of the measures submitted to the voters — a proposal for a constitutional amendment referred by the legislative assembly and two bills initiated by petition — were approved by the voters. At the election of 1906 eight measures — one bill referred by petition, three initiative bills and four initiative amendments — were approved, and three measures — two initiative bills and one initiative amendment — failed. Of the measures submitted at the election of 1908 — two amendments referred by the legislature, two acts referred by petition, five initiative bills and three initiative amendments — twelve in all, were approved, and the other seven — two amendments referred by the legislature, two acts referred by petition, and three initiative amendments — failed. Nine measures were approved in 1910 — one act referred by the legislature, four initiative bills, and four initiative amendments — and twenty-three failed, including four amendments and one act referred by the legislature, one act referred by petition, three initiative amendments, and fourteen initiative bills. At the election of 1912, eleven measures passed, including two amendments referred by the legislature, one act referred by petition, three initiative amendments, and five initiative bills; but

[1] *E.g.*, People's Power League, *Referendum Pamphlet*, 1912, pp. 34-5, 87-90. *Cf. Equity*, vol. 13, pp. 63-5 (1911), and, especially, W. F. Dodd, *Revision and Amendment of State Constitutions*, pp. 133-4, 185-200 (1910).

twenty-six measures failed, including four amendments referred by the legislature, two acts referred by petition, five initiative amendments and fifteen initiative bills. Four of the five acts referred by petition at the special election of 1913 were approved and the other rejected. Of the twenty-nine measures on the ballot at the election of 1914 — eight amendments and two acts submitted by the legislature, and twelve amendments and seven bills initiated by petition — only four were approved by the voters — two constitutional amendments submitted by the legislature and two initiated by petition.

In general, the greater the number of measures on the ballot the fewer in proportion are adopted at the election. But only four of the twenty-nine measures of 1914 were ratified, in comparison with the eleven of the thirty-seven measures of 1912.

Only fifty-one of the total of one hundred and thirty-six measures, or a little over one-third, were adopted by the voters. About the same proportion of statutes and of constitutional amendments were adopted, twenty-eight of the seventy-five statutes, and twenty-three of the sixty-one amendments. Further, it appears that eight of the twenty-seven measures submitted by the legislative assembly and eight of the fourteen measures referred from the assembly by petition, altogether sixteen of the forty-one measures, were adopted, and that thirty-five of the ninety-five initiative measures were adopted. That is, the promoters of initiative measures were sustained in nearly the same proportion of cases as was the legislative assembly.

The decreasing proportion of the measures adopted at the general elections is doubtless due chiefly to the voters' difficulty with the increasing burden of the ballot. "The people are tired," and many of them become more and more inclined to use their votes as a protest against the excessive use of direct legislation. The conservatives are congratulating themselves upon the fact that the abuse of direct legislation is thus "working out its own remedy."[1] But some meritorious and needed legislation has suffered from this attitude. "An overloaded ballot . . . is a menace to the fullest usefulness of direct legislation, for by presenting too great a task to the voters it invites a general determination to vote no regardless of the fact that many of the measures that are proposed may have considerable merit."[2]

But, as in the case of legislation by the representative assembly, the proper test of direct legislation does not lie in the *number* of measures enacted or defeated, but rather in the *character* of the measures enacted or defeated.[3]

4

The Rationality of the Vote

1. The Confusion of the Measure with the Referendum.

Voters have sometimes, perhaps often, confused the *referendum* with the *measure referred*, and so their votes have at times had the effect opposite to that intended. This situation has been considered serious enough to call for a proclamation of explanation of the matter to the voters by the secretary of state[4] and for numerous instructions by the press.

2. The Identification of Measures.

The inadequacy of ballot titles, especially considering the mass of measures submitted at the elections, in many cases has

[1] *Oregonian*, Nov. 6, 1914, p. 10, col. 1.
[2] Eugene *Register*, Nov. 7, 1914, p. 4, col. 1. *Below*, pp. 121-3.
[3] *Oregonian*, Jan. 26, 1911, p. 10, col. 3.
[4] "Probably the best guide for the voter to follow would be to ask himself the question: 'Am I in favor of the bill becoming a law?' If so he votes 'yes.' If he is not in favor of it becoming a law he should vote 'no.' The voter votes directly upon the measure before him, and not on the question of sustaining the referendum petition. Voters must bear in mind solely that if they are in favor of any measure they vote 'yes,' and if opposed to it they vote 'no.' This same question has arisen prior to other elections and it is not unlikely that many have voted contrary to their desires by reason of their not knowing how to properly mark the ballot." Ben W. Olcott, Secretary of State, Eugene *Register*, Nov. 4, 1913, p. 1, col. 5.

made the identification of measures on the ballot difficult,[1] and has thus caused confusion in voting. This has been true particularly in those cases in which two or more measures on the same subject have appeared on the ballot.

3. Knowledge of the Contents of Measures.

"We think the assertion may safely be ventured that it is only the few persons who earnestly favor or zealously oppose the passage of a proposed law initiated by petition who have attentively studied its contents and know how it will probably affect their private interests. The greater number of voters do not possess this information and usually derive their knowledge of the merits of a proposed law from an inspection of the title thereof, which is sometimes secured only from the very meager details afforded by a ballot which is examined in an election booth preparatory to exercising the right of suffrage."[2] "As a matter of fact, all our initiative laws are adopted or rejected on the sole basis of what can be expressed in the titles."[3] The actual amount of "law-making by titles" is doubtless greatly exaggerated by such statements, but it is certainly true that in some cases voters do, indeed, derive their knowledge of the contents of a proposed law "from an inspection of the title thereof."[4] And naturally voters have doubtless sometimes been thus mistaken as to the contents of measures before them. The amendment of 1910 to the local option liquor law, in spite of repeated warnings from press and pulpit, was certainly misunderstood, on account of its ballot title, by a large number of voters, and taken for a restriction of the liquor traffic instead of the opposite, and the amendment might not have been ap-

---

[1] *Above*, pp. 52-3. As an aid against confusion by the mass of measures on the ballot, it is very common for voters to take into the voting booth a "sample ballot" already marked, or a list of recommendations on measures clipped from a newspaper, or a marked list of the numbers of the measures to be voted on.

[2] *State* v. *Richardson, Oregon Reports*, vol. 48, pp. 309, 319 (1906).

[3] *Oregonian*, Nov. 25, 1911, p. 8, col. 1.

[4] And that inspection, too, apparently takes place only in the election booth in some cases. *Above*, pp. 95-6.

proved but for that error. Misleading titles in other measures — the Barlow road bill, the "taxpayers'" suffrage amendment — were apparently not so effective.[1]

In some other cases voters have been ignorant of essential provisions of the measures for which they have voted, at times because of their dependence on the title for their knowledge of the contents of the measure. And even the ballot title receives scant attention from many voters.

The case of the judicial amendment of 1910 is a striking illustration of this fact. This was popularly known as the "three-fourths jury amendment," and it is very probable that a very great majority of the voters were entirely ignorant of most of the other features of the measure. But the whole article of the constitution on the judiciary was involved. Says a justice of the supreme court (in office when the amendment was submitted): "Here is the situation: An important part of the constitution of this state has been changed, and no one . . . ever knew until after the vote was taken that it repealed an entire article of that most important document. It completely wiped out portions of that instrument to which no objection had ever been made, and without which it is impossible for the judicial arm of the state to get along only by presuming the existence of certain essential powers necessary to its proper exercise of the functions of the court." [2] As a matter of fact, the proposition had been discussed to some extent by the press, and even a glance over the ballot title should have disclosed proposals for important changes in the constitution. "The truth is, the issues involved and the consequences threatened, which were not of enough interest to such leaders of the bar as Judge Slater to cause them to read the newspaper discussions, were decidedly dull and abstruse to the ordinary voter. The voters wanted verdicts by three-fourths of the jury and they wanted technicalities swept away in consideration of appeals. They were told that the amendment would give them those two things. They decided

[1] *Above*, pp. 42–3. [2] W. T. Slater, *Oregonian*, Nov. 25, 1911, p. 8, col. 1.

the whole question and all its ramifications on the (to them) understandable factors it contained. They did not care for dry discussions of its other features. Generally they did not bother to read them." [1]

Another illustration of the concentration of the voters' attention upon one feature of a measure to the exclusion of other, and equally or more important features, is the vote on the "home-rule" tax amendment of 1910, above mentioned.[2] Both the poll tax and the home-rule provisions of that amendment were covered by the ballot title, and both were emphasized by the supporters of the amendment, but other very essential provisions of the measure were not indicated in the title. However, the poll-tax provision was probably the only part of the measure that was heeded by most of the voters. "We woke up to find that instead of abolishing [the] poll tax, we had passed a measure giving county home rule in taxation."[3] Approved by a majority of thirty-seven per cent of the votes cast at the election, the measure was repealed by an amendment at the next election by a majority of forty-four per cent.

The forms in which amendments to the constitution or statutes are drawn — the provision as amended being given without the original form [4] — must add to the errors caused by dependence on ballot titles and by inadvertence. The amendment repealing this "home-rule" provision [5] is a fine example of this form of legislation. And it is probable that on this account

[1] *Oregonian*, Nov. 25, 1911, p. 8, col. 1. See also F. V. Holman, *Some Instances of Unsatisfactory Results under Initiative Amendments of the Oregon Constitution*, pp. 39-46 (1910). [2] *Above*, p. 42.
[3] *Open Letter from Six Men of Oregon*, 1911. [4] *Above*, pp. 51-2.
[5] "For constitutional amendment to repeal all of section 1a of article IX except that part prohibiting poll and head taxes, in Oregon, and instead of the portions repealed to add a provision prohibiting the declaration of an emergency in any act passed by the legislature regulating taxation and exemptions."

"ARTICLE IX

"Section 1a. No poll or head tax shall be levied or collected in Oregon. The legislative assembly shall not declare an emergency in any act regulating taxation or exemption." *Senate Joint Resolution*, 1911, no. 19.

many who voted for the amendment did not know that they were voting for the repeal of home rule. Indeed some may have voted for the amendment solely because it contained a stricture upon the legislature's attaching emergency clauses to tax measures, which was substituted for the obligatory referendum in force before. And some may have thought they were abolishing the poll tax.

The "millage bill" of 1912 for the university and agricultural college, through no fault of either title or text, lost many votes in at least several parts of the state because it was understood by some to provide *mileage* for teachers or students. A great many voters, perhaps the most of them, were unaware that the presidential primary bill of 1910 contained a provision for "proportional representation," no mention of which was made in the ballot title.

The difficulty of the subject-matter of measures submitted [1] has doubtless often caused voters to vote contrary to their real intentions. It seems certain that the nature of the highly technical initiative freight-rate bill of 1912 was entirely misunderstood by great numbers of those who voted for it. The bill was framed in the interests of eastern and southern Oregon, and favored the development of jobbing centers in those sections in competition with Portland. But it was approved by the voters of every county of the state except two, and even by the voters of Multnomah county in which Portland is located, who gave over a fourth of the votes in favor of the measure, in spite of the fact that it had been condemned generally by the Portland press as unfair to that vicinity. It is very probable that most of those who voted for the bill believed it designed as a check upon the power of the railroads to the general advantage of the people of the state — some sort of an "anti-corporation" measure. The defeat in every county of the state except the county particularly affected and one other meeting the constitutional amendment submitted in 1914 which permitted the con-

[1] *Above*, pp. 37–41.

solidation of a city of over one hundred thousand population with the county was apparently due to mistake on the part of the voters as to the purpose of the amendment.

4. Attention to Legal Technicalities of Form.

The "anti-pass" bill of 1906 and the eight-hour labor bill of 1912, both initiated by petition and approved by the voters, were without enacting clauses, and thus, of course, were of no legal effect. This has often been given in evidence of the unfitness of the voters for participation in direct legislation. It is probably true that most of the voters had no knowledge of the defect in the measures or even knew that the enacting clause was essential. It is of course very probable that but very few voters indeed ever pay any attention to any formal technicalities in this connection.

5. The Vote on Subjects Unsuitable to Direct Legislation.

The special difficulty in the way of the voters' proper consideration of technical and complicated measures and measures of local interest submitted to them[1] has not only probably often caused mistakes in voting on the part of voters, but has probably to an extent nullified direct legislation in the case of some measures. Many persons, upon principle, habitually vote against any such measures if initiated by petition, and in favor of such measures if referred by petition, as a rebuke to those responsible for bringing unsuitable questions before the voters.

The technical nature of the subject was doubtless chiefly responsible for the defeat of various meritorious measures for the administration of tax reform.[2] The same cause contributed to the defeat of the "blue-sky" bill of 1912, also a meritorious measure. The extremely complicated character of the two radi-

---

[1] *Above*, pp. 37-41.

[2] The essential character of the approaches to the single tax proposed in Oregon have probably been pretty well understood, and rejected because of opposition to the principle involved.

cal proposals for the reorganization of the legislative assembly partially explains their rejection at the polls.[1]

Some technical and complicated measures have met approval doubtless for the reason that their general policy was of vital interest and well understood by the voters. The corrupt practices act, the employers' liability act, and the workmen's compensation act are illustrations in point. The extremely complex constitutional amendment for the reorganization of the judicial system of the state submitted by the legislative assembly was defeated probably not so much on account of its complexity [2] as for the reason that it provided for an increase in the number of the justices of the supreme court, for at the next election the similar measure initiated by petition but containing no provision for such increase was adopted.

The highly technical freight-rate bill of 1912 was adopted, probably, simply because it was erroneously believed to be an "anti-corporation" measure.

Local measures, of the merits of which the voters of the state generally can have little knowledge,[3] have generally suffered at the election. The approval of the Hood River county bill by the voters in 1908 apparently encouraged the "county-slicers" in submitting eight such bills at the next election, but every one of them was defeated. The same fate met a similar bill in 1912. "The people of the state will not vote to create new counties, because they are not familiar with local conditions and do not want to have such questions passed up to them." [4]

6. The Vote on Measures Submitted by Selfish Interests.

According to Jonathan Bourne's "friction theory of community endeavor" (as it has been dubbed) all attempts to pro-

---

[1] "How many of the complex and technical bills submitted were adopted? That is the real test. The people at the last election showed an increasing disposition to vote down bills dealing with such questions. . . . As the people become accustomed to use the new machinery they show increasing discrimination between subjects on which they can well vote directly and subjects which are better left to the legislature." *Oregonian*, Aug. 18, 1913, p. 6, col. 1.   [2] *Above*, pp. 37–8, 44–6.

[3] *Above*, p. 40.   [4] L. E. Bean, senate, *Oregon Journal*, Jan. 18, 1913, p. 3, col. 5.

I

mote narrow selfish ends by direct legislation are doomed to ultimate failure, and must result in a disposition to use the system for the public good. "Where individuals act collectively or as a community, — as they must under the initiative, referendum, and recall, — an infinite number of different forces are set in motion, most of them selfish, each struggling for supremacy, but all different because of the difference in the personal equations of the different individuals constituting the community. Because of their difference, friction is created — each different selfish interest attacks the others because of its difference. No selfish interest is powerful enough to overcome all the others; they must wear each other away until general welfare, according to the views of the majority acting, is substituted for the individual selfish interest. . . . Under the initiative, referendum, and recall there can be no class or community action against the general welfare of the citizens constituting the zone of action. The individual, through realization of the impossiblity of securing special legislation for himself and against the general welfare of the community, soon ceases his efforts for special privilege and contents himself with efforts for improved general welfare. Thus the individual, class, and community develop along lines of general welfare rather than along lines of selfish interest. . . . Community action determines the average of individual interests, and secures the greatest good for the greatest number, which is the desideratum of organized society. . . . Similar results are accomplished through the referendum."[1] This theory may not meet general acceptance, but, as a matter of fact, in the few instances where initiative or referendum movements have been promoted by selfish narrow interests[2] they have generally been defeated.[3]

[1] J. Bourne, *Initiative, Referendum and Recall, Atlantic Monthly*, vol. 109, pp. 122, 123–5 (1909). And see comment in *New York Evening Sun*, reprinted in *Oregonian*, Jan. 19, 1912, p. 10, col. 7.   [2] *Above*, pp. 113–15.

[3] Of course it is generally impossible to segregate the vote of the various interests at an election. But a very plausible explanation of the continuously adverse votes of some counties against the state university acts submitted to the people is the fact that

Where proposed legislation involves a conflict of interests between two classes of voters, the numerically larger class may have an undue advantage in the indifference of voters not directly interested, and thus attain their end to a considerable extent by weight of their own numbers — *i.e.*, by "brute force." [1]

7. The Vote on Conflicting Measures.[2]

"It has been amply illustrated in Oregon that when two or more bills of the same general purport but differing in details are presented all will be defeated, although a majority may favor the main issue involved." [3] The experience with the several initiative road measures of 1912 is the best justification of this doctrine. "Two years ago the legislature attacked the problem, and the net result of the deliberations was nothing at all. Last year a solution was attempted through the initiative, but the same influences that had defeated action in the legislature were found to be present. Warring factions arose, each firmly convinced that its plan, and its plan alone, would result in getting good results. Efforts were made to compromise, but without avail. Three programs finally went before the people and the result was that all were defeated." [4] "Too many measures disputing for votes on the same subject were submitted. The electors will nearly always vote right if given half a chance. They cannot pass measures satisfactorily if conflicting bills are presented to divide and confuse them." [5]

The defeat of both the university appropriation referendum bill of 1912 and the millage-tax bill, which was initiated at the same election because of fear of defeat of the former, was due

those counties contain colleges of their own, rivals of the university. See especially *Oregonian*, June 3, 1908, p. 8, col. 4. However, although this explanation may be true, wholly or in part, it should be noted that a greater number of other counties, with no such local institutions to favor, have always given majorities against the university.

[1] *Oregonian*, Oct. 4, 1911, p. 10, col. 1.   [2] *Above*, pp. 47–9.
[3] *Oregonian*, Apr. 14, 1913, p. 6, col. 2. See also especially *ibid.*, June 10, 1913, p. 10, col. 2.   [4] Eugene *Register*, Jan. 19, 1913, p. 12, col. 1.
[5] *Oregon Journal*, Nov. 9, 1912, p. 4, col. 1.

probably in some degree to confusion on the part of the voters induced by the conflicting measures.

The enactment by the people of *both* the Columbia river fishing bills of 1908 has been interpreted in different ways. For years previous the rival interests represented by the gill-netters of the lower Columbia and the wheelmen of the upper Columbia, respectively, had succeeded in the legislative assembly each in defeating the legislation proposed by the other. A decision by the voters of the state seemed the only solution, and hence each faction initiated a bill prohibiting the other's method of fishing. Both bills were approved, and the river was thus closed to commercial fishing.[1] Some interpreted the vote as evidence of the voters' ignorance of the nature of the bills.[2] But according to the other, and apparently true view, the voters knew what they were doing. "The electors, in an access of disgust, tinged with sardonic humor, passed both bills by different but decisive majorities." [3]

Although a number of other sets of conflicting measures have appeared on the ballot, in these cases the conflict probably had nothing to do with the result of the election. Indeed the conflict was not very clear to any one in some cases; and probably absolutely unknown in one case.

Unless the Columbia river legislation should be so interpreted, there has been only one case where confusion has actually been caused by the adoption of conflicting measures, and, in the absence of judicial interpretation, this case is still uncertain. But it would seem that the tax-exemption law of 1912 is in direct conflict with the constitution as amended at the same election. This conflict was apparently wholly unsuspected at the time of the election.

---

[1] See especially *Report of Oregon Conservation Commission*, 1908, pp. 119–20.

[2] See especially C. H. Carey, *New Responsibilities of Citizenship, Proceedings of the Oregon Bar Association*, 1908–10, pp. 18, 38 (1909).

[3] *Report of the Oregon Conservation Commission*, 1908, p. 119. See also W. S. U'Ren, reported in Chicago *City Club Bulletin*, vol. 2, p. 473 (1909); R. W. Montague, *Oregon System at Work, National Municipal Review*, vol. 3, pp. 256, 263 (1914).

The only (apparent) attempt to defeat reform legislation by proposing an alternative measure at the same election and confusing the voters confronted with rival measures [1] came to nothing. The bill providing for a commission for the investigation of the subject of employers' liability was defeated, and the employers' liability law was enacted.

The inability of the people to decide between conflicting measures may, as in the case of the road bills, throw back upon the legislative assembly the responsibility which was thrust upon the people on account of the failure of action by the assembly.[2]

In order to prevent the defeat of all rival measures in cases where voters have a difference of opinion as to the relative merits of the several measures, but prefer the enactment of any one of them rather than the defeat of all, it has been urged that voters should vote for *all* such measures.[3] But this might result in the serious confusion of the law. For the measure approved securing the highest affirmative vote does not as a whole become the law to the exclusion of other measures approved, but all measures approved go into effect except so far as they may be in conflict with provisions of measures receiving a higher number of affirmative votes.[4] "It ought to be plain that to vote yes on all bills dealing with the same subject would be as indefinite as enactment of laws by some form of lottery. The result would be a tangle that could be unraveled only after tedious recourse to the courts."[5]

8. Conservatism and Progressivism in the Vote.[6]

A combination of conservative and progressive or radical tendencies is indicated by the vote cast on the measures at the elections.

---

[1] *Above*, p. 49.   [2] *Below*, pp. 154–5.
[3] See especially report in *Oregonian*, Nov. 26, 1912, p. 10, col. 1.
[4] *Above*, p. 47.   [5] *Oregonian*, Nov. 26, 1912, p. 10, col. 2. See *above*, p. 48.
[6] "The composite voter whose mind and purpose are portrayed by these votes appears to be one jealous of his own rights and privileges, as most men are; resolute

Proposals for granting the suffrage to women were defeated at three succeeding elections before the suffrage was finally granted.

On the other hand, all the measures submitted for the avowed purpose of increasing the "people's power" have been approved by the voters, with the exception of the two amendments for the extensive reorganization of the legislative department, the amendment establishing proportional representation in the house of representatives, the amendment for the abolition of the state senate, and the bill providing for a board of people's inspectors and an official gazette. Moreover, measures deemed hostile to the "people's rule" have been defeated. The bills providing home-rule methods of creating new counties, etc., were defeated, probably because they would have made easier the creation of additional offices with additional taxation. The defeat of the non-partisan judiciary bill perhaps indicates some reaction against the independent attitude of the voters prevalent for some years.

The measures relating to the creation or regulation of public offices and institutions, or functions involving the expenditure of public money, have been in most cases defeated, and most of the measures designed to limit the expenditure of public money have passed.[1] The defeat of the two bills providing for the consolidation of certain state departments, in spite of the agitation — years old — for elimination and consolidation of offices, was

to see his government actually, as well as theoretically, deriving its just powers from the consent of the governed, and to see politics clean and fair; desirous of improvement of his institutions; open to thoughtful advice, and mindful of well seasoned opinion as to the means of betterment, but adverse to visionary innovations; reluctant to create new offices, and stingy with salaries to public officers, but yielding that point occasionally when involved with some higher good; nearly abreast of the best thought of the time in matters of social and industrial regulation, but lagging behind, and a bit muddled, in economics; and, until he reads the title clear of would-be spenders of the public money, saving with it to a fault." R. W. Montague, *Oregon System at Work, National Municipal Review*, vol. 3, pp. 256, 265 (1914).

[1] At the election of 1913 four of the five measures submitted involved additional expenditures and the four were approved by the voters. The other bill, not involving expenditures, was defeated.

probably due chiefly to the voters becoming generally aware that the real purpose of this legislation was not to secure economy in government but to legislate out of office individuals who had come into conflict with the real authors of these measures. However, one of the bills added a new function to the consolidated department. The defeat of the city-county consolidation amendment must have been due to ignorance of the nature of the proposal.

In view of the conservative attitude of the people toward public expenditures, thus made apparent, the customary attachment of the emergency clause [1] to certain appropriations by the legislative assembly is very significant. But although in cases of most of the measures the saving of money was probably the determining motive in the vote, in many cases other motives were controlling, Moreover, it should be noted that in recent years, especially during this period of the initiative and referendum, great developments have been undertaken very generally by the localities as well as by the state, with the result that the financial burdens have in many cases become far too heavy without the addition of further taxation, and that the expenditures proposed were doubtless, in some cases, for other reasons unwise.

Most of the "tax reform" measures have been defeated, probably in most cases on account of the technical nature [2] of the proposals.

All the measures concerned with the administration of the criminal law were adopted except the bill abolishing capital punishment and regulating the pardoning power and the bill providing for the sterilization of habitual criminals and other degenerates. The adoption of the amendment for the abolition of capital punishment, after the defeat of the similar measure at the preceding election, can doubtless be explained by the fact that women voted at the last election. Until the last election the vote on the measures dealing with the liquor traffic on the

[1] *Below*, pp. 138, 140.   [2] *Above*, pp. 37-41.

whole showed the people to be in favor of local option and opposed to state-wide prohibition. But the women's vote at that election was largely responsible for the decision in favor of state-wide prohibition.

The bill regulating the licensing of dentists (by lowering the standards) was rejected in spite of a strenuous campaign in its favor as a "trust-busting" measure.

Measures designed to regulate corporations and other interests have almost all been approved. The exception of the "blue-sky" bill was doubtless due to the proposal for the creation of a new department which it included.

The three most radical measures submitted for the benefit of the labor class — the eight-hour bill for female workers, the universal eight-hour amendment, and the unemployment amendment — were defeated, but the others passed. All the measures inimical to the labor interests were rejected.

Most of the county-division and county-boundary bills — involving questions of wholly local interest — were defeated.

It thus appears that all the most radical measures were rejected by the voters — the two proposals for the reorganization of the legislative assembly, the bill providing for people's inspectors and an official gazette, the amendment providing for the abolition of the senate, the "single-tax" measures, the sterilization bill, the women's eight-hour bill, the universal eight-hour amendment, and the unemployment amendment. Although the constitutional amendment permitting the use of proportional representation, and the presidential primary bill, in which the principle of proportional representation is applied, were accepted by the voters, they rejected the proposal to apply proportional representation to the composition of the house of representatives. Such a provision was also contained in the two rejected proposals for the reorganization of the legislative assembly.

On the whole it appears that the voters have shown a decidedly progressive attitude in direct legislation.

9. The Vote of the Uncertain Voter.

The voter who is uncertain as to the merits of measures submitted to his decision is confronted with two kinds of advice as to how he should act.

"When in doubt, note NO."[1] "When the ballot is so encumbered . . . the only defense of the voter who does not wish to run the risk of turning things topsy-turvy is to vote 'no' on all measures that he does not fully understand."[2] This principle is doubtless applied by some voters to both initiative and referendum measures alike, on the theory that by the approval of either they are assuming the responsibility for the enactment of law. But probably more voters make a distinction between initiative and referendum measures in this regard, and, while they reject initiative measures in the absence of positive evidence of their merits, place the responsibility for the measures referred principally upon the legislative assembly, and considering the approval by the assembly as *prima facie* evidence of their merits, vote, in the absence of evidence against their merits, for all measures passed by the assembly.[3]

"When in doubt, don't vote." "One sometimes hears it said that when in doubt you should vote 'NO.' This is one of the most pernicious fallacies developed under popular rule. If carried out it would block progress and make the rule of stupid standpattism effective. Because an individual has not sufficient intelligence, or is too lazy to consider a measure and make up his mind conscientiously, is no reason for standing in the path of more intelligent and more energetic people. A conscientious voter taking that attitude is hard to imagine. If a voter is worthy of citizenship he will either make up his mind one way or the other about a measure submitted and vote accordingly, or he will refrain from voting on it. He will refuse to

---

[1] "When in doubt, vote 'NO.' Vote 'NO,' unless you have been convinced by a personal investigation that the measure is for the public interest, and should pass." *Oregonian*, Sept. 25, 1912, p. 10, col. 1.

[2] Eugene *Register*, Sept. 1, 1912, p. 12, col. 2.

[3] *Oregonian*, Oct. 15, 1913, p. 10, col. 2; Nov. 14, 1913, p. 10, col. 2.

try to hold back the whole community on account of his own ignorance or apathy. He will refuse to nullify with his 'no' cast from ignorance, the intelligent 'yes' of some one who has given thought to the matter. He will refuse to shirk his own civic duty, and at the same time block the exercise of good citizenship by another. The advocate of the principle of voting 'no' when in doubt, advocates the rule of ignorance in an age of enlightenment."[1]

But, it is objected, "failure to vote simply reduces the opposition and virtually assists something which you might later wish you had resisted."[2] Further, it is said, this is "lawmaking by proxy." It operates to "relieve the people as a whole of the duty of deciding on any measure submitted for their action, and leaves it to a selected group and informed few, an assembly commissioned to decide questions or issues for the whole electorate. The Oregon system is for all the people, not a part of the people. If a part of the people only discharged their obligations as lawmakers, the system is a failure."[3] "If this delightful advice were accepted generally, it would mean that in order to get their pet plans enacted into law, the tinkerers and schemers would need only to word them in such a manner that understanding would be impossible, and then trust to their coterie of followers to cast the small number of votes that would be needed."[4]

In practice, a large majority of the measures submitted to the voters have failed, and the proportion of measures rejected has increased with the length of the ballot. But although a considerable minority of the voters have invariably failed to vote on all measures submitted, the fact that the average percentage of votes cast for measures at the several elections has varied little with the number of measures would, by itself, indicate that as the number of measures increases and the voters' difficulties in

---

[1] *Oregon Journal*, May 1, 1913, p. 8, col. 1.
[2] *Pacific Grange Bulletin*, vol. 5, p. 26, col. 2 (1912).
[3] *Oregonian*, Nov. 19, 1912, p. 12, col. 2.
[4] Eugene *Register*, Oct. 31, 1912, p. 4, col. 1.

the way of properly considering the measures are correspondingly increased the voters do not so much refrain from voting, but rather vote "No" in cases of doubt as to the merits of the individual measures.

10. The Vote as Protest.

Some voters, in cases where they consider that the system of direct legislation is being abused, on principle vote in favor of referred measures and against initiated measures, without regard to the merits of the particular measure.[1] But how extensively this practice prevails is wholly uncertain.

Some extreme conservatives, wholly opposed to the system of direct legislation, openly avow that they invariably vote to support the legislative assembly in case of referendum measures, and as invariably reject measures submitted under the initiative. But this class is apparently becoming smaller, and probably most of its members make the best of what they consider a bad situation, and discriminate among the measures submitted as other voters do. This class has its opposite extreme in a class of voters *supposed* to exist, who reject all measures coming from the legislative assembly and approve all measures submitted by initiative petition.

11. The Intelligence of the Vote in General.

Any estimate of the general intelligence of the voters in their actual dealing with direct legislation is likely to be colored very largely by mere theoretical considerations. Thus, doubtless the pessimistic view is induced very much by a preconceived belief that the people are incompetent in this direction —"that

---

[1] "Is not the voter justified in voting down the whole grist, and thus discouraging the industry? . . . Would it not be wise to kill all of those bills, good, bad, and crazy, and get rid of the abuse? If half of them are enacted, the rest will come up again." Salem *Capital Journal*, reprinted in *Oregonian*, Sept. 25, 1912, p. 10, col. 1. *Cf. Oregonian*, Oct. 30, 1913, p. 8, col. 2. "The way to rebuke reckless use of the initiative is to vote no, while the way to rebuke reckless use of the referendum is to vote yes." Eugene *Register*, Oct. 22, 1913, p. 4, col. 1.

the people cannot be trusted with legislative powers and that all legislation must be done by proxy."[1] And doubtless, too, the optimistic view is influenced by a preconceived belief that the people in their collective capacity are wholly or nearly infallible. "There is no infidelity in the collective citizen body. Its judgments are sound and its collective honesty complete. It has a sober sense, rational mental processes and its purposes are exalted. The whole trend of legislation by the electorate is for social and economic betterment. If a people are given the means of control, instead of having all control by proxy, state government will be swiftly purified. It has been so under direct legislation in Oregon, and it will be so in any state that adopts the system."[2]

In spite of the difficulties in the situation, the results of the several elections are, in general, competent evidence as to the intelligence of the vote cast. That the voters have done remarkably well under the circumstances is generally conceded, even by opponents of direct legislation, although there is of course much difference of opinion as to the relative merits of many individual measures that have been approved or rejected at the elections. "On the whole the people of Oregon have exhibited discernment and intelligence in separating the good from the bad or doubtful. If direct legislation has revealed fault it is not in the inconsiderate acts of the mass of voters, but rather in the selfish or experimental activity of minorities in holding up acts of the legislature desired by the people or in submitting laws that have no chance to gain the approval of the majority. Moreover, that fault is not with the principle, but with the unguarded, unrestricted manner in which it may be applied and is possible of correction."[3]

And whatever adverse criticism may be deserved by the action of the voters, it is believed that the results of direct legislation

---

[1] *Oregon Journal,* Nov. 2, 1907, p. 6, col. 3.

[2] *Ibid.,* July 3, 1910, sec. 2, p. 4, col. 1.

[3] *Oregonian,* Nov. 13, 1913, p. 10, col. 2. See also *ibid.,* July 21, 1909, p. 8, col. 2; Nov. 9, 1912, p. 8, col. 1.

at least compare favorably with those of representative legislation. "Upon all measures submitted to it, the electorate of Oregon has acted with a ripe and deliberate wisdom which compares favorably with the proceeding of the legislature."[1] "We are all under hallucination as to the wisdom of the average legislator. He has no monopoly of brains. He has no corner on honesty. He has no monopoly of legislative wisdom. . . . There is nothing hallowed about the Oregon legislature. There is no halo about the head of an average member. He is just a plain man and often a very common one."[2]

[1] *Oregonian*, Mar. 2, 1907, p. 8, col. 1.
[2] *Oregon Journal*, Nov. 21, 1912, p. 8, col. 2. See also especially *ibid.*, July 30, 1913, p. 6, col. 2.

CHAPTER XII

DIRECT LEGISLATION AND THE EXECUTIVE

It follows from a constitutional provision to the effect that "the veto power of the governor shall not extend to measures referred to the people," [1] that the veto power does not extend to initiative measures or to measures referred by the legislature, but that the possibility that measures passed by the legislature may be referred by petition does not exempt them from the governor's veto.[2]

Recently, on account of long contests in the legislative assembly over vetoed bills, it has been suggested that provision should be made for "a constitutional amendment which will automatically refer all vetoed bills direct to the people instead of back to the legislature," on the ground "that if there are sufficient flaws in a bill to merit the governor's veto, the people of the state should be given the right and privilege of sustaining or rejecting the veto instead of making it the bone of contention in a political fight in the legislature." [3] But under conditions usually present in Oregon, this would add greatly to the burden of the ballot. However, at times such a right for appeal would have saved the necessity of initiating a measure by petition.

---

[1] *Constitution*, art. 4, sec. 1 (1902).

[2] *Kadderly* v. *Portland, Oregon Reports*, vol. 44, pp. 118, 146 (1903); *State* v. *Kline, ibid.*, vol. 50, pp. 426, 430 (1907); *Oregon* v. *Pacific States Tel. & Tel. Co., ibid.*, vol. 53, pp. 162, 164 (1909). *Cf.* F. Foxcroft, *Constitution-Mending and the Initiative, Atlantic Monthly*, vol. 97, pp. 792, 793 (1906); G. A. Thacher, *Initiative and Referendum in Oregon, Proceedings of the American Political Science Association*, vol. 4, pp. 198, 202–4 (1907).

[3] Reported in *Oregon Journal*, Feb. 2, 1913, p. 5, col. 5. See also C. H. Carey, *New Responsibilities of Citizenship, Proceedings of the Oregon Bar Association*, 1908–10, pp. 18, 40 (1909).

Direct Legislation and the Executive

It has been noted above that the governor and other executive officers of the state have assumed the leadership in the submission of several important measures to the decision of the voters.[1] This seems to be but in keeping with the general tendency toward executive leadership in legislation.

The administration is further removed than the legislature from the action of direct legislation, but doubtless the responsibility of the administration is affected, for good or evil, in some degree as in the case of the legislature.[2]

[1] *Above*, pp. 12–13.   [2] *Below*, pp. 167–70.

CHAPTER XIII

THE DIRECT AND THE REPRESENTATIVE LEGIS-
LATURES

I

Direct Legislation and Representative Government

"It is difficult to conceive of any system of lawmaking coming nearer to the great body of the people of the entire state, or by those composing the various municipalities, than that now in use here."[1] But "the initiative and referendum amendment does not abolish or destroy the republican form of government, or substitute another in its place. The representative character of the government still remains. The people have simply reserved to themselves a larger share of legislative power."[2]

However, during the period of the operation of the system of direct legislation, there has been lack of confidence in the legislative assembly, encroachment upon the functions of the assembly by unnecessarily overloading the ballot with measures, and even a desire, on the part of some extremists among the advocates of direct legislation, entirely to abolish the assembly and place all responsibility for legislation directly upon the people.[3]

---

[1] *Kiernan* v. *Portland, Oregon Reports*, vol. 57, pp. 454, 472 (1910).

[2] *Kadderly* v. *Portland, ibid.*, vol. 44, pp. 118, 145 (1903). The constitutionality of the initiative and referendum was upheld in *Kadderly* v. *Portland, ibid.*, vol. 44, p. 118 (1903) and *Kiernan* v. *Portland, ibid.*, vol. 57, p. 454 (1910). In *Pacific States Telephone and Telegraph Company* v. *Oregon, United States Reports*, vol. 223, p. 118, *Lawyers' ed.*, vol. 56, p. 377 (1912), the question was considered to be of a political and not judicial nature, and the case was hence dismissed for want of jurisdiction. This case in particular aroused an intense interest in Oregon.   [3] *Below*, pp. 159–61.

2

The Two Legislative Bodies

"By the adoption of the initiative and referendum into our constitution, the legislative department of the state is divided into two separate and distinct lawmaking bodies. There remains, however, as formerly, but one legislative department of the state. It operates, it is true, differently than before — one method by the enactment of laws directly, through the source of all legislative power, the people; and the other, as formerly, by their representatives — but the change thus wrought neither gives to nor takes from the legislative assembly the power to enact or repeal any law, except in such manner and to such extent as may there be expressly stated. Nor do we understand that it was ever intended that it should do so. The power thus reserved to the people merely took from the legislature the exclusive right to enact laws, at the same time leaving it a coördinate legislative body with them. This dual system of making and unmaking laws has become the settled policy of this state, and so recognized by decisions upon the subject. Subject to the exceptions enumerated in the constitution as amended, either branch of the legislative department, whether the people, or their representatives, may enact any law, and may even repeal any act passed by the other." [1]

This, it has been contended, has brought the state into "a dangerous condition," and may lead to the final abolition of the legislature. "It is a condition similar to that which would occur if the sole legislative power of a state was composed of two houses which did not have to concur to enact a law, and each could enact laws to the exclusion of the other, 'and even repeal

---

[1] *Straw* v. *Harris, Oregon Reports*, vol. 54, pp. 424, 430 (1909). See also *Hall* v. *Dunn, ibid.*, vol. 52, pp. 475, 485 (1908); *Kiernan* v. *Portland, ibid.*, vol. 57, pp. 454, 480 (1910); *Bradley* v. *Union Bridge & Construction Co., Federal Reporter*, vol. 185, pp. 544, 546 (1911); F. V. Holman, *Some Instances of Unsatisfactory Results under Initiative Amendments of the Oregon Constitution*, p. 23 (1910).

any act passed by the other.' . . . Will not the legislature become as useless as a *vermiform appendix* is to a human being? It may have some functions, but it is apparently a nuisance. Would it not be wise to cut it out before it becomes dangerous?"[1] But the serious possibilities of conflict of the legislature with the people and the people with the legislature have not, as will appear,[2] been realized in actual experience with the system.

[1] F. V. Holman, *Some Instances of Unsatisfactory Results under Initiative Amendments of the Oregon Constitution*, p. 24 (1910).   [2] *Below*, pp. 159–66.

CHAPTER XIV

CHECKS OF THE LEGISLATIVE ASSEMBLY UPON DIRECT LEGISLATION

I

The Regulation of the Initiative and Referendum

"IF the legislature can restrict, limit or hamper the right of referendum which the people have reserved to themselves in the constitution, it practically annuls the amendment. Barrier after barrier could be placed around the steps necessary to invoke the referendum, until there would be so many barriers that they could not be surmounted, and the power of the referendum would be practically dead." [1] It is the fear of some such consequence that has brought the people generally to suspect the efforts made in the legislative assembly, session after session, to "tamper" with the system, and members of the assembly, whether friends or enemies of the system, have accordingly become very chary of such movements, which consequently, whatever their real merits, have almost always been defeated. This cautious attitude appears in the governor's message in 1911. "If imperfections [in the Oregon System] exist, these in time may be remedied or adjusted. But I hold that if changes must come, they should come at the hands of the friends of the law, and I say now that during my term of office I will zealously guard the integrity of these laws of the people and will combat any attempt to injure, infringe, or subvert them. The people of Oregon, at different times and in no uncertain tones, have declared for these laws, and no men or no hostile influence should

[1] Webster, quoted in *Oregon Journal*, July 2, 1907, p. 4, col. 1.

be permitted to attempt, in any manner, to wrest from the people their hard-won victory."[1]

But two years later the governor considered conditions safe enough to permit action by the assembly. "Oregon's system of popular government, having successfully withstood the attacks of its enemies, is here to stay. The time has come therefore when its friends should take steps to remove such defects as a fair trial has shown to exist."[2] And a demand for the improvement of the system is steadily becoming greater. "Everyone except the dyed-in-the-wool standpatters knows that there are defects in the Oregon System that ought to be remedied. Everyone except these typical old reactionaries knows that unless these defects are remedied in time the Oregon System of popular government will lose caste. This is not a day of hide-bound thinking. The demand of the times is for something better than we have, no matter how good the thing we have may be. . . . The real friends of popular government are not those who raise the long howl whenever any changes are suggested, but rather the ones who would apply the knife to real and pernicious evils."[3]

However, the generally prevailing attitude seems still to be against any substantial legislation in regard to the system, whether it comes from the legislative assembly or even from the direct action of the people.

2

Emergency Legislation

The original constitution of the state provides: "No act shall take effect until ninety days from the end of the session at which the same shall have passed, except in case of emergency;

---

[1] *Message of Governor West*, 1911, p. 38. See also *Governor's Message, House Journal*, 1913, p. 80. [2] *Ibid.*, 1913, p. 21.

[3] Eugene *Register*, Jan. 8, 1913, p. 4. col. 1. See also *Oregonian*, Dec. 28, 1912, p. 6, col. 2; Eugene *Guard*, Dec. 20, 1913, p. 4. col. 1.

Checks of Legislature upon Direct Legislation 133

which emergency shall be declared in the preamble or in the body of the law."[1] When the acts of the legislative assembly were made subject to the referendum in 1902, "laws necessary for the immediate preservation of the public peace, health, or safety" were excepted from this restriction.[2] Ten years later, as a substitute for a constitutional provision adopted in 1910, which required all tax laws to be referred to the voters, an amendment was approved at the election prohibiting the legislative assembly from declaring an emergency on "any act regulating taxation or exemption."[3]

It was early suggested that in view of the practice prevailing before the initiative and referendum amendment was adopted of attaching the emergency clause to measures without regard to the reality of the emergency, the legislative assembly might be able to evade the referendum;[4] but perhaps the prevailing opinion was to the effect that the decision of the assembly as to the existence of an emergency, under the referendum clause of the constitution, was not final.[5] All doubts about the legal power of the assembly in this respect were soon settled by the supreme court. "Action of the legislative and executive departments [upon emergency measures] is conclusive and final so far as their enactment is concerned. No power is reserved to the people to approve or disapprove them. They are not subject to the referendum amendment. . . . The legislative assembly may, in its discretion, put them into operation though the emergency clause . . . or it may allow them to become laws without an emergency clause, the necessity or expediency of either course being a matter for its exclusive determination. . . . As the legislature may exercise this power when a measure is in fact necessary for the purpose stated, and as the amendment does not declare what shall be deemed laws of the character

---

[1] *Constitution*, art. 4, sec. 28 (1859).   [2] *Ibid.*, art. 4, sec. 1 (1902).
[3] *Ibid.*, art. 4, sec. 1a (1912).   [4] *Oregonian*, Dec. 22, 1902, p. 6, col. 1.
[5] Governor Chamberlain, quoted in *Oregon Journal*, May 20, 1906, p. 20. col. 2; June 1, 1906, p. 3, col. 5.

indicated, who is to decide whether a specific act may or may not be necessary for the purpose? Most unquestionably those who make the laws are required, in the process of their enactment, to pass upon all questions of expediency and necessity connected therewith, and must therefore determine whether a given law is necessary for the preservation of the public peace, health, and safety. . . . It is a question of which the legislature alone must be the judge, and when it decides the fact to exist, its action is final. . . . But, it is argued, what remedy will the people have if the legislature, either intentionally or through mistake, declares falsely or erroneously that a given law is necessary for the purpose stated? The obvious answer is that the power has been vested in that body, and its decision can no more be questioned or revised than the decisions of the highest court in a case over which it has jurisdiction. Nor shall it be supposed that the legislature will disregard its duty, or fail to observe the mandates of the constitution. . . . If either of the departments, in the exercise of the powers vested in it, should exercise them erroneously or wrongfully, the remedy is with the people, and must be found . . . in the ballot box." [1]

Upon publication of the court's decision it was declared that the court had "devitalized" the referendum. "Most bills that

[1] *Kadderly* v. *Portland, Oregon Reports*, vol. 44, pp. 118, 146 (1903). See also *McWhirter* v. *Brainard, ibid.*, vol. 5, pp. 426, 429 (1875); *Briggs* v. *McBride, ibid.*, vol. 17, pp. 640, 647 (1889); *Dallas* v. *Hallock, ibid.*, vol. 44, pp. 246, 258 (1904); *Sears* v. *Multnomah County, ibid.*, vol. 49, pp. 42, 44 (1907); *State* v. *Cochran, ibid.*, vol. 55, pp. 157, 194 (1909); *Bennett Trust Co.* v. *Sengstacker, ibid.*, vol. 58, pp. 333, 342 (1911); *Reports of Attorney General*, 1903–4, pp. 52–4; 1904–6, pp. 137–9; 1906–8, p. 68; 1908–10, pp. 38–40, 57–8, 86–9. The same doctrine prevails in South Dakota and Arkansas. *State* v. *Bacon, South Dakota Reports*, vol. 14, p. 394 (1901); *State* v. *Moore, Arkansas Reports*, vol. 103, p. 48 (1912). *Cf. Oklahoma City* v. *Shields, Oklahoma Reports*, vol. 22, pp. 265, 300 (1908); *In re Menefee, ibid.*, vol. 22, pp. 365, 375 (1908); *Riley* v. *Carico, ibid.*, vol. 27, pp. 33, 37 (1910).

But in order to prevent the possibility of a referendum the assembly must positively declare that the act excepted comes with the exceptions stated by the constitution. "An emergency is declared," or other similar expressions are not enough. *Sears* v. *Multnomah County, Oregon Reports*, vol. 49, p. 42 (1907). Unless the emergency clause is so faulty that no *bona fide* claim can be made as to its validity, it is

shall be enacted in the legislature hereafter will contain emergency clauses, whether emergency exists or not, since they can thus escape referendum."[1] But, on the other hand, to permit the courts[2] to review the action of the legislature in this regard is certainly to "create confusion and doubt in every case of emergency."[3]

At the last session of the assembly before the referendum amendment went into effect emergency clauses were attached to over one-half of the laws which were passed. At the first session under the new system over one-fifth of the laws, and, at the special session held the same year, almost all the laws passed were so affected, as in the previous sessions, generally without any regard as to whether actual emergency existed or not. Thus was produced "the situation of a representative legislature forestalling and preventing the hostile action of the popular legislature operating by means of the referendum."[4] The emergency clause seems not to have been discussed at these sessions,[5] but the sudden reduction of the proportion of emergency measures of the regular session as compared with that of the preceding regular session must have some significance in this connection. When at the session of 1905 it appeared that the abuse of the emergency clause would nullify the people's power of referendum to a great extent,[6] Governor Chamberlain interfered,

---

presumed to be valid and must be so treated by officials until decided otherwise by the courts. *Report of Attorney General*, 1908–10, pp. 57–8. For an example of an emergency clause, see below, p. 140. [1] *Oregonian*, Dec. 27, 1903, p. 16, col. 1.

[2] Permitted in *McClure* v. *Nye*, California Appeals Reports, vol. 22, p. 248 (1913); *Attorney General* v. *Lindsay*, Michigan Reports, vol. 178, p. 524; *State* v. *Meath*, Pacific Reporter (Washington), vol. 147, p. 11 (1915). *Cf. Oregon Journal*, Mar. 8, 1915, p. 4, col. 1.

[3] Dissenting opinion, *State* v. *Meath*, Pacific Reporter (Washington), vol. 147, pp. 11, 19 (1915). *Cf. Oregonian*, Mar. 8, 1915, p. 6, col. 2.

[4] G. H. Burnett, *Recent Legislation*, Proceedings of the Oregon Bar Association, 1904–6, pp. 17, 24 (1904).

[5] *Cf.* Governor Chamberlain, quoted in *Oregon Journal*, May 20, 1906, p. 20, col. 2; June 1, 1906, p. 3, col. 5.

[6] *Cf.* especially *Oregon Journal*, May 17, 1906, p. 3, col. 1; Oct. 13, 1910, p. 8, col. 1.

and threatened to veto every bill to which an emergency clause was attached unless it was clearly apparent that an immediate emergency was actually present.

A very strict doctrine regarding the use of the emergency clause is contained in the governor's message. "The plain intent of this reserve power was to enable the people of the state to have referred to them directly for their approval or rejection any act of the legislature which in the opinion of at least five per cent of the legal voters should not find permanent lodgement on the statute books of the state, *except as to laws necessary for the immediate preservation of the public peace, health,* or *safety.*

"The supreme court of this state has held that it is the legislative province to declare in an emergency clause what acts are necessary for the immediate preservation of the public peace, health, or safety, and in the exercise of this power it seems to me great care should be used by the legislature to avoid attaching an emergency clause to any bill which is not clearly and distinctly for the purpose of preserving the public peace, health, or safety of our people.

"My attention has been called to the fact that many, if not a majority of the bills which have been introduced in both the house and senate have an emergency clause declaring such bills to be for the immediate preservation of the public peace, health, and safety of the people, thus, in effect, cutting off the right to have such laws referred to the people. As a matter of fact, no law can have for its object the immediate preservation of the public peace, unless it be to prevent invasion, insurrection, or war; no law can have for its object the immediate preservation of the public health, unless it be to prevent the introduction of some plague or the spread of some contagious or infectious disease; and no law can have for its object the immediate preservation of the public safety unless it be to prevent riot or mob violence, or something calculated to bring about great destruction to life or property.

"I am bound by the same oath of office as you and other officers of the state to support the constitution in letter and spirit, as I understand it, and following the construction heretofore given by the courts and the people to constitutional provisions like the one under consideration, I shall feel it to be my duty to refuse to give my assent to any act containing the emergency clause referred to unless it is clearly apparent that the emergency is immediate within the letter and spirit of this amendment to the constitution. The people of the state should have the right to avail themselves of the referendum clause in the constitution in all cases except those clearly intended to be embraced within the exceptions quoted."[1]

The governor's attitude dampened the ardor of the emergency-makers. In some cases emergency clauses were struck out of bills. In some cases, where the clause was objectionable to the governor, he vetoed the bill, and his vetoes were sustained. But, nevertheless, even a greater proportion of bills with emergency clauses became laws than at the previous session — nearly one-fourth of all the laws passed. And in many cases, of course, actual emergency was not present. In many cases emergency was not evident from a point of view much less severe than that announced in the governor's message. In strict accordance with that doctrine a real emergency will almost *never* arise. But neither Governor Chamberlain acted, nor have his successors acted in strict accord with that doctrine. Indeed, although it seems to be in harmony with the intent of the constitution, the doctrine is too strict for practical purposes. However, the conflict between Governor Chamberlain and the legislative assembly doubtless had much to do with the development of a strong public sentiment against the abuse of the emergency clause, and to the rapid decrease of that abuse by the legislative assembly.[2]

---

[1] Governor Chamberlain's *Message, House Journal*, 1905, p. 210. *Cf. Oregonian*, Jan. 28, 1915, p. 10, col. 2.

[2] *Cf. Oregon Journal*, May 22, 1908, p. 19, col. 6.

At the session of 1907 fewer emergency clauses appeared, and only one-tenth of the laws finally enacted carried such clauses. At the next session the proportion was still further reduced, and at the sessions of 1911 and 1913 not one-twentieth of the laws were passed with emergency clauses attached.[1] The large increase in the proportion of emergency laws at the session of 1915, to nearly one-fifth of the whole number of laws passed, was due, to a considerable extent, to the increase in the number of measures of the class to which emergency clauses are now most frequently attached — appropriation acts, chiefly those for the ordinary expenses of the state government — resulting from the policy of grouping fewer items in a single measure than had been customary in the past.

Public opinion in the state condemns the use of the emergency clause except for good reasons. "*Legislators must not trample on the referendum.* The legislature has no right to indiscriminately use the emergency clause. When that clause is attached to measures which are not required by any actual emergency, both the spirit and letter of the organic law are violated. . . . Emergency has a meaning that is patent to every legislator, and one so plain that it cannot be misunderstood or misconstrued." [2] Five candidates for the office of governor in 1914 promised in case of

---

[1] The unnecessary use of the emergency clause in an act containing provisions rejected by the voters at the election adds insult to injury. An amendment including, in addition to radical changes in the judiciary department, a provision for an increase in the number of the judges of the supreme court was rejected by the people in 1908; but at the next session of the legislature a bill was passed providing for the increase and an emergency clause was attached. "Does an emergency exist? Is there any acute crisis in our judicial affairs that justifies all this haste? There is not, of course. The 'crisis' and the 'emergency' are the people of Oregon, who voted down the same scheme last June, and will do it again if they have the opportunity. . . . But they are not to have the opportunity." *Oregonian*, Feb. 11, 1909, p. 8, col. 2.

Members of the legislative assembly responsible for the abuse of the emergency clause of course are not generally as outspoken as the member of the house who objected to taking the clause from his bill "for fear that the voters of Oregon would defeat the bill under the referendum." *Oregonian*, Feb. 11, 1909, p. 1, col. 7.

[2] *Oregon Journal*, Jan. 23, 1909, p. 6, col. 1.

Checks of Legislature upon Direct Legislation 139

election to use the veto power to prevent the abuse of the emergency clause.[1]

A consideration of the emergency measures of the session of 1915 will indicate the present attitude of the legislature in this regard.

A motive for the attachment of the emergency clause to the cession of jurisdiction over a park to the general government was to secure federal appropriations for the park for the present year. Without the emergency clause the two acts repealing provisions for the state census would not have gone into effect until after the taking of the census had begun. The provision for removing from the registration records the names of persons not citizens of the United States (recently disfranchised by constitutional amendment) was made effective immediately in order to put the records into proper condition for the early elections. The law regulating fishing in the waters over which the states of Oregon and Washington have concurrent jurisdiction was passed under an agreement with the legislature of Washington for the enactment of identical legislation, and hence delay to give opportunity for the referendum in this case was hardly practicable. The provision for a special election for referendum measures to be held in case any such measures should be filed would have of course been useless without the emergency clause. The immediate operation of the act relating to bounties for killing wolves, etc., was required as an aid in checking the spread of rabies in certain parts of the state. The amendment in reference to commitments to a reform school was badly needed to cure an accident

---

[1] "It is my earnest belief, and will be my policy if I am elected governor, that the spirit and letter of the constitution should be followed faithfully and fully and that the emergency clause must not be used 'except as to laws necessary for the immediate preservation of the public peace, health or safety.' It is my firm belief that . . . it is the unalterable duty of the chief executive to disapprove of the emergency clause when the actual emergency existing does not measure up to the meaning of the constitution in the fullest degree. I assuredly will disapprove the use of the emergency clause as a means of evading the operation of the initiative and referendum provisions." James Withycombe (elected), *Oregon Grange Bulletin*, Nov. 1914, p. 1. See statements of the other candidates, *ibid*.

in the law which prevented any commitment of a certain class of delinquents. The publication of the session laws, etc., would have been deferred very late if the provision for their publication had been delayed to give opportunity for a referendum.

None of the several acts permitting cities to manage waterworks jointly, regulating the merger of adjacent cities, changing the time of holding the circuit court in a certain district, authorizing cities to acquire grounds from cemetery associations, etc., authorizing counties to form joint road districts, relating to bids on public work, relating to public printing, changing the administration of a state irrigation project, was so urgently needed that the delay to allow opportunity for a referendum would have caused very serious inconvenience. However, although the attachment of the emergency clause was severely criticized in some cases, it is not probable that there was any desire to invoke the referendum on any of these acts.

But the act confirming the lease of certain state salt beds met opposition, and probably one motive for the attachment of the emergency clause was to escape the risk of a referendum. This was doubtless the chief motive for declaring an emergency in case of the act creating a new judicial district. In case of the law submitting appointive officers to the unqualified power of removal by the appointing authority, it was frankly admitted that the purpose of the emergency clause was to prevent the referendum of the law by those persons whose positions were endangered by the law.

Two-thirds of the emergency measures, forty-four out of the sixty-four, were appropriation acts, but most of these were for the ordinary expenses of the state government.[1]

[1] The customary form of emergency clause attached to such an appropriation act reads as follows: "It is hereby adjudged and declared that existing conditions are such that this act is necessary for the immediate preservation of the public peace, health and safety, and, owing to the urgent necessity of maintaining the public credit, an emergency is hereby declared to exist, and this act shall take effect and be in full force from and after its approval by the governor." *Laws*, 1915, ch. 301, sec. 3. For the view that the emergency clause may properly be attached to such acts

Other measures of the session in their original form contained emergency clauses, but the clauses were removed before enactment, in some cases at the instance of the governor.

Numbers of appropriation acts are thus withdrawn from the referendum by the use of the emergency clause at every session of the legislature. In case of appropriations for the ordinary expenses of the state government the inconvenience caused by waiting for the referendum period of ninety days to expire becomes serious hardship when the referendum is actually invoked.[1] But generally very large increases over the ordinary expenses of government have also been protected against the referendum by the attachment of the emergency clause.

Under present conditions it is true that "a weak-kneed governor and an unscrupulous legislature with a big working majority might render the referendum useless" by the abuse of emergency legislation.[2] But in case of abuse of the emergency clause, of course the people can resort to the initiative and thus undo what the legislature has done; and this has been threatened.[3] Further a too liberal use of the clause "may provoke the popular legislature to retort by labeling its legislation 'constitutional amendments,' and thus effectively prevent any change by the legislative assembly." [4]

On account of the abuse of the emergency clause there has been some movement to safeguard it with positive restrictions. The exemption of tax-measures from emergency legislation by a constituted amendment in 1912[5] was merely a substitute for the obligatory referendum on such measures. Among the numer-

---

see Governor's *Message, Senate Journal*, 1905, p. 1037. *Contra*, Governor's *Message, House Journal*, 1913, p. 1106. In several states such appropriations are excepted from the power of referendum. *E.g.*, California *Constitution*, art. 4, sec. 1 (1911); Washington *Constitution*, art. 2, sec. 1(b) (1912).

[1] *Report of Secretary of State*, 1904–6, pp. 17 a–19 a.

[2] G. A. Thacher, *Initiative and Referendum in Oregon, Proceedings of the American Political Science Association*, vol. 4, pp. 198, 204 (1907).

[3] *Oregonian*, Feb. 11, 1909, p. 1, col. 7; Feb. 12, 1909, p. 10, col. 3.

[4] G. H. Burnett, *Recent Legislation, Proceedings of the Oregon Bar Association*, 1904–6, pp. 17, 24 (1904). [5] *Above*, p. 133.

ous provisions for the reorganization of the legislative department in the amendments submitted in 1910 and 1912 there were provisions exempting other subjects from the operation of the emergency clause and requiring a three-fourths vote to declare an emergency. It was further provided that although emergency legislation passed by such vote should immediately go into effect, if a referendum petition should be filed against the law and the law be rejected at the election, it should thereby be repealed.[1] This meritorious amendment might have been approved if it had been submitted to the people by itself.[2]

It has even been suggested that the constitution might be amended to take away from the legislative assembly all power of declaring emergencies.[3] As above noted,[4] acts regulating taxation or exemption from taxation may no longer be withdrawn from the power of the referendum, and it seems probable that the continued complaint of the extravagance of the legislative assembly may result in a popular demand for some restriction of the use of the emergency clause in the appropriation of public money.[5] The freedom of the use of the emergency clause needs,

---

[1] *Referendum Pamphlet*, 1910, no. 360, sec. 1c, p. 187; 1912, no. 362, sec. 1c, p. 210; *below*, p. 256.

"No such emergency measure shall be considered passed by the legislature unless it shall . . . be approved by the affirmative votes of two-thirds of the members elected to each house of the legislature . . . and also approved by the governor; and should such measure be vetoed by the governor, it shall not become law unless approved by the votes of three-fourths of the members elected to each house of the legislature." Arizona *Constitution*, art. 4, sec. 1 (1911). "An emergency law shall remain in force notwithstanding such petition, but shall be repealed thirty days after being rejected by a majority of the qualified electors voting thereon. An emergency law shall be any law declared by the legislature to be necessary for any immediate purpose by a two-thirds vote of the members of each house voting thereon." Proposed Wisconsin *Constitution*, art. 4, sec. 1, rejected (1914). A separate vote on the emergency clause by a two-thirds vote of all the members of each house has been proposed for the enactment of an emergency law. Proposed Minnesota *Constitution*, art. 4, sec. 1c, rejected (1914).

[2] *Cf.* C. N. McArthur, *Oregonian*, Mar. 6, 1907, sec. 5, p. 11; *Labor Press*, Aug. 1, 1912, p. 4, col. 2.

[3] Reported in *Oregonian*, Dec. 23, 1903, p. 16, col. 1; Dec. 27, 1903, p. 16, col. 1. See also *Oregon Journal*, Feb. 27, 1914, p. 4, col. 2. [4] P. 141.

[5] *Cf.* A. D. Cridge, *Oregon Journal*, Mar. 8, 1913, p. 4, col. 4.

Checks of Legislature upon Direct Legislation 143

at least in the case of *increase* of expenditure, constitutional limitations.[1]

Abuses of the referendum encouraged by the laxity of the system of petition making have at times led to advocacy of the attachment of the emergency clause to defeat the abuses. "If the people of Oregon, or their representatives in the legislature, refuse or neglect to put proper safeguards around the initiative and referendum, the legislature will be justified in adding an emergency clause to every bill upon which there is reason to believe a referendum may be invoked." [2]

The delay of legislation caused by the operation of the referendum is a really serious matter. Under the present system legislation for which there is a wide popular demand may be held up for nearly two years. Three times the assembly has called special elections, wholly for decision upon measures referred by petition,[3] in order to lessen this difficulty. This policy of course causes additional expense to the state, but this is far more than balanced by the lessening of delay and by the reduction of the length of the ballot. It would be well either to

---

[1] "No law making any appropriation for maintaining the state government or maintaining or aiding any public institution, not exceeding the next previous appropriation for the same purpose, shall be subject to rejection or approval under this section. The increase in any such appropriation shall only take effect as in the case of other laws, and such increase, or any part thereof, specified in the petition may be referred to a vote of the people upon petition." Proposed Wisconsin *Constitution*, art. 4, sec. 1, rejected (1914). See also California *Constitution*, art. 17, sec. 2 (1911).

"Whereas the 'emergency clause' in the referendum law, as the law now stands, is liable to be improperly used; therefore be it *resolved* by this Grange, that we urge our senators and representatives to secure the passage of a law that will confine the use of the 'emergency clause' to cases in which the public peace or safety is in danger." Resolution of Clackamas County Grange, *Senate Journal*, 1905, p. 330.

[2] *Oregonian*, July 23, 1913, p. 8, col. 2.

[3] "This, I think, bad, as a hostile legislature could thus, by selecting an adverse time, hamper the measure proposed, etc. It's none of their business. They, of all others, should be required to keep their hands off. And as real emergency matters ought to be excepted, there is no objection to waiting till the next general election. This will give more time for the discussion, and there will be a full vote." R. B. Minor, *Oregon Law Criticized, Equity*, vol. 9, p. 9 (1907).

The constitutionality of such special elections has been established. *Equi* v. *Olcott, Oregon Reports*, vol. 66, p. 213 (1913); *Libby* v. *Olcott, ibid.*, vol. 66, p. 124 (1913).

make a permanent provision for special elections for the purpose within a reasonable period after the adjournment of the assembly,[1] or to change the time for the sessions of the assembly so that they will come in the same years as the general election.[2]

3

The Division of Legislative Measures

In order to discourage the use of the referendum, it is charged, the legislative assembly in some cases has distributed matter naturally covered by one act among several acts, and thus rendered petition making more difficult.[3] An act may be thus divided also with the hope that, should the several acts be referred, some of them will be approved though some may be rejected.

---

[1] *Cf.* especially *Oregonian*, Nov. 2, 1913, sec. 3, p. 6, col. 1; Jan. 16, 1915, p. 8, col. 3.

[2] *Cf.* Eugene *Register*, June 1, 1913, p. 12, col. 1; report in *Oregonian*, Jan. 20, 1915, p. 4, col. 3.   [3] W. S. U'Ren, quoted in *Equity*, vol. 15, p. 129 (1913).

CHAPTER XV

THE AMENDMENT AND REPEAL OF DIRECT LEGISLATION BY THE LEGISLATIVE ASSEMBLY

"ARE any and all acts by the people in whom sovereign power resides liable to be turned down by legislators who are mere representatives?"[1] The constitution is silent in the matter, but the supreme court has answered in the affirmative. "Our legislature . . . can, if it chooses, repeal all the laws (not included in constitutional amendments) enacted at the . . . election."[2] And likewise the legislature may legally enact any laws previously rejected by the people.[3] "If the people intended by the initiative or referendum to take from the legislature its power to legislate, why did they provide precisely the same method for popular enactment of a constitutional amendment and a statutory law? Yet the clear distinction is: In the one case there is specific inhibition upon legislative interference; in the other, the way is intentionally left open for legislative amendment, revision or repeal."[4] In fact it was clearly the intention of the promoters of the direct legislative movement to leave such powers with the legislative assembly.[5] But from the very first there has been a feeling of "delicacy in dealing with a law placed

---

[1] *Oregon Journal*, Feb. 12, 1911, sec. 2, p. 6, col. 1.

[2] *Kiernan* v. *Portland*, *Oregon Reports*, vol. 57, pp. 454, 480 (1910). See also *Kadderly* v. *Portland*, *ibid.*, vol. 44, pp. 118, 146 (1903); *State* v. *Schuler*, *ibid.*, vol. 59, pp. 18, 26 (1910). *Cf. above*, pp. 129–30.

[3] *State* v. *Cochran*, *Oregon Reports*, vol. 55, pp. 157, 195 (1909).

[4] *Oregonian*, Dec. 3, 1912, p. 8, col. 2.

[5] W. S. U'Ren, *Oregonian*, Feb. 9, 1913, sec. 3, p. 4, col. 4; W. S. U'Ren, quoted in *Oregonian*, July 9, 1904, p. 6, col. 1; *Oregon Journal*, Feb. 6, 1913, p. 5, col. 2. There was at least some contemporary opinion to the contrary. *Oregonian*, Dec. 27, 1903, p. 16, col. 2.

on the statute books through the initiative and referendum."[1] Logical consistency demands that action by the legislative assembly should be regarded as an interference with the popular will as much in the case of referendum measures as in the case of initiative measures adopted at the polls, and that negative majorities at the election should be regarded as much an instruction to the assembly as positive majorities. In fact, positive and negative majorities have been placed about on a par in this regard, but there has always been greater jealousy of interference with initiative than with referendum measures.

The proper attitude of the legislative assembly toward questions once decided at the polls is the subject of doctrines which vary all the way from the doctrine of absolute non-interference to the repudiation of the notion of the peculiar "sanctity" of direct legislation.

"I do not believe the legislature should amend any law that has been adopted by the people by the initiative."[2] "If an error has been made [by the people] let the people . . . correct it."[3] "As to measures that have been enacted by the voters, I shall oppose any changes except those that are clearly intended to aid the operation of the bill and make it more effective. As to measures rejected by the voters, I shall oppose their enactment by the legislature, and use the veto power on such measures if necessary."[4] Although there is opinion which favors the resubmission of a matter once determined by the people as an alternative to direct interference by the legislature,[5] such resubmission has been opposed as "tampering with the laws of the people."[6]

[1] Quoted in *Oregonian*, July 6, 1904, p. 6, col. 5.
[2] M. A. Miller, senate, *Oregon Journal*, Feb. 7, 1907, p. 10, col. 3.
[3] J. A. Westerlund, house of representatives, Eugene *Register*, Feb. 10, 1911, p. 1, col. 1.
[4] W. S. U'Ren (candidate for governor), *Oregon Grange Bulletin*, Nov., 1914, p. 1.
[5] E.g., *Governor's Message, Senate Journal*, 1913, p. 1036.
[6] Debate in senate, *Oregonian*, Jan. 30, 1913, p. 7, col. 1; Eugene *Register*, Feb. 8, 1913, p. 1, col. 7; Eugene *Guard*, Feb. 8, 1913, p. 13, col. 1.
Friends of the bill "contend that the moral conditions supersede any sentimental

Amendment and Repeal of Direct Legislation 147

More moderate views are thus expressed. "I believe [the] ... wishes [of the people] expressed at the ballot box should remain inviolate until changed by them, except only in case of some great ... emergency. I have always ... opposed any material change in the people's laws."[1] "If there is to be important change in the primary law, it should be made by the people."[2] Views shade off until there is no distinction made in this respect between direct and ordinary legislation. "Sometimes the people make mistakes. ... When the initiative was introduced that idea was carefully considered, and we thought that it might transpire that the people would enact laws with defects that would need to be remedied. They might make a serious mistake in passing a bill, and I do not see why the legislature should not change it. It has been said, somewhere, that man is prone to err, and the most of us do, sometimes."[3] "The legislature has its place in the political economy of the commonwealth and it is clearly its duty to correct errors in legislation, whatever the source of that legislation may be. All that is needed is to learn the lesson of experience, and to act honestly and courageously thereon; the people will sustain such action."[4] "If the people have been misinformed, or if time shows that they have made a mistake, or if the issue has not been presented to them in fair and simple terms, or if it be apparent that the people in defeating a measure preferred that the legislature

---

regard for an amendment passed by the people." *Oregon Journal*, Jan. 21, 1913, p. 1, col. 2. Further, it has been urged that when at an election voters have been *mistaken* as to the nature of a measure submitted, it is proper thus to allow them a resubmission of the question to correct their error. And when the suffrage was extended to women it was contended that the "home-rule" liquor amendment and the anti-capital-punishment bill should be resubmitted because they had not been passed upon by *all* the electorate.

[1] J. A. Carson and Jay Bowerman, *Senate Journal*, 1911, p. 65.

[2] *Oregon Journal*, Feb. 23, 1911, p. 8, col. 1. See also *Governor's Message*, *Senate Journal*, 1913, p. 1036.

[3] W. S. U'Ren, quoted in *Oregon Journal*, July 6, 1913, p. 5, col. 2. But see *above*, p. 146, note 4. See also W. S. U'Ren, quoted in *Oregonian*, July 9, 1904, p. 6, col. 1; letter in *Oregonian*, Feb. 9, 1913, sec. 3, p. 4, col. 4; F. M. Gill, *Oregonian*, Feb. 16, 1911, p. 10, col. 5. [4] S. A. Lowell, *Oregon Journal*, Nov. 29, 1912, p. 18, col. 4.

should handle the problem that particular bill presents, or if it appears that a popular law can be improved — in these events . . . the legislature is justified in amending 'people's laws' or enacting measures the people have disapproved."[1] Of course no one contends that the legislature has any "moral right to interfere wantonly with the people's laws, or any other laws."[2]

Even assuming that the voters generally make no mistakes at the election, majorities do not necessarily in all cases indicate public opinion either upon individual measures or upon the several provisions contained in some individual measures. For so far as the defeat of measures is due to negative votes cast as a protest against the *submission* of such measures, or is due to the habit of voting "no" on propositions not fully understood, the popular vote is no instruction whatever to the people's representatives. Further, when defeat is due to the presence of conflicting measures on the same ballot, it is difficult if not impossible for the legislature to obtain any guidance for action from the vote. Moreover, in the case of negative majorities it is generally impossible to be at all certain as to whether a measure has been rejected because all of its provisions were objectionable to the voters, or whether the voters objected only to one or more of the provisions. And a positive majority does not necessarily indicate the popular will as to the *whole* of a measure adopted at the polls. For the measure may have been adopted in *spite* of individual provisions obnoxious to most of the voters, or some provisions may have been entirely unknown to most of the voters.

It would seem that direct legislation has not been in operation here long enough to have allowed the development of a compromise theory admitting the "rigidity" of direct legislation, but limiting the duration of that "rigidity" to a reasonable length of time.

---

[1] *Oregonian*, Mar. 3, 1913, p. 6, col. 2. See also *ibid.*, May 3, 1904, p. 6, col. 3; Feb. 25, 1911, p. 8, col. 3. It has been observed that the solution of some legislative problems, as in the case of agreement with other states upon needed uniformity of laws, may necessitate the legislature's revision of direct legislation. *Oregonian*, Sept. 14, 1911, p. 12, col. 1.   [2] *Oregonian*, Feb. 17, 1911, p. 10. col. 2.

Public opinion apparently inclines to a more or less unqualified doctrine of non-interference, and, whether from conviction or from fear [1] of their constituents, or as a means of obstructing legislation, the members of the legislative assembly generally profess faith in this doctrine.

The controversy in regard to the "rigidity" of direct legislation has been somewhat confused with the controversy above [2] described in regard to changes in the system of direct legislation itself.

Whatever the merits of the doctrine of the "rigidity" of direct legislation, both the debates and the votes in the legislative assembly show much inconsistency in the application of the doctrine, and in many cases are evidence that the theory is used by members as a mere pretext to obstruct action not desired by them.

At the legislative assembly meeting next after the first exercise of direct legislation under the new system, an attempt was made to nullify the local-option law adopted by the people at the preceding election, but there was objection to undoing the work of the voters, and the matter was dropped. And since that time numerous proposals to interfere with the will of the people as expressed, positively or negatively, at the polls have been rejected by the assembly.

Although the attempt to nullify the local option law at the first session of the legislature held after its adoption failed, the law was abrogated to a certain extent at that session by the grant of special charters to several cities which conferred power upon three cities to regulate the sale of liquor. This was one of the reasons for the enactment by direct legislation, the next year, of a constitutional amendment prohibiting interference with municipal charters by the legislature. "The manifest pur-

---

[1] "Again I call you to beware. Two years ago I tried to monkey with one of the people's laws, and the voters of Jackson county and a couple of papers in Portland have not ceased to howl about it yet." J. A. Buchanan, house of representatives, Eugene *Register*, Feb. 10, 1911, p. 1, col. 1.   [2] Pp. 131–2.

pose of the people in the passage of this constitutional amendment was to prevent the co-ordinate branch of the statute-making power from passing local laws, the effect of which was to evade the general laws initiated by the people."[1] The local option law was later amended to change the time of election, and to penalize officials for failing to perform their duties under the law.

The direct primary law of 1904 has been amended by a number of laws enacted by the assembly, but these amendments, with one exception, consist either in changes in the mere administrative details of the law or in extending the scope of the law. In 1911 the governor vetoed a bill providing for "second-choice" voting at primary elections, partly for the reason, he declared, that it "tampered" with a law which the people had approved.[2] The veto was sustained. But at the session of 1915 the law was very materially amended to permit candidates to substitute the declaration of candidacy and payment of a fee in lieu of the petition required by the original law.

In 1913 the assembly sustained the governor's veto of a bill which made some substantial changes in the principle of the presidential primary law of 1910 — changes not tending, he asserted, "to aid or make more effective" the principles on which the people's law was based.[3] But at the next session important changes were made in the law by eliminating the provisions for "proportional representation" and payment of delegates' expenses to constitutional conventions, in spite of the fact that in the meantime the people had rejected a measure one purpose of which was the elimination of these same provisions.

The amendment of the public utilities act of 1910 by the assembly in 1915 merely extended the provisions of that law, and added penalties for its enforcement. The workmen's compensation act of 1913 was much "strengthened" by the as-

---

[1] *State* v. *Schluer, Oregon Reports*, vol. 59, pp. 18, 33 (1911). See also *Hall* v. *Dunn, ibid.*, vol. 52, pp. 475, 485 (1908).   [2] *House Journal*, 1913, p. 80.
[3] Governor West's *Message, Senate Journal*, 1913, p. 1036.

sembly at the session next following. The amendment of the eight-hour labor law at the same session expressly to exclude from its operation state institutions and departments removed a doubt as to the proper interpretation of the law.

A law of 1909 which provided for two additional judges for the supreme court was severely criticized on the ground that the people had at the preceding election rejected a constitutional amendment containing a similar provision. "The legislature that the people directly elected at the same time that they condemned the increase in supreme court judges, was one of the most dishonorable legislatures that ever afflicted a state. It cared nothing for the expressed will of the people at the polls, and duly proceeded to pass a measure providing for two additional supreme court judges in open defiance of people and law. . . . The increasing of the supreme court bench was an assault upon the people."[1] And the grievance was the greater because the law passed with the emergency clause attached.[2] But the measure rejected by the people had, in addition to the provision for an increase in the number of judges of the supreme court, "provided for an entire and radical change in the whole method of electing judicial, county, and precinct officers," and this, and not the provision for additional judges, may have been the cause of the defeat of the measure.[3] It seems to have occurred to nobody to object to the act of the legislature of 1913 which provided a further addition of two justices to the court.

The two gross-earnings tax laws of 1906 were repealed "by inference" by legislation enacted in 1907 and 1909, but the members of the legislature were doubtless at the time unaware of this effect of their action.

The people rejected the referendum act of 1908 providing for appropriations for local armories through four years, but nevertheless the legislative assembly has made appropriations for such armories at almost every session since. However, the appro-

[1] *Oregon Observer*, reprinted in *Oregonian*, Nov. 1, 1909, p. 6, col. 6.
[2] *Above*, p. 138. [3] *State v. Cochran*, *Oregon Reports*, vol. 55, pp. 157, 195 (1909).

priations have been smaller and have been made conditional upon further local appropriations.

The two initiative laws of 1908 closing the Columbia river to commercial fishing were repealed by the legislative assembly at its next session. But whether the people intended their action to be final in this case is uncertain.[1] Moreover, the needed uniformity of fishing regulations for the Oregon and the Washington sides of the river could hardly have been accomplished except through the action of the legislatures of the two states.[2]

The corrupt practices act approved by the people in 1908 was amended five years later by the assembly, but only in the way of making the law more effective.

The action of the assembly of 1913 in passing, over the governor's veto, the repeal of the initiative law of 1910 which closed the Rogue river to commercial fishing caused a great deal of controversy. The governor considered it to be an unwarranted interference with direct legislation. "Since the election of 1910 another election by the people has been held in 1912, and there was no effort put forth to have the law either amended or repealed at this later election."[3] But, on the other hand, it was declared that the repeal was justified as "righting" a "wrong," "correcting" a "mistake."[4]

Although initiative bills providing methods for the reorganization of new counties had been rejected at the two preceding elections, the assembly enacted a bill on this subject in 1913. But the bill of 1910 had contained provisions also on other matters,

---

[1] *Above*, p. 116. "The legislature of 1909 enacted a new fish law to extricate the fishing interests of the Columbia river from the impossible situation into which they had been driven by the enactment through the initiative of two conflicting laws in 1908. Did the legislature violate its plain obligation to the people?" *Oregonian*, Feb. 17, 1911, p. 10, col. 2.   [2] *Cf. ibid.*, Sept. 14, 1911, p. 12, col. 1.

[3] *House Journal*, 1913, pp. 1251–2. In answer to the assertion that this was a local matter and therefore never should have been submitted to the people of the state, the governor pointed out that this bill had carried in the localities directly concerned. *Ibid.*

[4] *Oregonian*, Feb. 28, 1913, p. 10, col. 2; F. M. Gill, *ibid.*, Feb. 16, 1911, p. 10, col. 5.

Amendment and Repeal of Direct Legislation 153

and the provisions for county organization both in this bill and the bill of 1912 were different from those of the bill enacted by the legislature.

The fact that the "millage bill" of 1912 for the university and the agricultural college was rejected at the polls was urged against the enactment of the two millage laws for those institutions at the next session of the legislative assembly. "At the last election the people voted down the millage tax, and their decision should be considered final at this time."[1] Likewise objection was made to the appropriations made by the assembly in 1913 for the university because the people had rejected the university appropriations submitted at the last election. But the appropriations allowed by the assembly were much smaller than those rejected by the people, and the millage laws enacted by the assembly omitted the provision for the consolidation of the management of the two institutions contained in the bill submitted to the people.

A "blue-sky" law was enacted by the assembly in 1913, although such a provision had been defeated at the polls at the preceding election. Objection was raised. "It is too much like a bill turned down by the people. I say this bill should be put up to the people . . . who are as intelligent as we are, and some a good deal more so."[2] But, on the other hand, action by the legislature was approved. "The rejection by the people of the 'blue sky' bill submitted to popular vote under the initiative should not be taken by the legislature as implying that the people do not desire a law designed for substantially the same general end. The initiative bill was rejected mainly because it was not deemed a proper subject for the initiative, partly because some of its provisions did not meet with general approval. . . . The people of Oregon never intended to grant immunity from punishment to stock and bond swindlers, nor

---

[1] G. W. Weeks, quoted in *Oregonian*, Jan. 9, 1913, p. 12, col. 4.
[2] L. G. Lewelling, house of representatives, *Oregon Journal*, Feb. 16, 1913, p. 9, col. 3.

to leave the field open to those swindlers who chose to take the risk of punishment."[1] The "self-supporting" feature of the law enacted probably most commended it to opponents of the initiative law, in which this feature was lacking.

At the election of 1912 the people adopted two constitutional amendments placing limitations of indebtedness for public roads upon the state and the counties respectively, and at the same time rejected two rival bills, one providing for a state highway department, and the other for a state road board and the issue of state road bonds, and three rival measures providing for the issue of county road bonds. The interpretation of the will of the people under such circumstances is a matter of difficulty. One interpretation is simply that the people were generally opposed to the expenditure of money for such purposes. "The vote cast upon road bonding and taxation bills . . . should be conclusive proof that a vast majority are opposed to bonding and increased taxation in any form, and are satisfied with the present system of building roads."[2] But it is certain that the defeat of legislation was due, to some extent at least, to the presence of rival measures on the ballot, which divided the friends of good-roads legislation against themselves. Contrary to the opinion of some that "the people had shut off the legislature from passing good-roads legislation," "it was agreed by a large majority of the members [of the senate] present that the people, in rejecting what road bills they did at the last general election and accepting the two constitutional amendments placing limitation on bonded indebtedness for good-roads purposes, practically put it up to the legislature to carry out some comprehensive good-roads plan."[3] The controversy ended by the enactment of two road bills, one providing for the issue of county bonds, but differing from all of the county bills rejected by the people, and the other for a state highway com-

[1] *Oregonian*, Jan. 6, 1913, p. 6, col. 2.
[2] G. C. Mitty, *ibid.*, Dec. 21, 1912, p. 10, col. 7.
[3] *Ibid.*, Jan. 28, 1913, p. 6, col. 3.

mission differing from both of the rejected state road measures. It was considered that it would be unwise to make provision for state road bonds in view of the recent action of the people, but the law enacted provided for a state road fund and state taxation for road purposes.

A number of measures rejected by the voters at the polls have been resubmitted to them by the legislature in the original or a modified form.

It thus appears that little undue interference with direct legislation has been effected by the legislative assembly.

However, for years there has been some agitation for constitutional restrictions upon the power of the legislature over the "people's laws," even to the extent of prohibiting any interference whatever by the legislature.[1] And both in 1910 and 1912 an amendment, including many other matters, proposed that no statute or resolution approved by the vote of the people should be amended or repealed by the legislative assembly except by a three-fourths vote of all members of each house of the legislature.[2] It failed of adoption, but was confused with so many

---

[1] Reported in *Oregonian*, Jan. 2, 1907, p. 38, col. 3; May 12, 1910, p. 7, col. 3; *Oregon Journal*, Jan. 27, 1915, p. 2, col. 3.

[2] *Referendum Pamphlet*, 1910, no. 360, sec. 1c, p. 187; 1912, no. 362, sec. 1c, p. 210. "Neither the legislative assembly, nor any city council or other representative or legislative body, shall have the power to amend or repeal any law, or part thereof, or any ordinance or resolution, or part thereof, that has been, or that hereafter may be, approved and adopted by the vote of the people of this state, or if it be a local measure, then by a vote of the people of the locality to which it applies. No such measure shall be amended or repealed in any manner other than by a majority of the legal voters who vote on this question for such amendment or appeal [repeal]." *House Joint Resolution*, 1915, no. 10. *Cf.* Arizona *Constitution*, art. 4, sec. 6 (1914). "No act, law or amendment to the constitution, adopted by the people at the polls under the initiative provisions of this section, shall be amended or repealed except by a vote of the electors, unless otherwise provided in said initiative measure; but acts and laws adopted by the people under the referendum provisions of this section may be amended by the legislature at any subsequent session thereof." California *Constitution*, art. 4, sec. 1 (1911). "No act, law, or bill approved by a majority of the electors voting thereon shall be amended or repealed by the legislature within a period of two years following such enactment." Washington *Constitution*, art. 2, sec. 1c (1912). See *above*, p. 174, note 2.

other subjects in the same measure that the attitude of the voters on this provision is uncertain. The absolute prohibition of interference with the people's laws by the legislative assembly, in view of emergencies which are likely to occur, would be unwise.[1] But with either absolute or partial limitation there would be created "a secondary constitution to which legislative enactments must conform," and thus would arise uncertainty as to the technical validity of many statutes.[2] Moreover, such restriction would tend to the unnecessary increase of the number of measures on the ballot.[3] And it would seem that public opinion, unaided by constitutional restriction, has generally been effective enough to secure reasonable protection against abuses by the legislative assembly in this regard. Indeed, undue caution in action on the part of the assembly might result in the obstruction of progress in legislation.

But friends of direct legislation still scent danger to the "people's laws" from interference on the part of the legislative assembly, and recently extracted pledges from candidates for the office of governor to use the veto power for the protection of the people's laws.[4]

[1] *Cf. Oregonian*, Sept. 14, 1911, p. 12, col. 1.
[2] *Ibid.*, Sept. 14, 1911, p. 12, col. 1.
[3] R. G. Calvert, *ibid.*, Jan. 29, 1915, p. 1, col. 7.
[4] "It is my firm belief that the chief executive should be in warm sympathy with the laws enacted by the people. . . . I will disapprove of any action aimed or designed against any law enacted by the people." James Withycombe (elected), *Oregon Grange Bulletin*, Nov., 1914, p. 1. See also *above*, p.146, note 4.

CHAPTER XVI

PUBLIC OPINION BILLS

No provision has been made by law in Oregon for "public opinion bills," whereby the voters may indicate their desire for the enactment of certain legislation by the assembly;[1] but the legislative assembly has been in effect thus instructed in some instances.

The anti-pass bill of 1906 was adopted by a large majority vote at the election, but, in the absence of an enacting clause, the law was void. It was hoped by its supporters that the large majority of votes for the bill would be "accepted by the legislature as a command to enact an effective anti-pass law";[2] and when the legislature met, although it had rejected such a bill at the preceding session, it enacted a law substantially the same as that adopted at the polls. Again, in 1912 the eight-hour labor law, adopted by a smaller majority than that received by the anti-pass law, lacked an enacting clause, and again the legislature obeyed the instructions from the polls. "Senator Smith . . . who introduced the bill, said he believed it could be made clearer by amendment, but he proposed it now without the change of a word because the people had passed upon it. Sarcastic remarks were made by several senators, who declared they were not in sympathy with the bill, but would vote for it because the people did."[3]

---

[1] *Cf.* Illinois *Laws*, 1901, p. 198; *Hurd's Illinois Revised Statutes* (1912), secs. 428–9; *Ohio Constitution*, art. 2, sec. 1b. (1912); Massachusetts *Acts and Resolves*, 1913, ch. 819.   [2] W. S. U'Ren, *Oregonian*, June 27, 1906, p. 14, col. 4.

[3] *Oregon Journal*, Feb. 4, 1913, p. 1, col. 1. "Stewart in explaining his vote against the bill declared that he did not agree that the people cannot make mistakes and believed that the people, or a large majority of them that voted in favor of it, were laboring under a misapprehension as to its contents." *Oregonian*, Feb. 5, 1913, p. 6, col. 3.

The question of the voters' "instructions" came up again at the same session in a different manner. The legislature of 1911 had enacted a law putting the state printer on a flat salary and otherwise changing the organization of this office at the expiration of the incumbent's term. Then followed an initiative bill designed to put the law into effect at once, but the bill was defeated at the election. The vote was interpreted, on the one hand, as a direction for a repeal of the law, but, on the other hand, as a mere concession to the incumbent.[1] The law of 1911 was repealed by the assembly, and a substitute with some changes enacted.

Penal provisions were purposely omitted from the "state-wide" prohibition amendment of 1914. But the adoption of the measure at the election was interpreted as a command to the assembly to provide proper supplemental penal legislation. "It is the mandate of the people that the liquor traffic be abolished and it is the duty of the legislature to make the voice of the people effective."[2] The proper interpretation of the mandate was the subject of dispute, and opinions differ as to whether the requirements of the mandate were fulfilled by the statute finally enacted.

[1] *Oregon Journal*, Jan. 16, 1913, p. 4, col. 1.
[2] Ben Selling, representative elect, reported in *Oregonian*, Nov. 8, 1914, sec. 1, p. 10, col. 3.

CHAPTER XVII

COMPETITION WITH THE LEGISLATIVE ASSEMBLY

"In the most enlightened view and purpose, substitution of representative government by a pure democracy is not contemplated in adopting the principle of direct legislation. The principle is best defined as a supplementary power given to the people to use at times when the legislative branch of the government fails in what its authors actually intended it to be — actually representative."[1] "We shall not abandon the representative system of government, of course; we will only check and correct it, and bring it back to its true foundation principle, that representatives should truly, conscientiously and purely represent the masses of the people."[2]

This is the theory, but in practice, as has been indicated,[3] direct legislation has become more than a "supplementary" institution. Thus, it is asserted, the "negation of representative government" results. "It was not intended that representative government should be abolished by the new system; but it has been abolished by it."[4] "The assumption that representative government is a failure is responsible for this state of things."[5] But, as explained above,[6] the "sins of the legislators," whether "sins of omission" or "sins of commission," whatever their extent, are not the only causes of the multiplicity of measures submitted to the people.

[1] *Oregonian*, Jan. 3, 1913, p. 8, col. 2.
[2] *Oregon Journal*, Mar. 12, 1905, p. 4, col. 1.   [3] *Above*, pp. 78–82.
[4] *Oregonian*, Mar. 10, 1908, p. 8, col. 1.   For the development of a "round-about representative government," see *above*, pp. 98–9.
[5] *Ibid.*, Apr. 12, 1908, sec. 3, p. 6, col. 1.   [6] Pp. 82–5.

However, that this assumption is to a considerable extent justified, that the shortcomings of the legislature are the chief cause of activity in direct legislation, is often declared and widely believed. "Where a large number of measures appear on the ballot it is both a demonstration of the interest of the people in getting good government and of the inefficiency and incompetence of their representatives."[1] "The point has been reached where legislatures are little trusted. Legislation has been juggled and trifled with until most people have lost faith in the delegated body. So many incompetents and nincompoops have been sent to Salem along with good men to make laws that when a good job of constructive legislation is wanted the measure is framed and put before the people. This accounts for most of the measures on the ballot."[2] "It is manifest that the public has largely lost confidence in the body. The action of past assemblies has been such that there is little public faith in the capacity and good purpose of the representative system. No less than this is shown in the almost universal protest that has gone up from every section of the state against the proposed special session. The situation largely explains why so many measures are proposed by the initiative. The public seems, after use of both plans, to have more faith in the initiative and in the judgment and capacity of the people than in the legislative body and the judgment of its delegated representatives. The view is so general and so marked that there are frequently heard expressions favoring ultimate abolishment of the legislature."[3] "Why a legislature, anyhow, in a state where the people have the law-making power?"[4]

---

[1] W. S. U'Ren, reported in *Oregonian*, Dec. 8, 1912, p. 13, col. 1.

[2] *Oregon Journal*, May 11, 1912, p. 4, col. 1.   [3] *Ibid.*, Oct. 2, 1911, p. 8, col. 2.

[4] Oregon City *Courier*, quoted in *Oregonian*, Dec. 2, 1913, p. 10, col. 2. "We have nearly reached the conviction that the legislature is unnecessary. I would not be at all surprised if soon a bill would be initiated doing away with the legislature altogether. An amendment to the resolutions adopted [by the Central Labor Council] last night, was that we favor the abolishing of the legislature, but this amendment was overruled because of the feeling that such an expression was premature. But it

The fact that measures appear on the ballot which have previously failed in the legislature is of course no condemnation of the legislature unless those measures are meritorious. Indeed, in some cases, the appeal from the legislature to the people has been caused by the refusal of the legislature to be influenced by pernicious special interests.

Over half of the initiative measures which have appeared on the ballot may fairly be said to have been presented, in one form or another, first for action by the legislative assembly, and only after failure of enactment there to have been submitted to the people. But many of these measures have been reform measures, and, as shown by the large majority received at the election, measures demanded by public opinion. However, other measures which the assembly has refused to pass have also failed to receive the popular approval. "If inefficiency and irresponsiveness to public will on the part of the law-making body had been responsible for the large number of measures presented in the recent campaign, the fact would have been shown in the adoption of a large percentage of those measures. As the people declared they did not want two-thirds of them, how is the legislature at all to blame for not enacting them?"[1]

Where the defeat of meritorious legislation by the legislative assembly cannot be urged as an excuse for placing a measure on the ballot, it has been declared that it is not even worth while to submit propositions of some kinds to the assembly. "Should the legislature undertake the passage of such a ["blue-sky"] law the legislators would be besieged by lobbyists who would seek to so alter the bill as to leave it valueless. It would come through the mill so emasculated as to be of no service to the people."[2]

---

is coming." William McKenzie, union labor leader, quoted in *Oregon Journal*, Sept. 23, 1911, p. 1, col. 5. "In time the people may strip the legislature of every power it once enjoyed, leaving it but a place in memory, and themselves exercise directly within the state all of the powers formerly committed to the legislature." *Kalich* v. *Knapp, Pacific Reporter* (Oregon), vol. 145, pp. 22, 26 (1914)

[1] *Oregonian*, Nov. 24, 1912, sec. 3, p. 6, col. 3.

[2] *East Oregonian*, reprinted in Eugene *Guard*, Oct. 25, 1912, p. 4, col. 3.

The large number of measures on the ballot is, especially under the conditions prevailing in the making of petitions, no certain evidence of desire on the part of the people as a whole to "supersede representative government." "While the submission of thirty-seven measures in one election may, on its face, seem to show a tendency toward democracy, the freedom with which the principle is applied cannot be ascribed to desire by the people to supersede representative government. Rather it is due to the ease with which laws may be initiated or referred. The fact that they are on the ballot is not proof that the people desired to pass on them, for the test of public opinion in this direction must rest wholly in the action taken at the polls."[1] And by their action at the polls the people have sustained the legislature in case of eight of the fourteen acts subjected to the referendum by petition, while only thirty-five of the ninety-five initiative measures have been approved at the elections.

The quality of the representation in the legislative assembly can of course be improved by the election of better men by the voters. "Those who would abolish the legislature and let the people make the laws must remember the people named and chose the members of the legislature, and a stream cannot rise above its head. The people are ruling."[2] "The legislature is what the people make it. They have the ballot. They have the votes. They do the electing. They get what they vote for. ... The people themselves must shoulder the responsibility for legislative follies. The legislature is of their own making, and when they howl at the legislature, they are only howling at themselves."[3]

Competition with the legislative assembly has been charged as due not only to the quality of the membership of the assembly, but also to its present form of organization and to the legislative processes now prevailing. Some proposed radical changes in

[1] *Oregonian*, Jan. 3, 1913, p. 8, col. 2.   [2] *Ibid.*, Feb. 25, 1913, p. 8, col. 4.
[3] *Oregon Journal*, Sept. 25, 1912, p. 6, col. 1.

the organization of the assembly by way of proportional representation and the abolition of the senate would, it is urged, "make the legislature as progressive as the people of the state," and thus greatly reduce the necessity of resort to direct legislation.[1] The division of the legislative session into two periods, one exclusively for the purpose of the introduction of measures, and the other for the enactment of measures into law (and for both the introduction and enactment of measures appearing during the session to be demanded by public opinion), would, it is believed, by allowing public criticism of the legislative program during the recess, make the legislature more responsive to public opinion, and thus tend to reduce the amount of direct legislation.[2] But there is probably much more agreement as to the necessity of rational reforms for efficiency, for the absence of which the legislative assembly is itself wholly responsible.[3]

Of course under the present system the governor shares the responsibility for proper legislation with the assembly, and thus comes in for some criticism in connection with discussion of responsibility for the extensive use of direct legislation.[4]

---

[1] People's Power League, *Referendum Pamphlet*, 1912, pp. 220, 222.

[2] "Whereas, It is the desire of the twenty-seventh assembly of the state of Oregon to be responsive to the will of the people in the enactment of meritorious legislation demanded by them, thereby to prevent crowding of the ballot in the future with initiative measures, now, therefore, Be it resolved, the senate concurring, That the twenty-seventh legislative assembly of the state of Oregon, now in session, fully realizing our duty and responsibility to the people, do declare, that we are ready, able and willing to enact any meritorious legislation that may be brought to us from the people, to the end that such matters may be disposed of with due care and dispatch, and to the further end that the ballot at the next ensuing general election in the state of Oregon shall not be crowded with more measures — with or without uncertain meanings and design — than the people of the state of Oregon can properly and carefully consider and vote upon.

"That the people are therefore requested to present all measures to said legislative assembly at as early a date as possible so that the same may be given due consideration." *House Joint Memorial*, 1913, no. 1, passed by the house of representatives, but not by the senate. *House Journal*, 1913, pp. 153–4.

[3] See especially *Oregon Journal*, Jan. 10, 1913, p. 8, col. 1.

[4] *E.g.*, *Oregonian*, Oct. 29, 1912, p. 10, col. 2.

Without any lack of confidence in the legislative assembly, direct legislation may be substituted for representative legislation in cases where it is practically certain that measures if enacted will be referred by petition.[1] But, of course, in such cases, the voters are without the advantage of the discussion of the merits of the measures by the assembly.

Upon the theory that direct legislation is to be used only as a check upon or a supplement to legislation enacted by the legislative assembly, it has been proposed to limit by law the use of the initiative to cases where the legislature has refused to act. "No bill should ever be allowed to be placed upon the ballot by the initiative unless a bill having the same general objects or containing the same subject-matter had first been introduced in the legislature and had there failed of passage. . . . If a new law is enacted, the place to have it enacted is in the legislature. . . . [It will receive discussion in the legislature] as well as from the press and public; by such discussion its crude features will be eliminated, its weak points probably discovered and the whole measure strengthened and worked over into a more acceptable form. Then, if through any undue influence it fails to pass, it can be placed before the people with much better chance of its being a 'safe' project and being understood by the average voter."[2] In accord with this view it has been definitely proposed that initiative measures shall, under provision of law, be presented to the legislative assembly first, and that the assembly shall have the power either to adopt the measures as submitted, or to offer a competing measure and submit both measures together to the popular vote.[3] Precedents of several other

---

[1] *Cf. Oregonian*, Oct. 23, 1912, p. 10, col. 7.

[2] A. T. Buxton, reported in *Oregonian*, Mar. 24, 1908, p. 6, col. 1. See also especially *Oregon Journal*, May 1, 1909, p. 6, col. 3. For the view that legislation is likely to be the worse for its revision by the assembly, see *above*, pp. 28–9.

[3] W. S. U'Ren, *Results of the Initiative and Referendum in Oregon, Proceedings of the American Political Science Association*, vol. 4, pp. 193, 197 (1907); A. T. Buxton, quoted in *Oregonian*, May 15, 1908, p. 6, col. 3; C. H. Chapman and others, *Introductory Letter*, 1909, pp. 6, 1–2; report in *Oregonian*, Sept. 9, 1909, p. 8, col. 2.

Competition with the Legislative Assembly 165

states point in this direction,[1] and such provision has already been made in case of initiative ordinances of Oregon cities.[2]

"The plan has its attractions. . . . The number of initiative measures would be cut down if the legislature acted both in harmony and good faith, but if obstructive in tendency or contentious in spirit, each measure petitioned for would bring forth two at the election following the session of the legislature. Alternative or rival measures . . . tend to defeat each other, even though a majority of the voters favor the basic principle involved in each."[3] However, it would seem that this objection might be removed, as above[4] suggested, by a system of preferential voting or alternative measures.

[1] *E.g.*, Washington *Constitution*, art. 2, sec. 1 (a) (1912).
The proposed Wisconsin provision is a new departure. "The people reserve to themselves power . . . to propose laws and to enact or reject the same at the polls. . . . A proposed law . . . shall consist of a bill which has been introduced in the legislature during the first thirty days of the session, as so introduced; or at the option of the petitioners, there may be incorporated in said bill any amendment or amendments introduced in the legislature. . . . Upon petition filed not later than four months before the next general election, such proposed law shall be submitted to a vote of the people. . . . The petition shall be filed with the secretary of state and shall be sufficient to require the submission by him of a measure to the people when signed by eight per cent of the qualified electors," etc. And similar provisions for constitutional amendments. Proposed Wisconsin *Constitution*, art. 4, sec. 1; art. 12, sec. 3, rejected (1914).

[2] "If any ordinance, charter or amendment to the charter of any city shall be proposed by initiative petition, such petition shall be filed with the city clerk . . . and he shall transmit it to the next session of the city council. The council shall either ordain or reject the same, as proposed, . . . and if the council shall reject said proposed ordinance or amendment, or shall take no action thereon, then the city clerk, . . . shall submit the same to the voters of the city or town. . . . If the council reject such ordinance or amendment, or take no action thereon, it may ordain a competing ordinance or amendment, which shall be submitted by the city clerk . . . to the people of the said city or town, at the same election at which said initiative proposal is submitted." *Laws*, 1907, ch. 226, sec. 12; *Lord's Oregon Laws*, sec. 3482.

[3] *Oregonian*, July 26, 1913, p. 6, col. 1. See *above*, p. 49.

[4] Pp. 49–50. It has been suggested that the legislative assembly might well be empowered to amend initiative measures in order to improve their form, without destroying the "sense or purpose" of the original. "Obviously some safeguard should be thrown around the initiative measures proposed to the legislature if amendments by that body were to be permitted. Why not permit amendment of the phraseology of such bills and refer them to the supreme court for decision as to whether the sense

But whatever the amount of competition with the legislative assembly, from the ever-increasing amount of legislation enacted by the assembly — one hundred and fifty-two laws in 1901, three hundred and forty-nine laws in 1915 — it is clear that there is no danger that the representative legislature will be superseded by the direct action of the people.[1]

or purpose of the original has been destroyed? A court opinion that the legislature had not emasculated the bill should serve as well as submission of the matter to the people. The referendum would protect the public from the imposition through the imperative mandate of laws it did not desire." *Oregonian*, Mar. 27, 1911, p. 6, col. 3.

[1] *Cf.* R. W. Montague, *Oregon System at Work, National Municipal Review*, vol. 3, pp. 256, 268 (1914).

CHAPTER XVIII

THE EFFECT OF DIRECT LEGISLATION ON THE CHARACTER AND ACTIVITY OF THE LEGISLATIVE ASSEMBLY

"THE first noticeable effect was a large decrease in the number of paid lobbyists at the next session of the legislative assembly in January, 1903, and the comparative number of charges that the action of members on any bill had been influenced by money. The legislature made mistakes, but no one charged it with being corrupt. It was generally conceded that the absence of corrupting influences was largely due to fear that the referendum would be demanded on any legislation obtained by such methods."[1] And although the paid lobby is still much in evidence and charges of actual corruption of members of the legislature are occasionally made, some of them, at least, upon good grounds, present conditions are in very great contrast with the disgraceful conditions which existed prior to the adoption of the system of direct legislation. "The fact that legislative measures can be reviewed by popular vote is a club that makes legislators behave themselves. The fact that if the legislature does not pass a good measure the people can and will, is the most powerful influence in the world to compel legislators to enact good laws. . . . It steadies the legislature and keeps it strictly sane. It keeps that body from becoming puffed up and enables it to more distinctly hear the wishes of the people. It is a safety valve against legislative follies, a guarantee against legislative extravagance and a sign post pointing members to the path of duty."[2]

[1] W. S. U'Ren, *Operation of the Initiative and Referendum in Oregon*, Arena, vol. 32, p. 128 (1904). See also W. S. U'Ren, *Oregonian*, Apr. 29, 1907, p. 5, col. 7.
[2] *Oregon Journal*, Sept. 18, 1909, p. 4, col. 1.

But the popular control over the legislative assembly which has been made more effective by the operation of the direct primary, established two years after the adoption of the initiative and referendum, has doubtless had very much to do with the change in the character of the assembly, and it is impossible to divide the honors in this connection between direct nomination and direct legislation. Further, it is impossible to say how much of the reform has been due to the change in public sentiment rather than to the operation of the new instruments of government.

However, the legislative assembly has by no means yet reached perfection under all these influences combined, and indeed the enthusiasts for direct legislation are the loudest in their complaints of the "unrepresentative" character of their representatives in the assembly.[1]

Although it is probably generally conceded that the initiative and referendum have been powerful instruments in the development of *negative* virtue in the legislature, there is a difference of opinion as to their influence for *positive* virtue.

Of course, under the system of direct government, in a sense, the people are responsible for *all* legislation. "With this power, it necessarily follows that the people themselves must assume the responsibility not only for laws which are written in our statute-books and which ought not to remain there, but for failure to enact those laws which ought to be enacted. . . . Blame for bad laws was accustomed in those days to be visited upon the legislature, but now responsibility rests with the people themselves."[2] It is constantly asserted that under the present system legislatures evade responsibility for legislation and shift it upon the people. "If men in public office are not to have stamina enough to consider well the best interests of their constituents and, having decided, act courageously, then they had better resign office, or else the whole representative system ought to be

---
[1] *Above*, pp. 82–5, 159–60.
[2] Governor Chamberlain, reported in *Oregonian,* Apr. 27, 1906, p. 6, col. 1.

done away with and all legislation and administration be performed by the people direct, with whatsoever success might be possible."[1] And it must be admitted that evidence of a tendency to avoid responsibility does at times appear in the legislative assembly. On the other hand, however, there is more evidence of an increased sense of responsibility there — for what is done, due, in part, to the referendum, for what is not done, due, in part, to the initiative.[2] "We have had some experience with the referendum, and we should go slow."[3] "Shall we put this before the people ourselves, or shall we ask the people to place it on the ballot by petition of eight per cent of the voters?"[4] But there is danger that the clamor of special narrow interests will be mistaken by the legislative assembly for public opinion, and, in fact, during the session of the assembly disappointed advocates or opponents of legislation, however broad or narrow the interests they represent, are constantly threatening to invoke either the initiative or the referendum.

The constitutional provision which permits the legislative assembly to submit statutes to the people of the state for approval or rejection [5] is vicious in that it may tempt the assembly

---

[1] Eugene *Register*, Jan. 5, 1913, p. 12, col. 2. See also J. N. Teal, *Practical Workings of the Initiative and Referendum in Oregon*, Proceedings of the Cincinnati Conference for Good City Government, 1909, pp. 309, 311; S. A. Lowell, *Oregonian*, Jan. 25, 1913, p. 6, col. 5.

[2] *Cf.* R. W. Montague, *Oregon System at Work*, National Municipal Review, vol. 3, pp. 256, 268 (1914).

[3] C. Schuebel, house of representatives, *Oregon Journal*, Feb. 17, 1913, p. 4, col. 2.

[4] A. H. Eaton, house of representatives, Eugene *Guard*, Feb. 8, 1913, p. 13, col. 1.

The ever-increasing amount of legislation enacted by the legislative assembly (*above*, pp. 78–80) might appear to be evidence against any tendency of the assembly to shift its responsibility upon the people. But, although the increase in the volume of legislation might be interpreted to prove that the assembly does not refrain from action in view of the power of the people to obtain desired legislation independently of the assembly through the initiative, it might as well be interpreted to indicate that the assembly is becoming less conservative and tending to cast the final responsibility for action upon the people in view of their power to nullify undesired legislation by the referendum. However, this increase in the volume of such legislation has doubtless been due mostly, if not wholly, to causes unconnected with direct legislation.

[5] *Constitution*, art. 4, sec. 1 (1902). *Above*, pp. 9–10.

to shift the responsibility for the enactment of legislation, for which it has been chosen, back upon the electors, and also to add to the already overloaded ballot. The action of the legislature is practically a substitute for an initiative petition whereby the legislature may suggest rather than enact legislation, and thus become in this regard a mere "probouleutic" assembly.

However, so far the possibilities of evil of this power of referendum have been little realized. The two statutes submitted in this manner at the election of 1914 are the first of the kind, and they come within the class only by a technical construction of the law. They had both been submitted to the people before and had been rejected, and hence, on the principle of the practical "rigidity" of direct legislation, could not consistently have been finally enacted by the legislature.[1]

---

[1] *Above*, pp. 132–44. *Cf.* proposed Wisconsin constitutional amendment prohibiting the legislature from referring statutes to the voters. Proposed Wisconsin *Constitution*, art. 4, sec. 1, rejected (1914).

CHAPTER XIX

THE REFERENDUM AS A SUBSTITUTE FOR CONSTITUTIONAL LIMITATIONS UPON THE LEGISLATIVE ASSEMBLY

NUMEROUS limitations upon the power of the legislature have been considered in the past an absolute necessity on account of the actual or possible mistakes or abuses of power by the legislature. The legislature has thus been unable, in many matters, to institute reforms except by the submission of constitutional amendments to the people, and the people, on the other hand, have had to vote upon questions which in some instances they would doubtless have preferred to leave to the judgment of the legislature if they had had any power to correct the action of the legislature in case correction might be really needed. The check upon the legislature now secured through the referendum makes unnecessary many of the present limitations, and this opens the way for entrusting more power to the legislature. The substitution, to some extent, of the optional for the obligatory referendum would bring a very great advantage, especially in case of technical measures of legislation, which the voters are likely to reject when submitted to them for the simple reason that they do not understand them.[1] Further, in removing some of the sources of possible conflict between constitutional and statutory provisions, this reform would, so far, substitute the legislation of the assembly for the jurisdiction of the courts, and thus favor *policy* rather than *technicality* in legislation.[2]

---
[1] *Above*, pp. 37–41, 112–13.
[2] "The judicial control over legislation is not in any case an unmixed blessing, because it decreases legislative efficiency and as employed to the present time has

The amendment of the constitution adopted in 1912, which removes to a considerable extent the limitations imposed upon the legislative assembly in the organization of the judicial department of the state government, is in accord with this idea.

often checked for many years needed reforms which the courts have been forced to accept in the end, but the state judicial power over legislation when employed as frequently and as irresponsibly as during the past thirty years, can hardly be considered an instrument of very great value. In fact the referendum has in some cases been advocated because of the belief that it will weaken or destroy this very power."
W. F. Dodd, *Revision and Amendment of State Constitutions*, pp. 254-5 (1910).

CHAPTER XX

DIRECT LEGISLATION AND THE COURTS

I

The Interpretation of Direct Legislation

POPULAR legislation, like ordinary legislation enacted by the representative assembly, is of course interpreted and applied by the courts, and the courts necessarily in some cases of crudely constructed measures "practically legislate amendments by decisions."[1] And since statutes adopted by the people are in general subject, from the standpoint of *law*,[2] to the restrictions imposed by the constitution upon ordinary legislation, there is a possibility also that the courts may find popular legislation to be unconstitutional, although so far, in actual practice, this possibility has scarcely been realized at all. There is a tendency to jealousy of any interference with the "people's laws" on the part of the courts, as on the part of the legislative assembly.[3] "Of course there is going to be trouble over the enforcement of the workmen's compensation act, which has just been adopted by such an overwhelming majority by the people of the state. . . . The next step will be to call upon the courts for a judicial decree, and by the time they get through juggling with it, it will be hard for the people to recognize the law they have so unanimously adopted. . . . It is to be hoped that in case the decision as to the enforcement of the law is thrown into the courts that the legal wise-acres will have judgment enough to listen to the

[1] F. V. Holman, *Some Instances of Unsatisfactory Results under Initiative Amendments of the Oregon Constitution*, p. 2 (1910).
[2] *Below*, pp. 180–1.   [3] *Above*, pp. 145–56.

advice of the people."[1] Indeed much objection has been raised even against instituting court proceedings to keep off the ballot measures not conforming to the technical requirements of the law,[2] and measures the petitions for which have been tainted with fraud.

2

"*The Recall of Judicial Decisions*"

Some time before the announcement of Roosevelt's proposition for "the recall of judicial decisions," it had been suggested in Oregon that the system of direct legislation might *logically* be extended by "an amendment providing referendum votes on decisions of the supreme court."[3] In the legislative assembly of 1913 there was a futile attempt to embody a modification of Roosevelt's plan in a constitutional amendment. "Whenever the highest court of the state shall declare an act of the legislature affecting either social or industrial conditions to be void on the ground that authority to enact it had not been delegated by the people to the legislature, the question shall be submitted to a vote of the electors at the next general election thereafter, unless the legislature shall provide for its submission at an earlier date as follows: 'Shall chapter . . . become a law?' and if the majority of the votes cast for and against the

[1] Eugene *Guard*, Nov. 7, 1913, p. 4, col. 1. See also Eugene *Register*, Dec. 3, 1913, p. 4, col. 1; *Oregon Journal*, Apr. 3, 1914, p. 6, col. 1. "When a majority of the electors voting at a state election shall by their votes signify approval of a law or resolution, such law or resolution shall stand as the law of the state, and shall not be overruled, annulled, set aside, suspended, or in any way made inoperative except by the direct vote of the people." Nevada *Constitution*, art. 19, sec. 2 (1904).

[2] "No law or amendment to the constitution initiated and approved by the electors as herein provided, shall be held unconstitutional, or void on account of the insufficiency of any initiative petition; nor shall the repeal of any law submitted by the referendum petition be held invalid for such insufficiency." Minnesota *Constitution*, art. 4, sec. 1 (d), rejected (1914). See W. F. Dodd, *Revision and Amendment of State Constitutions*, pp. 228–36 (1910); *Oregonian*, July 28, 1915, p. 6, col. 2.

[3] F. V. Holman, *Some Instances of Unsatisfactory Results under Initiative Amendments of the Oregon Constitution*, p. 46 (1910).

proposition shall be in the affirmative, it shall take effect ten days after the completion and certification of the official canvass of the votes, the same excepting with respect to the time it takes effect, as if its enactment had been authorized by the constitution, which shall be deemed amended so as to authorize it, and it shall be subject to amendment and repeal the same as other laws." [1]

On account of the practical obliteration of differences between constitutional and ordinary statutory law under the system of initiative legislation in Oregon,[2] it would seem that a provision for the "recall of judicial decisions" would add absolutely nothing to the power which the people already possess. "If the Oregon supreme court declares unconstitutional a law the majority of the people want, we can write that law into the constitution by initiative just as easily and by the same process that we write an ordinary statute."[3] The people may thus easily change the constitution "piece-meal," to nullify, for the future, the effect of a specific judicial decision, or "wholesale," to change a broad principle of constitutional law.[4] It is probably for this

---

[1] *House Joint Resolution*, 1913, no. 12. See *Oregonian*, Feb. 5, 1913, p. 8, col. 2; *Oregon Journal*, Feb. 6, 1913, p. 4, col. 4.

"None of the said courts except the supreme court shall have any power to declare or adjudicate any law of this state or any city charter or amendment thereto adopted by the people in cities . . . as in violation of the constitution of this state or of the United States; provided that before such decision shall be binding it shall be subject to the approval or disapproval by the people. . . . All such laws or parts thereof submitted as herein provided when approved by a majority of the votes cast thereon . . . shall be and become the law of this state notwithstanding the decision of the supreme court. . . . All such charters, or amendments thereto, . . . when approved by a majority of the votes cast thereon . . . shall be and become the law of this state and of said city . . . notwithstanding the decision of the supreme court." Colorado *Constitution*, art. 6, sec. 1 (1914).

[2] *Below*, pp. 180–4. See A. L. Lowell, *Government and Parties in Continental Europe*, vol. 2, pp. 296–7 (1896); W. F. Dodd, *Revision and Amendment of State Constitutions*, pp. 252–8 (1910). [3] *Oregonian*, Mar. 1, 1912, p. 10, col. 3.

[4] That the "recall" of decisions allows gradual and partial reform in place of change of general principles by constitutional amendment, has been considered, from a generally *conservative* point of view, to be a disadvantage rather than an advantage. "The impatient man, in his haste to undo an individual wrong, thus would leave the

reason that there has been little popular interest here in this innovation of government.

general wrong unredressed. The patient man, who strikes at the root of an evil, uses the individual wrong as an ax wherewith to hew out the roots and to bring down the whole evil growth. Not because recall of decisions impairs the dignity and independence of the courts; not because it is necessary to right judicial wrongs, but because it is reform by piecemeal, is the measure unwise. We had better by far wait longer and make a complete job of the reform." *Oregonian*, Dec. 9, 1913, p. 10, col. 2. See also *ibid.*, Nov. 2, 1913, sec. 3, p. 6, col. 4.

CHAPTER XXI

DIRECT LEGISLATION AND THE CONSTITUTIONAL CONVENTION

A BILL providing for a constitutional convention was defeated in the legislative assembly of 1905, three years after the system of direct legislation was adopted. Those back of the movement were suspected of the intention of securing the abolition of the initiative and referendum,[1] but doubtless opposition was caused also by a belief that under the system of direct legislation the constitutional convention is a superfluity.[2] In order to safeguard the new system, the People's Power League in 1906 was instrumental in placing on the ballot a constitutional amendment providing that "no convention shall be called to amend or propose amendments to this constitution, or to propose a new constitution, unless the law providing for such convention shall first be approved by the people on a referendum vote at a regular general election."[3] This was adopted by the people.

In 1909 a bill calling a constitutional convention passed the legislative assembly and, under the law, was submitted for the decision of the people. The friends of the movement urged the necessity of a systematic revision of the "ancient" constitution, in place of the "piece-meal" methods prevailing. "Shall we continue, at a great expense, to attempt, in the present spasmodic, erratic and unsystematic manner to revise a faulty constitution? Shall we continue, at each succeeding election, to vote upon amendments proposed by any manner or group of men? Shall we continue to

[1] See especially *Oregon Journal*, Jan. 27, 1905, p. 4, col. 1; Feb. 1, 1905, p. 5, col. 5.   [2] *Cf.* C. E. Ladd, quoted in *Arena*, vol. 29, p. 271 (1903).
[3] *Constitution*, art. 17, sec. 1 (1906).

adopt proposed amendments without amendment or debate? Shall we continue to allow our constitution-making to be done by self-appointed law-makers who are responsible to nobody? Would it not be better to submit the whole question to a body of sixty men, selected according to law, and then at the polls pass upon the results of their deliberations? Would it not be better to follow some well-defined plan than continue to patch our constitution piece-meal and at random, where those who prepare the amendments are generally unknown and responsible to no constituency?"[1]

But the motives of the advocates of the convention were suspected. "It was urged by those who were responsible for the passage of the bill calling for the convention that our constitution was coming to be a motley affair and was sadly in need of complete revision. It is probable that the average citizen has not felt the urgent need of this revision to the same extent as the professional politician who finds many of the opportunities and much of the boodle of his former occupation cut off by the present provision of the constitution giving the people a direct control of the affairs of the government. This is the bright particular spot in the present constitution at which these revisionists are aiming. It is the elimination of this feature which they hope to secure by the adoption of a new constitution. Most of us have been laboring under the impression that when anything particularly wrong should be found in our constitution we have a comparatively easy method of remedying the difficulty; we have felt that we had reached a point beyond the necessity of a constitutional convention. Not so the politician, and those who look to him to promote their interests. They want to do away with the initiative and referendum. At first they hoped to do it through the courts. They realize the hopelessness of taking it directly to the people, at least at the present time. But the constitutional convention could be packed and

[1] C. N. McArthur, *Need of a Constitutional Convention, Proceedings of the Oregon Bar Association*, 1908–10, pp. 148, 157.

manipulated just as the old political conventions were, and made to give us a new constitution with direct legislation left out or so arranged as to destroy its effectiveness. It is true, the matter would still have to be submitted to the people and, if it were unsatisfactory, they would have an opportunity to reject it. . . . There is one safe plan to be followed . . . that is to leave the thing alone. If we got a new constitution and it was unsatisfactory, we might be able to vote it down and we might not."[1]

Some persons went further and declared that there was really no intention of allowing the people to decide on the new constitution. "The plan is to have a new constitution made and 'proclaimed' by the convention as the constitution of Oregon, without permitting the people to vote on that new constitution. In that way . . . the convention can make a new constitution for Oregon, leaving out the initiative, referendum and recall, and thus take from the people the power they now have to manage their public affairs."[2]

That there was any real intention of bringing about the promulgation of a constitution without a vote of the people is almost impossible; but a great many voters believed this to be the case, and, perhaps chiefly for this reason, the proposition for a convention was overwhelmingly defeated at the election. However, there was at least some hope among conservatives that Oregon could be induced to "shake off a large part of her progressive garments."[3]

[1] A. T. Buxton, *Pacific Grange Bulletin*, Aug., 1909, p. 3, col. 4.

[2] People's Power League, *Referendum Pamphlet*, 1910, pp. 18, 19. See also *Oregon Journal*, Apr. 4, 1909, p. 8, col. 1; resolution of State Grange, *Oregonian*, May 16, 1909, p. 6, col. 1. The decisions of courts of other states holding valid constitutions "proclaimed" by constitutional conventions were cited. On this subject see especially J. A. Jameson, *Constitutional Conventions*, 4th ed., pp. 414, 490–503 (1887); C. S. Lobingier, *People's Law*, pp. 330–7 (1909).

[3] Reported in *Oregon Journal*, Feb. 21, 1909, p. 8, col. 4.

CHAPTER XXII

DIRECT LEGISLATION AND THE STABILITY OF GOVERNMENT

THE original constitution provided for the submission of proposed constitutional amendments by the majority vote of all members elected to each of the two houses of two successive legislative assemblies to the electors, and required for ratification of the amendment, the vote, apparently, of a majority of all the electors voting at the election.[1] This was a very slow and cumbersome procedure compared with that provided in 1902, whereby constitutional amendments may be submitted to the people in the same way as other measures by initiative petition.[2] But since 1906 the approval by the legislative assembly at one session has been sufficient for the submission of amendments to the voters. Further, since 1906 the majority for ratification of such measures has been the same as in the case of measures submitted by the initiative, a majority of the votes cast on the measure.[3]

As a general rule, initiative statutory measures are, technically, subject to the same constitutional limitations as are statutes enacted by the legislative assembly,[4] although in a few

[1] *Constitution*, art. 17, sec. 1 (1859). See *State* v. *Swift, Indiana Reports*, vol. 69, p. 505 (1880); *In Matter of Denny, ibid.*, vol. 156, p. 104 (1900); T. M. Cooley, *Constitutional Limitations*, 7th ed., pp. 892–3 (1906); Lobingier, *People's Law*, pp. 326–30 (1909). [2] *Ibid.*, art. 4, sec. 1 (1902).

[3] *Ibid.*, art. 17, sec. 1 (1906). For opposition to this amendment as increasing the instability of the constitution, see *Oregonian*, May 28, 1906, p. 6, col. 6.

[4] *Kadderly* v. *Portland, Oregon Reports*, vol. 44, pp. 118, 146 (1903); *State* v. *Richardson, ibid.*, vol. 48, pp. 309, 318 (1906); *State* v. *Langworthy, ibid.*, vol. 55, pp. 303, 308 (1910). "The limitations expressed in the constitution, on the powers of the general assembly to enact laws, shall be deemed limitations on the power of the people to enact laws." Ohio *Constitution*, art. 2, sec. 1 (1912).

matters the restrictions apply only to action by the assembly.[1] But it is evident that this technical limitation can easily be evaded. "Under the system now prevailing, a clause of the organic act appears to control only the legislative assembly, since it requires no more effort nor any greater care to amend a clause of the constitution than it does to enact, alter, or repeal a statute, for a majority vote is sufficient to give sanction to a bill, and no greater vote is required to amend the fundamental law. . . . As a majority vote of the qualified electors by an exercise of the initiative power can enact a statute, they can, by giving such a law an appropriate article and section and entitling it an amendment of the constitution, make it a part of the fundamental law and render the supposed stability of the organic act subject to sudden and serious changes."[2]

It had early been suggested that this would become a general practice. "In order . . . to escape conflict with the constitution, many proposed bills are likely to be adopted as parts of the constitution, whereas they should properly be enacted as statutes, if enacted at all. This possibly leaves many persons to lament that the barriers between the constitution and the statutes no longer exist."[3] But, as a matter of fact, there has been very little statutory matter formulated into constitutional amendments for this reason, or, at least, chiefly for this reason.

---

[1] In practice, new-county statutes are the only examples of such initiative legislation. A constitutional amendment of 1910 made the referendum on tax bills passed by the assembly obligatory, at the same time that it exempted from constitutional limitation tax measures referred to the people either by the legislature or by initiative petition (*Constitution*, art. 9, sec. 1a (1910)), but this was repealed two years later. *Constitution*, art. 9, sec. 1a (1912).

[2] *State* v. *Schluer*, Oregon Reports, vol. 59, pp. 18, 27 (1911).

[3] *Oregonian*, Dec. 27, 1903, p. 16, col. 1. *Cf.* W. F. Dodd, *Revision and Amendment of State Constitutions*, pp. 252–8 (1910).

When a bill is in conflict with existing provisions of the constitution, it has been contended that the constitution must be amended before the bill can be submitted to the voters; but doubtless the better view is that an act will be valid if passed simultaneously with the constitutional amendment. *Cf. Oregonian*, May 10, 1912, p. 12, col. 1. However, in the analogous case where a law has been declared by the courts to be unconstitutional and the constitution has been later so amended that such a

But, under the circumstances, it seems absurd that a mere detail of the *form* of a measure should be of such consequence.[1]

However, it is clear that so far as *initiative* legislation is concerned, there is practically no constitution in Oregon. "The constitution of Oregon is only a check or restriction on the legislature. The people's will rises above it." [2] "There is no constitution, for it is subject to such flux and change as no longer to be the mainstay of our government." [3] "The only constitutional protection enjoyed by the people of this state to-day lies in the federal constitution, but as that instrument bears only indirectly upon important questions . . . it is quite evident that in all ordinary matters of government the people of Oregon are practically without constitutional protection." [4]

Not only on account of such practical absence of constitutional limitations upon initiative legislation, but on account of the extreme ease of working the initiative and referendum, these institutions have been branded as "revolutionary." "They violate the very principles upon which and for which organized society forms a constitution. . . . They upset society. . . . They have the effect practically of abolishing constitution and laws altogether; or at least keeping people who would defend the stability and orderly progress of society, always on guard, always under arms, for their defense." [5] "Why . . . should the state be kept in continual turmoil and uproar, to hold a check

---

law could be enacted, the weight of decision favors the view that the law declared void must be reënacted in order to be valid. But the authority of the United States supreme court is to the contrary. See especially *Cyclopedia of Law and Procedure*, vol. 8, p. 768; T. M. Cooley, *Constitutional Limitations*, 7th ed., pp. 259–60 (1903).

[1] *Cf. Oregonian*, May 10, 1912, p. 12, col. 1.

[2] *Oregonian*, Dec. 22, 1912, sec. 3, p. 8, col. 3.

[3] C. H. Carey, *New Responsibilities of Citizenship, Proceedings of the Oregon Bar Association*, 1908–10, pp. 18, 33. "The people inaugurated constitutional government, and have not yet abandoned the constitution they promulgated in the beginning." *Andrews v. Neil, Oregon Reports*, vol. 61, pp. 471, 474 (1912).

[4] C. N. McArthur, *Need of a Constitutonal Convention, Proceedings of the Oregon Bar Association*, 1908–10, pp. 148, 154. See also *Oregonian*, Mar. 19, 1908, p. 8 col. 1; Jan. 18, 1909, p. 6, col. 2; July 6, 1909, p. 8, col. 1; F. V. Holman, *Chicago Civic Federation Bulletin*, no. 3, p. 12 (1911). [5] *Oregonian*, Feb. 18, 1908, p. 8, col. 1.

Direct Legislation and Stability of Government 183

upon this dangerous system, and often be plunged into terror about it?"[1]

The rights of the minority are declared to be in constant danger from the system. "It is an evil [of] our initiative and referendum, that a slender majority can on the exciting impulse of a single election now ride rough-shod over all the rights of a minority, even to sweeping away any or all of the elementary constitutional safeguards which the experienced wisdom of ages have established as supposed permanent guarantees of the rights of individuals, and of minorities, against sudden encroachments of majorities. . . . Nobody knows when it may go off next, nor where it may strike."[2]

And indeed some of the best friends of the system of direct legislation are of the opinion that at least constitutional amendments can be made too easily under the present law. "It is a fact that as matters now stand, the constitution can be amended far too easily for the safety and security of the state. I venture to call attention to this matter again this year merely to suggest that it would be well for friends of the system to give consideration to means of its modification in this particular before more sweeping changes are forced by its enemies."[3] And doubtless more friends of the system occasionally long for a "closed season" against its operation. There is additional cause for such an attitude in the fact that questions "settled by the people" in some cases do not *remain* settled, but come up before the legislature or the people again and again in the original or a somewhat modified form.

The various proposed checks upon the use of the initiative and referendum have been discussed above.[4]

It is true that under the old system the constitution was changed but once in the period of forty-three years, and that it

---

[1] *Oregonian*, July 21, 1909, p. 8, col. 2. See also *ibid.*, July 5, 1912, p. 10, col. 1.
[2] M. C. George, *Oregonian*, Mar. 23, 1908, p. 9, col. 2.
[3] Master of the State Grange, reported in *Oregonian*, May 13, 1909, p. 6, col. 3. See also *Oregon Journal*, Nov. 22, 1908, sec. 5, p. 6, col. 2. [4] Pp. 84–5.

has been changed twenty-three times in one-fourth of that period while the new system has been in operation, and that, in all, during the latter period, sixty-one amendments to the constitution have been proposed, twenty-three submitted by the legislative assembly, and thirty-eight initiated by petition. But of the twenty-three amendments adopted [1] by the voters only nine — all initiated by petition — can be considered of really fundamental importance — those (1) providing for the majority vote to be required for the adoption of amendments submitted by the legislature and for an obligatory referendum on acts calling a constitutional convention, (2) home-rule charters for cities, (3) the local initiative and referendum, (4) the recall, (5) authorizing proportional representation, (6) county home-rule in taxation, etc., (7) three-fourths verdict and reorganization of the judicial system, (8) woman's suffrage, and (9) the substitute for county home-rule in taxation. Moreover, of the thirty-eight attempts to amend the constitution which have failed, only eight — the two propositions for the "wholesale" reorganization of the legislative department of the state, the two "single-tax" propositions, with, perhaps the fifteen-hundred-dollar tax exemption and the sur-tax amendments, submitted together, and together an analogue to the "single-tax" amendments, the universal eight-hour labor amendment, and the Socialists' proposal for a department of public works for the benefit of the unemployed — have been very "radical," and not all of these have been really "disturbing." And none of the statutory law, enacted, or merely submitted, has been very "radical."

However, it is asked, "is change a crime? Must states and nations not go forward? China clung to the same old order several thousand years. . . . Is that the way we ought to do?" [2]

[1] Five of the amendments adopted originated in the legislature, and the other fourteen were submitted by initiative petition.
[2] *Oregon Journal*, Dec. 17, 1912, p. 8, col. 2.

CHAPTER XXIII

DIRECT LEGISLATION AND POLITICAL PARTIES

"It is one of the greatest merits of the initiative and referendum that it makes possible a clear separation between local and national issues. Under the older system . . . the people could express their opinion upon such a matter as the Barlow road purchase only by their choice of legislators. In determining this choice, numerous other questions necessarily played a part. . . . The method of initiative and referendum permits each voter to express his individual opinion upon every question standing entirely by itself and without admixture of personal or partisan bias. It absolutely separates the business department of legislation from the personal or partisan side. . . . Under the old system he [the voter] could not vote for his opinion upon this matter of pure business without voting against his party. This was a real misfortune, and it greatly contributed to dishearten the common man with politics. . . . It was all promises and no performance. Under the Oregon system the voter acts directly upon results. The individual feels his manhood as he could not under the purely representative method." [1]

But the very general realization of the absence of party issues in state politics, the declining faith in the reality of national party distinctions, and the separation of national and local politics encouraged for some years by the direct, or practically direct, system of election of United States senators, have so largely operated toward the substitution of "business" for partisan politics in elections that the actual effect of direct legislation in this connection is obscured. And its effect upon party

[1] *Oregonian*, June 10, 1906, p. 6, col. 5.

organization is also uncertain. "Party political organizations are in failing health. The absolute power to decide all questions by 'Be it enacted by the people of the state of Oregon,' and to decide many questions at one election and each separately on its own merits appears to be fatal to the perfection of party discipline and organization."[1] But certainly the practical annihilation of party organization has been due more to the operation of the direct primary, a child of direct legislation, than to the operation of direct legislation itself.

It was predicted that with the power of initiative and referendum reserved to the voters they would be, as in Switzerland, "no longer obliged to defeat a useful public servant for re-election and thus destroy his political career in order to overrule his vote or opinion on some one question," no matter how important it might be.[2] And perhaps in actual practice the Swiss precedent is to some extent followed in Oregon.

[1] W. S. U'Ren, *Oregonian*, Apr. 29, 1907, p. 5, col. 7.
[2] W. S. U'Ren, *Initiative and Referendum in Oregon, Arena*, vol. 29, pp. 270, 273–5 (1903).

CHAPTER XXIV

STATE DIRECT LEGISLATION AND FEDERAL MATTERS

"A NATIONAL initiative and a national referendum is the logical and necessary sequel of a state initiative and a state referendum." [1]

But whatever the desirability or practicability of "compounding the American people into one common mass" for the purpose of direct legislation, there is no reason why voters of the state may not be vested with more power over federal legislation than they exercise at present. Before the direct election of United States senators by the voters of the states was provided for by the amendment of the federal constitution, direct election was accomplished in Oregon, and later in other states, by a system under which candidates for the legislature pledged themselves to vote for the people's choice of senators, and, when elected, kept that pledge. The same principle is contained in the presidential primary law. This principle might well be applied to advance popular control over the federal constitution and statutes. Candidates for congress and the legislative assembly might thus be practically required to pledge themselves to further or to oppose federal legislation, statutory or constitutional, in accordance with the wishes of the voters of the state as expressed on the particular questions submitted at the election.[2]

[1] *Oregonian*, July 3, 1911, p. 6, col. 2. "We are very much interested in seeing this spread [of the initiative and referendum] to other states, because we do not get the full benefit of it until we have it nationally." W. S. U'Ren, reported in Chicago *City Club Bulletin*, vol. 2, p. 478 (1909). [2] See *below*, p. 193.

CHAPTER XXV

THE POPULARITY OF DIRECT LEGISLATION

THE constitutional amendment of 1902 establishing the initiative and referendum was adopted by the overwhelming vote of 62,024 to 5668.[1]

But there is still opposition[2] to the system. Some of the opposition is doubtless due, partly to objections to direct government upon general principles, and partly to the natural objections of interests whose policies have been thwarted by the system; but probably it is due, at least as much, to the abuses which the system has suffered in practice. However, all the opposition together is probably comparatively insignificant, and the general popularity of the system well established. It is universally admitted that there are faults in the system, but the principle of the system is very generally accepted.

"Withal, it cannot be said that faith in the principle has been shaken among even a reasonable proportion of the voters. Rather the weaknesses of the present laws governing the use of the initiative and referendum are recognized and admitted. Some improvement is needed." [3] "The Oregon system is not in the balances. It is here to stay. The people rule ... in Oregon through the Oregon system, and they have no wish or desire or purpose to go back to old methods." [4] "Dissenters must reconcile themselves the best way they can to living under the new system. Adjustment may come slowly in some instances, but it will come in course of time." [5]

---

[1] Seventy-two per cent of those voting at the election voted on the amendment. And see *above*, pp. 3-5.

[2] It is perhaps significant in this connection that the amendment of 1906 extending the initiative and referendum to the localities was adopted by a vote of only 47,678 to 16,735. And see *above*, pp. 177-9. [3] *Oregonian*, July 5, 1912, p. 10, col. 1.

[4] *Ibid.*, May 8, 1912, p. 10, col. 2. [5] *Ibid.*, Feb. 21, 1912, p. 10, col. 1.

PART II
THE RECALL

THE RECALL [1]

THE "final crowning act to complete the temple of popular government here," as it was described,[2] was the adoption of the "recall" by a constitutional amendment in 1908.[3] As in the case of the initiative and referendum, the "recall" or "imperative mandate" had been advocated for years in Oregon before its final adoption. The constitutional amendment which was finally submitted to the people was initiated by the People's Power League under the leadership of W. S. U'Ren. It was approved by a majority of 43,948 to 26,778.

"The recall is neither more nor less than a special election to determine whether an official shall be superseded before the ordinary expiration of his term."[4] The constitutional provision[5] allows the recall of any elective public officer in the state[6] by the voters of the district from which he was elected. The recall is begun by the filing, with the proper state or local authority, of a petition demanding the recall, signed by twenty-five per cent of the number of electors who voted in the district at the preceding election for justice of the supreme court.[7] The petition must set forth the reasons for the demand. The

[1] Revised from *American Political Science Review*, vol. 6, pp. 41–53 (1912).

[2] *East Oregonian,* reprinted in *Oregon Journal,* Jan. 1, 1907, p. 6, col. 6.

[3] *Constitution,* art. 2, sec. 18 (1908). [4] *Oregonian,* Feb. 24, 1913, p. 6, col. 4.

[5] *Constitution,* art. 2, sec. 18 (1908). *Cf. House Joint Resolution,* 1907, no. 18. There has been some uncertainty as to the proper interpretation of the law, but the interpretation here given is that followed in practice.

[6] As a part of the plan for the reorganization of the legislative assembly submitted to the people by the People's Power League in 1910 there was included a plan for the recall of either or both houses of the assembly. *Referendum Pamphlet,* 1910, no. 360, sec. 3, pp. 189–90. See also C. H. Chapman and others, *Introductory Letter,* 1909, pp. 16–18; People's Power League, *Introductory Letter,* 1911, p. 12, sec. 3b.

[7] See *above,* p. 6, note 1.

officer may avoid a recall election by resignation. If he does not resign within five days after the petition has been filed, a special recall election is called. The "special" election is sometimes held at the same time as a general or a primary election.[1] On the "sample ballot" the reasons for demanding the recall as set forth in the petition and the officer's justification of his course in office are printed, in neither case to the extent of more than two hundred words. Until very recently, "the conception of a recall election has been that it is simply a requirement that the incumbent shall run against one or more candidates for his office before his term has expired."[2] But a decision of the supreme court of 1914 requires the question of recall and the question of succession to office in case of recall to be submitted separately on the ballot.[3] The incumbent is still virtually a candidate for re-election without nomination, since others may be nominated for the office, and the person receiving the highest number of votes cast at the election is declared elected, whether he is the person whose recall is demanded or another.[4] No petition may

[1] Saving of expenses can of course be effected by holding a recall election at the same time as a regular election. A motive for holding a separate election for the purpose may be that fewer persons would vote at a special election than at a general election and that while opponents of the officials attacked would turn out in force, many of their supporters would stay at home. *Cf. Oregonian*, Mar. 14, 1914, p. 4, col. 2; Apr. 24, 1914, p. 4, col. 3. [2] *Oregonian*, Oct. 22, 1914, p. 10, col. 2.

[3] "In our judgment the simple and natural construction of this section is that . . . there are two questions to be decided by the electorate: First, the principal one, of whether the people will recall said officer; and, the second, of who shall be his successor, which is subsidiary and conditional upon the determination of the first adversely to the incumbent of the office. The essence of the section is the recall of an officer. This accomplished — and not until then — it becomes necessary to consider who shall take his place, and this is determined by the selection of one from among whatever number of candidates may offer themselves for the place." *State* v. *Barbur, Pacific Reporter* (Oregon), vol. 44, p. 126 (1914).

[4] Should there be no other candidate at the election except the incumbent, he would retain his office in spite of a majority vote for his recall. And even where other candidates appear, "the paradox may happen that the recall will in effect defeat itself," because "it is possible that . . . the plurality of votes, although a very small minority of the total, may go to the individual who first held the office in question." *State* v. *Barbur, Pacific Reporter* (Oregon), vol. 144, pp. 126–7 (1914). See also **John Pipes**, reported in *Oregonian*, May 17, 1912, p. 8, col. 5.

be circulated against an officer until he has held office for six months, except in the special case of a member of the legislative assembly, in which case it may be filed within five days from the beginning of the first session after his election. After one recall election no additional recall petitions may be filed against the same officer during the same term unless the petitioners pay into the public treasury the amount of the expenses of the preceding recall election. Although the constitution expressly authorizes legislation for the "payment by the public treasury of the reasonable special election campaign expenses" of the officer subjected to a recall election, no such legislation has yet been enacted.[1]

It has been proposed to extend the recall by extra-constitutional provision, to include United States senators and representatives.[2]

There was much uncertainty as to whether the constitutional amendment providing for the recall was legally effective without further legislation until the supreme court decided, in 1914, that the amendment is self-executing.[3] It is still uncertain as to whether school directors can legally be recalled in the absence

[1] *Constitution*, art. 2, sec. 18 (1908). *Cf. House Joint Resolution*, 1907, no. 18.

[2] In 1911 there was some talk of recalling a representative in congress on account of improper personal conduct, but of course in view of the fact that the house of representatives is final judge of the qualifications of its own members, the recall amendment could not be applied in this case. See especially *Oregonian*, Aug. 12, 1911, p. 6, col. 5; *Oregon Journal*, Aug. 13, 1911, sec. 2, p. 4, col. 4. The representative agreed to waive any technical objection that might legally be made to holding a recall election, and pledged himself to resign if the recall election did not give him a majority of the votes cast. *Oregon Journal*, Aug. 14, 1911, p. 1, col. 2. But nothing came of this proposition. A bill which failed of enactment in the legislative assembly of 1913 required that any candidate for the United States senate or the house of representatives should, at the time of filing his declaration of intention to become a candidate, sign one of two statements, one promising to resign upon an adverse majority vote given at a recall election, the other refusing to resign in such a case. *House Bill*, 1913, no. 236. This is in line with the extra-constitutional machinery formerly used for the direct election of United States senators and still used for the direct nomination of president. Compare the statutory provisions for the "advisory recall" of United States senators, representatives, and district judges, in Arizona *Laws*, 1912, chs. 56, 65. See also Michigan *Constitution*, art. 3, sec. 8 (1912); Michigan *Laws*, 1913, no. 325, sec. 2.

[3] *State v. Harris*, *Pacific Reporter* (Oregon), vol. 144, p. 109 (1914).

of supplementary legislation. All of the supplementary bills introduced into the legislature have failed of enactment.[1]

"Office holders are not now chosen for a definite period but only so long as seventy-five per cent of the people are satisfied with the way in which they discharge their official duties. . . . It is necessary to have a system of some strength and stability, or disintegration and disorder are likely to result. . . . Under this recall system, we may be thrown in the throes of a bitter campaign at any time, in city, county or state."[2] But these possibilities have not been very far realized.

While the constitutional amendment providing for the recall was yet before the people, the recall of a member of the city council of Portland was discussed, to be attempted if the amendment should be approved at the election. But apparently the first serious attempt to recall an officer was made in Medford the next month after the amendment was adopted. This was blocked by a decision of the circuit court holding that the amendment was not operative without additional legislation.

The first actual recall election in Oregon occurred the next year, when the mayor of Junction City was removed. It was charged in the recall petition that the officer was inefficient, immoral, untruthful, and arbitrary in the exercise of his authority; but a motive which was influential at least to some extent was the hostility of certain property owners caused by the mayor's action in opening streets which they had illegally closed.

The same year the mayor and all five of the councilmen of Estacada were recalled.[3] The petition declared that the

[1] *Senate Bill*, 1911, no. 223; *Senate Bill*, 1913, no. 221; *Senate Journal*, 1913, pp. 1029–30; *Senate Bill*, 1915, no. 61; *Senate Joint Resolution*, 1915, no. 8.

[2] Eugene *Guard*, Oct. 14, 1911, p. 4, col. 1.

[3] This was the result according to the actual returns. But the canvassers — the recalled officers — denied the legality of the election (they and their followers generally had therefore not participated in the election), and refused to canvass the returns. The decision of the court in mandamus proceedings brought to compel such canvass was delayed until it became useless by the intervention of the regular municipal election. At that time all the recalled officers stood for re-election and were all defeated.

officers had managed the affairs of the city in an unsatisfactory manner, illegally diverted public funds, repudiated the city debt, etc. But the real cause of the recall movement was simply a factional fight waged by two banks and their respective supporters, which had divided the city against itself ever since the second bank was organized, and which ceased only with the merger of the two banks.

In the same year the recall of the mayor and three of the councilmen of Union was prevented only by these officers' going "through a regular routine of resigning and electing themselves to other offices."[1] While the ground for the recall was asserted to be unsatisfactory administration, diversion of public funds, needless expenditures, abuse of the emergency clause in the enactment of ordinances, impairment of the public credit, etc., the movement was really the outcome of a struggle between those who opposed and those who favored the stringent enforcement of the prohibition law. The officers attacked represented the prohibition ticket which had won at the preceding election.

In 1910 the mayor of Ashland was subjected to a recall election, but the election resulted in his favor. The petition charged him with incompetency, improper expenditure for street improvements, unwarranted removal of a city employee, and favoritism in committee appointments, although the real ground of the agitation seems to have been opposition to his progressive policy in regard to public improvements.

The next year a member of the city council of Portland was recalled by the voters of his ward. Although the petition for

[1] After the recall petition was filed, the mayor resigned and was elected recorder by the council. One of the councilmen named in the recall petition resigned and was elected mayor by the council. The other two councilmen concerned resigned, and were re-elected by the council. By this process a recall election at the time was avoided. And any further attack was prevented, because the date of the regular election came within the six months' exemption period which followed. "So you can see how easy it is to avoid the recall if the people interested will work together," said one of those who worked together in this case. At the regular election the whole ticket which these officers represented — some of them stood for re-election — was defeated on the recall issue.

his recall declared simply that the councilman did not "faithfully and efficiently represent" the interests of his ward and city, the motives behind the recall were various. The officer had been inconsiderate in dealing with some of his constituents who desired his influence in securing certain action by the council. He had fathered an ordinance deemed by the labor unions prejudicial to their interests, and he was opposed by their adherents on this account. Their candidate won in the recall election. Further, the councilman had advocated the location of a sewer outlet in a certain locality, and had thus aroused the opposition of some property owners. One of them was a candidate at the recall election. The councilman had also incurred the enmity of a corporation attorney by charging the latter with an attempt to bribe him to drop some legislation detrimental to the interests of the company. The attorney was very active against the officer in the recall campaign. It was also claimed that several corporations which had suffered from legislation originating with the officer were partly responsible for his defeat.

In 1913 the county judge of Klamath county was successful against a recall election. The reasons for the demand of the recall are declared in the petition to be the following: "unlawful, unwise and inefficient management of county finances; the incurring of a large amount of unlawful indebtedness; unnecessarily increased taxation, waste of money in county expenses; favoritism in contracting with and employing relatives of members of the county court and certain firms and corporations at a financial loss to the county; unlawfully issuing and selling warrants of the county at a discount; carelessness and inefficiency in auditing bills against the county; accepting employment from corporations whose interests are opposed to the public interests and at far greater salaries than that paid by the county; inefficient and unsatisfactory service as a county judge; failure to get value received for money spent for roads, though petitioners are not opposed to good roads; lack of ability, as shown in the past to expend future levies for roads; inability to construct a new courthouse with economy and a due regard for cost though petitioners are not opposed to the new courthouse and are indifferent as to its location, but only insist that it shall be built economically and that its cost shall not be excessive, which the past actions of said officer indicate that he will not be able to do." But the recall movement was apparently to a considerable extent the outcome of an old local factional fight involving much personal enmity.

The same year the county judge and the two county commissioners of Clackamas county were defeated at a recall election. The petitioners charged that the officers had been careless and extravagant in the management of the county business — more particularly, that they had paid three hundred and fifty dollars for the examination of a bridge without inviting competition, replaced a bridge in good condition with a steel bridge instead of making the few repairs necessary on the old bridge, built many bridges without due publicity and without asking for competitive bids, contracted for cruising timber at an excessive rate without giving notice that the contract was to be let — and had failed to comply with the law defining their duties in regard to roads and bridges. But it is somewhat significant that the leader in the recall movement was a bridge-builder who had failed to secure any of the bridge contracts.

In the fall of the same year the county judge and county commissioners of Hood River county were compelled to face a recall election, upon charges including extravagance in the employment of a county roadmaster,[1] unnecessarily expending large sums of money for improperly oiling roads, paying unitemized claims against the county, and paying a high price for an improperly constructed bridge. Here the leader of the recall movement had been the county judge's opponent at the recent primary election, and it is said that most of the road supervisors of the county were opposed to interference by a roadmaster,

[1] It seems that the recall movement would have been dropped if the court had dismissed the roadmaster in accordance with a petition, "insolently refused."

and aided in the agitation for the recall of the court. At the election all three of the officers were removed.

Failure "to faithfully represent" the people of their respective wards and of the city were the charges in the petitions which resulted in forcing two members of the city council of Salem to face a recall election held in the same fall. The movement was due wholly to another member of the council, who had been disgruntled by the action of these members in opposing his policies. Both officers were sustained by large majorities.

Several recall elections occurred the next year. First, two members of the city council of Medford were thus removed from office, on charges that they did not truly represent their constituents and were generally incompetent and were guilty of extravagance. Very much complaint of the officers' general incompetence and some charges of petty grafting had been made. The interests of one of the councilmen, a saloon keeper, did not accord with the strict enforcement of the liquor law, and the attack was first directed against him. The recent increase in the city taxes accelerated the movement.

A short time later two directors of the Quincy school district in Columbia county were recalled,[1] chiefly because of these officers' refusal to discharge a teacher accused of teaching socialistic doctrines to her pupils. The petition charged the directors with retaining the teacher, knowing her to be "a person unfit and unsuited for the position" by reason of violation of the statutes and the rules of the state board of education in "neglecting to inculcate in the minds of her pupils correct principles of morality and a proper regard for the government under which they live"; and with violation of the law in failing to display an American flag on the school grounds, in employing one of the directors for making repairs on the schoolhouse, and in employing his wife as janitor of the building. The first official act of the new board was to discharge the teacher.

---

[1] The adherents of the officers removed declared that the recall election was illegal, and did not participate in the election of their successors at the later election.

The petition for the recall of a city councilman of Waldport, ousted the next month, charged him with "inability to conduct the affairs of his office in a fair and impartial manner." The charge, being interpreted, is, apparently in part, voting for the issue of a saloon license to an outsider offering more favorable terms than a local applicant.

The county judge of Curry county the same year was subjected to a recall election upon the charge that he had been instrumental in the expenditure of public money "in ways unauthorized by law and of no benefit to the people," that he had disregarded the "rights of petition of the taxpayers" for the appointment of certain county officers, and that he had failed to conduct the county business on business principles, "to the great loss of the taxpayers." However, the real motive for the movement was revenge against the judge for his part in protecting the county treasury against some of the "recallers" and in disappointing others of them in their hopes for appointment to office. The judge was sustained at the election.

All of the members of the Columbia county court were defeated at a recall election held a few weeks later. The petitions alleged that the officers had been "selfish and extravagant in the management of the county business," and in proof of the charges declared that the court had ordered a road built which would be of "no practical benefit to the public," that they had purchased an expensive machine without advertising, and that they had not complied with statutes governing road administration. But the recall was wholly the outcome of a quarrel between two sections of the county in regard to the route which should be followed in road construction, and it was instituted by the section not favored by the court's decision.

At the same election the county attorney was recalled[1] on charges that he had not conducted his office "for the best interest

[1] The recall of the county attorney was nullified by the supreme court's decision to the effect that in his case the recall petition had not been filed in accordance with the requirements of law. Later he resigned.

and welfare" of the county, in that he had been "derelict in his duties," and had "allowed personal matters to interfere with the sound judgment at all times necessary in the duties of a prosecuting attorney," and that he had "allowed personal preferences and prejudices to influence him in his conduct as a public officer." As a competent observer puts it, "the real cause for his recall was the arbitrary manner in which he discharged the duties of his office, in utter disregard of everything and everybody, even of the decisions of the lower courts."

The recall election which has so far aroused most public attention was held in Portland the next month, when the mayor and two of the city commissioners were sustained. The mayor was charged, in the recall petition, with illegally retaining his position as manager of an insurance company since his election to the office of mayor, lack of efficiency and stability, discharge of competent city employees contrary to the spirit of the civil-service law, and extravagance in the management of the city business. The commissioners were charged with extravagance in administration, administration detrimental to the business and industrial life of the city, lack of efficiency, stability and good judgment, and discharge of competent city employees contrary to the spirit of the civil-service law. But the real motive for the recall movement had nothing whatever to do with these charges. The movement began virtually with the election of the officers, and continued, with a mysterious interval of quiescence, for months. The parties responsible for the movement long remained concealed, and only a few of them later became generally known. Their chief, and probably their only motive for action was, apparently, desire for the spoils of office. The officers were sustained by overwhelming majorities at the election.

Two weeks later the mayor of Florence was recalled. The petition declared that he was "an unfit person" to hold the office by reason of his having illegally authorized the destruction of a certain building belonging to a private citizen, and, when judgment for damages occasioned by such action was obtained against him by the owner, having authorized and voted for the payment of the judgment out of the city treasury (in fact the judgment was obtained against the mayor and another officer in their official capacities and the city council authorized the payment of the judgment); and by reason of "sundry other illegal acts" committed by him. The owner of the building was responsible for the recall movement, but some hostility to the mayor's policy in regard to public improvements and some old factional differences contributed to its success.

At the end of the year the county attorney of Tillamook county was recalled. The petition charged him with incompetence and neglect of official duties, resulting in unnecessary expense to the county. The greatest grievances were, apparently, that he "mixed with the saloon element," and formulated faulty indictments, purposely, it was believed, in a number of criminal cases.[1]

The next recall election was held late in the summer of the present year. At this time the county attorney of Wheeler county was the object of the attack. It was charged in the recall petition that the officer was corrupt and incompetent, that his free indulgence in strong drink interfered with the performance of the duties of his office, that he failed to enforce the local option law, that he did not enforce the laws impartially, and that his incompetence caused the county a great deal of unnecessary expense. Whatever the truth of these charges, apparently the recall movement was due, in large part, to personal spite against the officer. He was successful at the election.

In the seven years since the recall amendment was adopted seventeen recall elections have been held. All but six of them have resulted in the defeat of the officers attacked. Thirty-

---

[1] Charges against the officer were preferred before the grand jury, but the jury favored removal by recall rather than by court procedure, and the members themselves circulated the recall petitions.

four officers have been involved, and only nine of them have been allowed to retain office.[1] Some of the charges stated in the petitions in these various cases could be substantiated, but others could not. It has been made apparent that the reasons for the demand for removal did not usually disclose the real motives, or all of the real motives for the demand. All the officers involved have been local officers. The county judges were attacked as administrative rather than as judicial officers.[2] All of the cities, except Portland, are small, the largest containing nine thousand people, and the smallest about two hundred and fifty. The population of the counties involved varies from something over two thousand to nearly thirty thousand. The school district contains about five hundred people.

In addition to the movements which have resulted in actual recall elections, many more or less serious attempts to bring about recall elections have failed.[3]

Mayors of cities have thus been attacked on charges of neglect of the interests of a particular district of a city; of an "open-town" policy; of presence in a barroom after legal hours; of failure to enforce city ordinances against vice, extravagant expenditure of public funds without accounting therefor, etc.; of usurpation of the power of the council, misstatement of the proceedings of the council, etc., and total unfitness for office on account of lack of education and ability; because of permitting public speaking on the streets and of retaining a police force alleged to be corrupt; on charges of failure to enforce the city ordinances.

[1] Many very erroneous statements as to the frequency of the use of the recall in Oregon have been made even by Oregonians. *E.g.*, "There has never been an official recalled in this state." *Governor's Message, Senate Journal*, 1913, p. 1030. And it is possible that the statement of the recall elections given in the text is not absolutely complete.

[2] A judge and two commissioners constitute the "county court." Judicial functions are performed by the judge alone. The judge acts with the commissioners in the administration of the county business.

[3] The evidence available in many of these cases is very fragmentary and unsatisfactory.

Attempts have been made to remove a city councilman, on the charge of having ceased to reside in his ward, although the real cause was probably that he voted to license a hotel bar, and there was hope of electing as his successor one who would favor a "dry" town; another councilman, on the charge of incompetency, disregard of the wishes of his constituents, arbitrary and unreasonable action, personal interest in certain franchises, and having ceased to reside in his ward, although his activity in the removal of some officers really started the recall movement (one of the deposed officers aided in circulating the recall petition); another councilman, more than once, for refusal to aid some of his constituents in securing certain desired local improvements at the hands of the council; another, because of his official opposition to the widening and extension of a certain street; another, for voting for a public utility franchise in opposition to a demand for municipal ownership of that utility; another, on charge that he failed to represent his constituents, but used his office for his political and personal advantage, that in the council he had favored commercialized vice, that he aided in the repeal of an initiative bill-board ordinance, and that he had been negligent, careless and indifferent in the discharge of the duties of his office. Councilmen have been attacked also for voting for a "blanket" franchise; on the charge of holding up certain improvements and delay in submitting a new charter.

An attempt to remove a school director was made because of his activity in locating a school building contrary to the desire of certain petitioners and in retaining, also contrary to the desire of petitioners, a teacher who had dismissed some students for disorderly conduct (the father of one of these students managed the circulation of the recall petition). Two other school directors were attacked on charges of inefficiency and of irregularities in the awarding of contracts. In a later case where the recall petition declared the reason for the recall of three school directors to be, first, their refusal to acknowledge a petition, favored by most of the patrons of the district, for the retention of one teacher at an increased salary and the reduction of the salary of another teacher, and, second, their making contracts with a teacher extending beyond the directors' term of office, the trouble was started by the directors' support of the teacher last mentioned, who had dismissed a pupil for refusal to "salute the flag." A quarrel in another district over the question of the district's paying the tuition of students going from this district to a high school in another district was the cause of a recall movement against the two directors who favored payment of tuition.

A movement to recall a county assessor was based on charges of incompetence, unequal assessment, and casting aspersions upon the motives of the taxpayers protesting at a public meeting against his assessments, and attempting to intimidate them; but some of the trouble was caused by the assessor's enforcement of the law requiring full valuation in assessment.

Attempts to recall members of county courts, including county judges in their administrative capacity,[1] have been made on charges of incompetence, ignoring the express choice of the majority of the taxpayers in the appointment of road supervisors, and squandering money in unscientific road construction (the increase of the county tax levy and failure properly to care for certain roads seem here to have been the greatest grievances); because their new organization of road construction took considerable authority from the road supervisors, and perhaps because of enmity created by the removal of a supervisor; because residents of one district disapproved of the commissioners' improvement of the roads in another; on charges of wasteful expenditure of public funds, failure to publish claims allowed against the county, giving county work in return for political favors, and, in case of one of the commissioners involved, buying supplies as a private dealer and selling them to the county at greatly increased prices, and forcing county employees to trade at the commissioner's store (it is claimed that political enmity was back of the recall movement); for accepting a road

[1] *Above*, p. 202, note 2.

not coming up to the specifications of the contract (the commissioner was believed to be financially interested in the contract); on charges of having been extravagant, unbusinesslike and careless in the administration of county affairs; on charges of favoritism in the award of contracts and carelessness in the management of the county business.

The recall of one district attorney was sought because of his discrimination between the rich and the poor, protection of gambling houses and saloons in their violation of the law, using his official position to serve his own selfish interests, etc.;[1] that of another chiefly because of his neglect to enforce the laws controlling vice and the sale of liquor.

An attempt was made to recall a state senator, who, it was charged in the petition, used his office for personal and political ends, was attorney for various interests inimical to the public interests and thus unable impartially to represent his constituents, had supported a bill for one of these interests which abrogated a law enacted by the people, and voted for the appropriation of the people's money for unnecessary and extravagant uses.

A recall movement directed against a sheriff came from I. W. W.'s and others disaffected especially by reason of the sheriff's enforcement of the law regarding public speaking on the streets.

Soon after the recall amendment was adopted there was some talk of recalling a circuit judge because of his decision sustaining the legality of a provision of a city charter which allowed the sale of intoxicants. But no serious attempt to recall a judge was made until three years later, when a petition for the recall of a district judge was widely circulated, charging him with giving, in a notorious murder case, partial instructions which biased the jury in favor of the defendant. Later *lawyers*

---

[1] Recall proceedings in this case were delayed by court proceedings until the officer's term had expired. But he was a candidate for re-election at the primary election, and was defeated. It is very probable that a recall election would have resulted in his removal.

started a recall movement against a municipal judge upon the charges of bringing convictions without complaints, of favoritism, of illegally releasing prisoners after sentencing them to long terms, of decisions contrary to the precedents of the court, including precedents set by himself.

"The judiciary is not so intimately associated with the daily life of the average voter as is the municipal administration."[1] "Experience teaches that if any one needs protection from the abuse of the recall it is the short-term servant of the people whose acts are more intimately within the knowledge of the people than the acts of the judiciary."[2] "Court decisions in which the people generally take a living, active interest are rare — extremely rare. Acts of administrative officers overshadow them. The latter deal with everyday events with which the people are familiar and concerning which the people are more willing to risk their own judgment. The decisions of widespread importance generally concern the constitutionality of some police measure or involve the validity of some important governmental function. The public inclination, if the decision does not accord with public ideas, is to accept the decision, provided confidence in the court has not theretofore been weakened, and to seek a change in the easily-molded constitution. . . . There has been less trifling with the recall in Oregon as applied to the judiciary than to any other branch of elected public service. It always will be so. The principle is preserved, however, as a useful implement for use in a possible genuine emergency. The fact that its application is rare speaks well not only for the sanity of the people, but for the integrity of the courts. Whatever misgivings there may be in Oregon over any phase of the Oregon system, they concern the judicial recall probably less than any other."[3]

In some of the foregoing cases other officers would have been included in the attack, but escaped because they had not

[1] *Oregonian*, Apr. 6, 1911, p. 8, col. 1.   [2] *Ibid.*, Feb. 8, 1911, p. 8, col. 3.
[3] *Ibid.*, Apr. 26, 1914, sec. 3, p. 6, col. 1.

yet held office for the minimum period of six months, or because the officers' terms would soon expire in any event, or because the "recallers" considered it best to concentrate their efforts.

In addition to the more or less serious recall movements, numerous threats of recall have been made, probably most of which nobody has taken seriously.

The failure of the large number of recall movements to result in an election has been due to various causes. Some of the movements have been stopped before election on account of opinion or decision to the effect that the constitutional provision for recall was not self-executing but required additional legislation to put it into effect;[1] and this doubtless prevented the beginning of more, and perhaps many more recall movements. Some of them have come to an end by reason of lack of funds. Others have started so near, or continued until so near the expiration of the officer's term that the continuance of the agitation has been discouraged. Probably in most cases failure has been due to the general lack of sympathy with the movement. Some of the officers attacked have evaded the danger of a recall election by giving heed to the "recallers'" demands as to official action. Others have resigned from office to save themselves from apparently certain defeat at a recall election.

In many cases of recall movements the grounds for recall were doubtless insufficient. Of course the operation of personal and factional interests cannot be prevented in a recall election any more than in any other election.

What are the proper grounds for the recall of an official is a question upon which there must be much difference of opinion. It has been strongly urged here that an officer should never be recalled except upon charges of misfeasance or malfeasance in office.[2] And the most ardent advocates of the recall recognize

---

[1] *Above*, pp. 193–4.
[2] *E.g.*, *Oregonian*, Apr. 6, 1911, p. 8, col. 1. See Washington *Constitution*, art. 1, sec. 33 (1912).

the fact that it should be used with caution. "The recall is a good weapon, but one to be sparingly used. . . . There should be but rare or occasional use of it, but the people would better keep it laid up in their toolhouse to use in case of emergency."[1] More specifically, "it was designed as a reserve power of the people, to be used only against flagrantly incompetent, corrupt or despotic officials, or those who proved false to their platform pledges."[2] "Mere difference of view on what some people think they ought to do on a public matter is not sufficient reason for using the recall. The recall was never intended for such use."[3] "Frequent or foolish use of the recall would create sentiment against it, and might result in its abandonment. Its own friends would forsake it if by its over-employment it should keep communities in a state of turmoil and strife."[4]

The subject of the proper grounds for a recall has been discussed in Oregon chiefly in connection with criticisms of the attempt to recall a circuit judge. The following comments were made in this connection by a strong advocate of the recall as an instrument of government. "In reality it is not Judge Coke that the good people of Roseburg are after. Their real fury is against McClallen, but for the moment it is Judge Coke that is in sight. The public sympathizes with them in their indignation. McClallen shot down a highly esteemed citizen. He escaped punishment. The indignation of the Roseburg people is a natural sequence. But it was not Judge Coke that pulled the trigger of the murderous revolver. McClallen did that. It was not Judge Coke that fixed the requirements of the jury instructions at the trial. It was the law of the land that did that. Parts of the very instructions used were the dictum of the Oregon supreme court in the Morey case. On sober second thought, the Roseburg people must realize that fury is being visited on the wrong man. It was McClallen that killed a citi-

[1] *Oregon Journal*, Mar. 1, 1910, p. 8, col. 2. [2] *Oregonian*, May 21, 1913, p. 12, col. 1.
[3] *Oregon Journal*, Feb. 25, 1914, p. 6, col. 2.
[4] *Ibid.*, Aug. 16, 1911, p. 6, col. 1.

zen. In a Portland case where the instructions on vital points were the same as Judge Coke's the jury convicted. Had the two cases been tried contemporaneously, would the friends in one instance have used the recall because one court convicted and used it in the other because there was an acquittal? . . . Under the recall, the people would place Judge Coke on trial. They would also have to try the McClallen case in full. They would have to know all the facts in detail to pass an intelligent opinion. They would have to have the law points explained. They would have to hear the instructions. They would have to study the decisions and precedents. They would also have to try the supreme court of Oregon, for the supreme court, in the Morey case, affirmed, in effect, the vital instructions given by Judge Coke. They would have to pass on the question of whether the supreme court was right or wrong. In short, they would have to supersede the supreme court and perform the functions of super supreme justices. In exercising the recall in such an instance, the electors of the second district would, in effect, assume all the functions of one of the coördinate branches of the state government of Oregon, setting aside the judiciary for the moment and making each elector in the second district a super supreme judge, exercising power above the judiciary and above the constitution itself. . . . The people are not in position to pass upon the legal questions involved in the instructions to a jury. They cannot be constituted and do not want to be constituted a super supreme court, superseding and setting aside the constitutional supreme court. They are sane and sound in their judgments on ordinary issues, but they never have claimed nor never will claim that they are all skilled in the law. . . . In the very nature of things, it is as the confusion of tongues at the Tower of Babel for an electorate of laymen to attempt determination of whether a judge is right or wrong on a legal question. . . . If a judge goes on the bench in a state of intoxication; if a judge permits a railroad attorney to finance his campaign . . .; if a judge becomes a known corruptionist, a political trickster or dissolute in his habits, then he is within the scope of what prudent men accept as possible reason for invoking the recall."[1]

A short time before this recall movement began it was said: "The presence in the Oregon constitution of the judicial recall for more than two years and the failure here to experience the dire results predicted by the eastern press is fairly conclusive of one of two things. Either judges are very rarely compelled, in deciding cases in accordance with the law and evidence, to ruffle public sentiment, or else the public is capable, even though ruffled, of discerning between a strict judicial duty and venality or incompetence. . . . But so far the recall has not been used . . . against the judiciary. True, we have never had a Schmitz liberated through sheerest technicalities nor the popular will grossly subverted. We believe, however, that if the courts declared some popular law unconstitutional, the people would not seek to recall the court in the absence of evidence of corruption, but would amend the constitution through the initiative. . . . Probably the recall will never be invoked in Oregon against a judge unless corruption is charged."[2]

It might be contended that where the movement against a member of the judiciary is organized and guided by *lawyers*, as in the case of the municipal judge, there is possibly less danger that the "electorate of laymen" will go wrong in determining the question of recall.

It has been objected that the law does not limit the statement of reasons for the demand of recall to "justifiable" reasons,[3] and that it thus opens the way for grave abuse. Some change here might well enough be made, but how effective any such limitation as to reasons would be is doubtful, since, in practice,

[1] *Oregon Journal*, July 7, 1911, p. 8, col. 1; July 13, 1911, p. 8, col. 1; June 19, 1911, p. 8, col. 1; Sept. 8, 1911, p. 8, col. 3. "If the decision is indicative of gross ignorance or corruption . . . the judge ought to be recalled." *Oregonian*, Apr. 26, 1914, sec. 3, p. 6, col. 1. [2] *Oregonian*, Feb. 18, 1911, p. 8, col. 3.

[3] Malfeasance or misfeasance in office. Washington *Laws*, 1913, ch. 146, secs. 11, 13.

as has been observed,[1] the actual reasons for the recall movement may be different from the reasons named in the recall petition.

It is possible that a recall petition, based upon good grounds or not, may be circulated, and then when completed or nearly completed, be put in "cold storage" to await a more convenient opportunity for a sudden assault upon the officer involved. And, whether or not the petitions were originally circulated with this end in view, there are cases in which the uncertainty of the officer's position has been thus continued for a considerable period of time. "A plan of securing petitions and holding them indefinitely, to be filed at the whim of a few wire pullers, is absurd. Such a program could be employed to bully and control officials. No little group of men should be permitted to hold such petitions in their hands, to be used as a means of influencing affairs at the city hall. No more dangerous program could be introduced into municipal or other government. Recall petitions should be filed and an election be brought when sufficient names are secured, or they should be destroyed. Possession of them by designing men for long periods, is an unjust and dangerous business. It gives them a power that should not be allowed to exist in organized government."[2] This abuse could be prevented by a provision of law requiring that the petitions should be dated the day of their first circulation and be filed within a certain period after that day.

In general, the recall campaigns are carried on much in accordance with the methods prevailing in case of direct legislation.

The management of recall movements has been undertaken either by organizations already in existence — labor unions and various kinds of civic betterment clubs — or by temporary groups, large or small, formed for the occasion, or by individuals. Sometimes mass meetings have been called and committees appointed to conduct the campaign, or one member of a group has been designated for this purpose. In cases where large numbers of signatures are required on the petitions sometimes paid man-

[1] *Above*, p. 202. [2] *Oregon Journal*, May 10, 1914, sec. 2, p. 4, col. 1.

agers have been employed. The petitions are circulated either by paid circulators or gratuitously by persons sufficiently interested in the cause. They are circulated, as in the case of initiative and referendum petitions, at all sorts of places. The expenses are paid by private subscription. In some cases counter-petitions have been circulated against proposed recalls.

As in the case of direct legislation,[1] there has been some concealment of the parties actually responsible for recall movements, and gross frauds have been perpetrated by some circulators of recall petitions. And, in general, the abuses prevalent in the circulation of recall petitions are the same, in kind though apparently not in extent, as in the circulation of petitions for direct legislation.[2]

As a check upon abuse of the recall, some of its leading advocates have considered that it might be well to amend the law to increase the percentage of signatures now required for the filing of petitions.[3] But this would seem to be unwise.[4] A more rational change would be to reform the method of securing the signatures. Although it is probably true that people do not sign recall petitions thrust before them on the streets and elsewhere as readily as they do initiative and referendum petitions,

[1] *Above*, pp. 13–16.

[2] *Above*, pp. 65–8.

In upholding the character of the circulators employed in a certain recall campaign the manager wrote: "One of the most active solicitors for signatures is a widow, the mother of three young boys dependent upon her for support. Her taxes on her little home, her street assessments and other obligations weigh upon her slender resources heavily. . . . Another is a modest little woman with an invalid mother to support. Another is the wife of a mechanic. Both are trying to pay for little homes in the country. Another is a young woman trying to help out a family purse that has been well flattened out these recent months by high taxes and misfortunes. Others are volunteers among the most respectable in the city, who are working for what they consider a good cause." A. D. Cridge, *Oregonal Journal*, Feb. 25, 1914, p. 6, col. 5.

A councilman reports that an agent of a corporation *threatened* to circulate recall petitions against him with the aid of the many employees of the company unless he dropped certain proposed legislation hostile to the interests of the company.

[3] A bill introduced in the legislative assembly of 1913 prohibiting giving or accepting pay for securing names to recall petitions failed of enactment. *Senate Bill*, 1913, no. 221. *Cf.* Washington *Laws*, 1913, ch. 146, sec. 16. [4] *Above*, pp. 62–4.

nevertheless under the present system there is great probability that accommodating persons will by their signatures aid a movement for the merits of which they care nothing.[1] For this reason, and also as a guard against fraud, the circulation of petitions, whether paid or voluntary, should be prohibited, and provision made for signature at public offices or other proper places. "The only possible excuse for the recall is that it should be spontaneous and that each signer should be sufficiently interested to go to some public office and sign the petition — not wait to have it shoved into his hand with a 'Sign here' from a 5-cents-a-name getter."[2] But the requirement for signature at a public office or other proper place should doubtless be accompanied with a reduction of the percentage of signatures now required for filing petitions.[3] In general, the recall needs the same safeguards as does direct legislation.

The expenses of the recall election — both to the public and to candidates — have doubtless had considerable effect in discouraging recall movements. The six-months' exemption provision has operated as a check in at least several cases, and possibly some danger of action for libel — threatened in a few cases — has sometimes discouraged the circulation of petitions. The difficulty of persuading suitable candidates to oppose the incumbent has prevented action in some cases. Especially is this the case of course where officers are attacked without good cause. "Is there wonder that self-respecting men refuse to become recall candidates against them? The very injustice of the thing would bring odium upon the recall candidates, drive thousands of votes to the present officials and throw the recall into disrepute."[4] Where the offense has been a

---

[1] "A man may go down the street any time and get signers to a petition to hang some one. There is always a large per cent of the people against any officer." J. C. McCue, house of representatives, *Oregonian*, Feb. 21, 1907, p. 7, col. 1.

[2] *Oregonian*, Aug. 23, 1913, p. 8, col. 4. See also *Oregonian*, Mar. 22, 1912, p. 12, col. 2. *Above*, pp. 74–6. See Washington *Laws*, 1915, ch. 55, sec. 4.   [3] *Above*, p. 75.

[4] *Oregon Journal*, Apr. 25, 1914, p. 4, col. 1. See also *Oregonian*, Apr. 26, 1914, sec. 3, p. 6, col. 1.

legislative act the possibility of invoking the referendum has doubtless diminished demand for recall to some extent. The "unwholesome notoriety" brought upon the community by recall movements has doubtless had some conservative effect. "The good sense of the electors" is of course the chief reliance of the advocates of this instrument of government against any danger from its unwarranted use.

When the official attacked is recalled at the election, it may be impossible to determine whether he was deposed upon the grounds, asserted or real, which caused the demand for the recall. For at the election he must, under the present provisions of the law, at the same time justify his official conduct, compete with the political ambitions of the other candidates, and face any personal opposition by the voters. There "are represented as important factors in the recall . . . caprice of the public, immaterial and extraneous issues,[1] politics, personal revenge and deliberate misrepresentation. . . . It is unjust, it is degrading, it is inimical to his independence, that he should be compelled to defend his acts or policies or decisions with one hand and combat political ambition and personal popularity of candidates who may oppose him with the other."[2] This is the case especially where, as has sometimes occurred, there are several candidates for the same office at the recall election.

Of course no provision of law can entirely segregate the proper issue of the recall election, but something may be done in this direction by changing the law so that only the question of the recall of the officer shall come officially before the voters at the election. "Divorce . . . can probably only come through making the recall a real impeachment by the people on specific charges of misconduct and on them alone, without the selection of a successor of the accused officer being involved in the pro-

[1] "The candidate for county judge, in answer to many questions, admitted that he knew nothing about the facts of the recall petition, and agreed with the county court in building the road through St. Helens, for which the court is being recalled." *Oregonian*, Sept. 20, 1914, sec. 1, p. 16, col. 5.

[2] *Oregonian*, Aug. 30, 1911, p. 10, col. 1; Aug. 16, 1911, p. 8, col. 1.

ceeding."[1] The succession to office should be determined in the same manner as in the case of vacancies in office caused by death or resignation.[2] A later special election would not serve the purpose. For it is usually inexpedient to circulate recall petitions before a suitable opposition candidate is found, and thus the issue of candidates and the issue of the recall would necessarily be confused as much as under the present system.[3]

The recent change in the form of the recall ballot, whereby the question of recall and the question of succession to office are separately stated, and the people thus enabled "to vote directly upon the unadulterated question of recalling an incumbent of a public position,"[4] is a distinct aid, when there are several candidates, toward making the recall a more efficient means of deciding the issue properly involved. In one election under the old form, where several opponents to the incumbent appeared, he was defeated by a candidate who received 1185 out of a total of 4237 votes, only twenty-two more than received by the incumbent.[5] The chances of the failure of the election really to decide the recall issue would be reduced, without separating the two questions on the ballot, by the substitution of some form of majority vote, for the plurality vote allowed to decide the election. The "preferential" system of voting has been adopted

[1] *Oregonian*, Aug. 30, 1911, p. 10, col. 1.

[2] *Cf. ibid.*, Oct. 31, 1911, p. 10, col. 3; May 22, 1914, p. 10, col. 2. So provided by Washington *Laws*, 1913, ch. 146.

[3] The Quincy district directors were recalled at one election, and their successors chosen at another. But the supporters of the recalled officers maintained that the recall was illegal, and refused to participate in the second election. The Michigan statute requires the question of recall and the question of succession to office to be decided at separate elections. Michigan *Laws*, 1913, no. 325. See also proposed Minnesota *Constitution*, art. 7, sec. 10, rejected (1914).

[4] *State* v. *Barbur*, *Pacific Reporter* (Oregon), vol. 144, pp. 126, 127 (1914).

[5] The California plan (California *Constitution*, art. 23, sec. 1, 1911), which separates the two questions on the ballot, but which does *not* allow the incumbent to become a candidate, makes matters worse than they were under the old-style Oregon ballot. "It is stated by the proponents of the California recall that under that system a majority vote is required to recall an official. There is another way of stating this proposition. A majority in an election is one vote more than half the total vote cast. If it requires a majority to recall an official it also is essential that an official

for the election of the Portland mayor and commissioners.[1] In the past "recallers" have, apparently, generally been anxious enough to unite all opposing forces lest a multiplicity of candidates might operate to the *advantage* of the incumbent.

The interest of the voters in some recall elections has been intense — in a few cases the vote cast at the election being in excess of the registered vote; but in others there has been much apathy on the part of the voters — less than a third of the registered vote being cast in some cases.[2] In some cases the election has come at the same time as a general or a primary election, or measures have been submitted to the voters at the same time, and thus other interests have been involved.

"The merit of the recall lies in its swift and admirable method of removing from office the corrupt or grossly unfaithful incumbent. It acts when his malfeasance or misfeasance or crimes or misdemeanors become generally known. His trial neither awaits the legislature, there to displace other legislative functions, nor encounters the law's delays, nor is it postponed until his term expires. It is a workable substitute for impeachment and other

under recall must gain a majority of the votes in order to hold his job. He may have been elected by a bare plurality, but if his policy in office is attacked by recall petition, a plurality in the recall election will not save him. He must then defeat his combined opponents. . . . Instead of removing the recall from political manipulation, the Cailfornia plan would only thrust it deeper in the mire. No matter what the charge recited in the recall petition, its filing would be an invitation to the office-hungry to seek the job of the officer attacked. The more candidates the better chance each would have, and the greater the chances that the incumbent would be removed." *Oregonian*, Oct. 31, 1911, p. 10, col. 3.

[1] The People's Power League of Oregon in 1912 suggested a modification of the California plan in providing for a system of preferential voting on candidates at the recall election and thus avoiding plurality elections. People's Power League, *Introductory Letter*, 1911, pp. 9–10, 24. Further, see W. S. U'Ren, *Text for Recall Amendment*, Equity, vol. 13, p. 8 (1913).

[2] "The duty to vote on such issues is as grave as duty to vote at a general election. The people in adopting the recall expressed a willingness to sit as jurors on the efficiency of their servants if called upon to do so by a small percentage of their number. . . . No matter what merit there may have been in this particular recall the indifference of the large body of voters therein will give encouragement to selfish or venomous effort on the part of a few to instigate recall proceedings against worthy officials." *Oregonian*, Aug. 18, 1913, p. 6, col. 2.

ponderous, obstructive and ineffective methods of ridding office of undesirables." [1]

Opinions widely differ as to the effects of the institution upon the conduct of officers. On the one hand it is claimed "its mere availability is a deterrent to sane officials to keep within the bounds of official duty." [2] On the other hand it has been said that "the recall . . . exerts no corrective influence over officials that the laws against official corruption and the controlling power of public sentiment do not." [3] In fact it seems that at least on some occasions the serious threat of a recall has prevented, or has helped to prevent, official "sins of commission"; and it may be, of course, that much official corruption or delinquency has been prevented by a deterrent influence of the recall law. But, on the other hand, the possibility of a recall has probably caused some "sins of omission."

Where the recall issue is a permanent one, as it has been in some cases, of course a recall election only furnishes additional opportunity for the temporary settlement of that issue. Limited to such cases, this opinion is correct: "In a state where there are frequent elections — for most officials the term is but two years — the 'recall' established by law is frequent enough. If the people are dissatisfied with the official they need not re-elect him." [4]

But the terms of office in Oregon are now generally too short, and the adoption of the recall has opened the way for an increase in the length of terms [5] — an important reform apparently otherwise impossible. And another reform, the movement for which is continually becoming stronger, the "short ballot," would not be practicable without this means of correcting the possible abuse of power concentrated in the hands of few officials. The "short ballot" would, on the other hand, by fixing

---

[1] *Oregonian*, Feb. 24, 1913, p. 6, col. 4.
[2] *Oregon Journal*, Aug. 16, 1911, p. 6, col. 1.
[3] *Oregonian*, Feb. 25, 1910, p. 10, col. 2. [4] *Ibid.*, Oct. 26, 1909, p. 10, col. 2.
[5] "Adoption of the recall system has counteracted all necessity for short terms in county office." *Oregonian*, Nov. 1, 1914, sec. 3, p. 6, col. 1.

more definitely the responsibility for official conduct, render the recall a much more effective instrument of government.

Apprehensions of recall have had apparently no effect in discouraging candidates, whatever the quality, from seeking office.

It has been feared that the possibility of getting rid of obnoxious officials by recalling them might tend to make the voters more careless in the choice of officials. "The fact that an officer can be recalled will tend to lessen the care that should be exercised in his selection, which will lead to farther recall, thus setting up a vicious circle."[1] But it can hardly be said there is any evidence that carelessness of the voters is thus increased, although it is true that voters are at times urged by the press to give careful consideration to the merits of candidates and not to trust to the possibility of recall after their election in case they should be mistaken in their choice.

The discord apparent in recall movements, and the actual or threatened violence which has accompanied a few of them, cannot be justly charged as caused by the recall.

Even if there were no inherent difficulties — in fact to some extent insurmountable — in the way of knowing adequately the effects of the recall in operation, our experience is yet too limited to justify any positive general conclusion as to the merits of the institution. As above observed, the legal status of the recall provision has been until recently uncertain, and it is impossible to say to what extent this uncertainty has prevented the use of the recall[2] for good or for evil. But it is certain that the recall has been greatly abused. It has often been denounced in strong terms by its opponents, although they, like the opponents of the system of direct legislation, have now, apparently, for the most part, accepted the inevitable. It has been as often extravagantly praised by its friends; but, whatever are its merits, the democratic character of the recall has very much more to do with its popularity than any of its practical results thus far in evidence.

---

[1] J. R. Kendall, *Oregonian*, Aug. 4, 1911, p. 6, col. 6.   [2] *Above*, pp. 193-4, 207.

PART III

APPENDIX

APPENDIX

I. BIBLIOGRAPHY

American Commonwealth Where the People Really Rule, Arena, vol. 35, pp. 523–6 (1906).
ALBERTSON, R., *New Oregon Law, Arena*, vol. 38, pp. 98–100 (1907).
ALBERTSON, R., *Oregon Aroused, Arena*, vol. 39, pp. 227–8 (1908).
ALBERTSON, R., *Oregon Election, Arena*, vol. 40, pp. 245–6 (1908).
BARNETT, J. D., *Operation of the Recall in Oregon, American Political Science Review*, vol. 6, pp. 41–53 (1912).
BONYNGE, R. W., *Political Innovations, Forum*, vol. 45, pp. 645–50 (1911).
BOURNE, J., *Functions of Initiative, Referendum and Recall, Annals of the American Academy of Political and Social Science*, vol. 43, pp. 3–16 (1912).
BOURNE, J., *Initiative, Referendum, Recall, Case and Comment*, vol. 18, pp. 293–8 (1911).
BOURNE, J., *Initiative, Referendum and Recall, Atlantic Monthly*, vol. 109, pp. 122–31 (1912).
BOURNE, J., *New Independence, Collier's*, vol. 45, p. 13 (1910).
BOURNE, J., *Oregon's Struggle for Purity in Politics, Independent*, vol. 68, pp. 1374–8 (1910).
BOURNE, J., *People's Rule in Oregon, Equity*, vol. 12, pp. 97–8 (1910).
BOURNE, J., *Popular Government in Oregon, Outlook*, vol. 96, pp. 321–30 (1910).
BOURNE, J., *Popular versus Delegated Government, Senate Doc.*, No. 524, 61st Cong., 2d Sess. (1910).
BOURNE, J., *Practical Conservation of Popular Sovereignty, Twentieth Century Magazine*, vol. 3, pp. 132–4 (1910).
BOURNE, J., *Where the People Rule, Columbian Magazine*, vol. 3, pp. 821–32 (1911).

BOYLE, J., *Initiative and Referendum*, 3d ed. (1912).
BURNETT, G. H., *Recent Legislation*, Proceedings of the Oregon Bar Association, 1904–6, pp. 17–25.

CADMAN, J. P., *Oregon Democracy in Action*, Public, vol. 14, pp. 40–2 (1911).
CAREY, C. H., *New Responsibilities of Citizenship*, Proceedings of the Oregon Bar Association, 1908–10, pp. 18–41 (1909).
CHAMBERLAIN, G. E., *Speech in the Senate of the United States*, Apr. 17, 1911.
CRIDGE, A. D., *Lessons of the Election*, Equity, vol. 17, pp. 54–7 (1915).
CRIDGE, A. D., *Why so Many Measures in Oregon*, Equity, vol. 14, pp. 132–3 (1912).

DECOU, E. E., *Oregon: The Home of Direct Legislation*, World To-day, vol. 15, pp. 857–60 (1908).
Democracy and the Referendum in Oregon, Review of Reviews, vol. 35, pp. 748–51 (1907).
Direct Legislation, Review of Reviews, vol. 38, pp. 20–1 (1908).
Direct Legislation in Oregon, Arena, vol. 38, pp. 80–5 (1907).
Direct Legislation Methods, Direct Legislation Record, vol. 8, p. 18 (1901).
DUNIWAY, R. R., *Direct Legislation Revolutionary*, Case and Comment, vol. 18, pp. 319–23 (1911).

EATON, A. H., *Oregon System* (1912).
EGGLESTON, W. G., *People's Power in Oregon*, World's Work, vol. 22, pp. 14353–9 (1911).
EGGLESTON, W. G., and others, *People's Power* (1910).
EGGLESTON, W. G., and others, *People's Power and Public Taxation*, 3d ed. (1910).

FORD, H. J., *Facts about the Oregon System*, Journal of Accountancy, vol. 12, pp. 85–94 (1911).
FOXCROFT, F., *Constitution-Mending and the Initiative*, Atlantic Monthly, vol. 97, pp. 792–6 (1906).
FOXCROFT, F., *Initiative — Referendum in the United States*, Contemporary Review, vol. 99, pp. 11–19 (1911).

FULTON, C. W., *People as Legislators, North American Review*, vol. 185, pp. 69–74 (1907).

GALBREATH, C. B., *Provisions for State-Wide Initiative and Referendum*, Annals of the American Academy of Political and Social Science, vol. 43, pp. 81, 91–8 (1912).

Government by the People in Oregon, Equity, vol. 12, pp. 143–6 (1910).

HAYNES, G. H., *Education of Voters, Political Science Quarterly*, vol. 22, pp. 484–97 (1907).

HAYNES, G. H., *"People's Rule" in Oregon, Political Science Quarterly*, vol. 26, pp. 32–62 (1911).

HAYNES, G. H., *People's Rule on Trial, Political Science Quarterly*, vol. 28, pp. 18–33 (1913).

HEDGES, G. L., *Where the People Rule* (1914).

HENDRICK, B. J., *Initiative and Referendum and How Oregon Got Them, McClure's Magazine*, vol. 37, pp. 234–48 (1911).

HENDRICK, B. J., *Law-Making by the Voters, McClure's Magazine*, vol. 37, pp. 435–50 (1911).

HENDRICK, B. J., *"Statement No. 1," McClure's Magazine*, vol. 37, pp. 505–19 (1911).

HOLLINGWORTH, C. M., *Oregon Plan* (1911).

HOLMAN, F. V., *Results in Oregon, Chicago Civic Federation's Bulletin*, No. 3, pp. 10–22 (1911).

HOLMAN, F. V., *Some Instances of Unsatisfactory Results under Initiative Amendments of the Oregon Constitution* (1910).

HOWE, F. C., *Oregon the Most Complete Democracy in the World, Hampton's Magazine*, vol. 26, pp. 459–72 (1911).

Independent Voting in Oregon, Review of Reviews, vol. 34, p. 143 (1906).

KENNAN, G., *Direct Rule of the People, North American Review*, vol. 198, pp. 145–60 (1913).

KING, J., *Concerning the Cost of Petitions, Equity*, vol. 14, pp. 18–22 (1912).

KING, J., *How Oregon "Stood Pat," Twentieth Century Magazine*, vol. 4, pp. 114–20 (1911).

KING, J., *Oregon Makes Answer, La Follette's Magazine*, Dec. 31, 1910.

KING, J., *Safeguarding Petitions, Equity*, vol. 16, pp. 80–5 (1914).
KITTLE, W., *Putting Government in People's Hands, La Follette's Magazine*, vol. 2, pp. 7–8 (1910).

LA ROCHE, W. P., *Constitution and Convention, Proceedings of the Oregon Bar Association*, 1908–10, pp. 139–47.
LOWELL, A. L., *Public Opinion and Popular Government* (1913).
LOWELL, S. A., *Direct Legislation, Proceedings of the Oregon Bar Association*, 1898–9, pp. 60–71.

MCARTHUR, C. N., *Need of a Constitutional Convention, Proceedings of the Oregon Bar Association*, 1908–10, pp. 148–65.
MCCALL, S. W., *Representative as Against Direct Government, Proceedings of Ohio State Bar Association*, 1911, pp. 67–89.
MCCALL, S. W., *Representative as Against Direct Government, Atlantic Monthly*, vol. 108, pp. 454–66 (1911).
MCCULLOCH, C. H., *People's Rule in Oregon, Arena*, vol. 41, pp. 461–6 (1909).
MINOR, W., *Closing Address, Proceedings of the Oregon Bar Association*, 1908–10, pp. 166–76.
MONTAGUE, R. W., *Oregon System at Work, National Municipal Review*, vol. 3, pp. 256–83 (1914).
Most Important Political Event of the Year, Arena, vol. 36, pp. 186–8 (1906).

News from Oregon, Direct Legislation Record, vol. 3, p. 18 (1901).

OGBURN, W. F., *Initiative and Referendum Tested in Hard Times, Survey*, vol. 33, 693–4 (1915).
OGBURN, W. F., *Methods of Direct Legislation in Oregon, Publications of the American Statistical Association*, N.S., vol. 14, pp. 136–55 (1914).
OGBURN, W. F., *Social Legislation on the Pacific Coast, Popular Science Monthly*, vol. 86, pp. 274–89 (1915).
Oregon, Direct Legislation Record, vol. 7, pp. 69–70 (1900).
Oregon Election, Equity, vol. 10, pp. 67–70 (1908).
Oregon and Genuine Representative Government, Twentieth Century Magazine, vol. 2, pp. 261–2 (1910).
Oregon to the Front, Equity, vol. 6, pp. 25–6 (1906).

Oregon Vote, Equity, vol. 6, pp. 25–6 (1906).
OWEN, R. L., *Code of People's Rule*, Senate Doc. No. 603, 61st Cong., 2d Sess. (1910).
OWEN, R. L., *Oregon System in Practice, Journal of Accountancy*, vol. 12, pp. 101–3 (1911).

PAINE, R. T., *Lincoln's Ideal Carried Out in Oregon, Arena*, vol. 40, pp. 283–6 (1908).
PEASE, L., *Initiative and Referendum — Oregon's "Big Stick," Pacific Monthly*, vol. 17, pp. 563–75 (1907).
People's Power League, Introductory Letter, 1911.

RAINE, W. M., *Referendum at Work, World To-day*, vol. 11, pp. 1268–72 (1906).
Responsible Government, Outlook, vol. 89, pp. 363–4 (1908).

SCHAFER, J., *Oregon as a Political Experiment Station, Review of Reviews*, vol. 34, pp. 172–6 (1906).
SHIBLEY, G. H., *Initiative and Referendum in Practical Operation, Arena*, vol. 40, pp. 142–50 (1908).
SHIBLEY, G. H., *Judges Attack Oregon Amendment for Majority Rule, Arena*, vol. 30, pp. 613–6 (1903).
SHIBLEY, G. H., *Majority Rule System, Arena*, vol. 31, pp. 284–5 (1904).
SHIPPEE, L. B., *Oregon's Initiative and Referendum Again, Atlantic Monthly*, vol. 109, pp. 429–32 (1912).
SHIPPEE, L. B., *What of the Legislature? Overland Monthly*, vol. 60, pp. 62–8 (1912).
Singular Political Situation, Outlook, vol. 89, pp. 313–4 (1908).
SMITH, C., and EDWARD, H. P., *Behind the Scenes at Salem* (1911).
SNOW, C. M., *Letting the People Speak, Harper's Weekly*, vol. 55, Apr. 22, 1911, p. 9.
STEFFENS, L., *U'Ren, The Law-Giver, American Magazine*, vol. 65, pp. 527–40 (1908).
STICKLEY, G., *New Methods of Getting the Government Back into the Hands of the People, Craftsman*, vol. 20, pp. 192–6 (1911).
Strengthen the Oregon Plan, Independent, vol. 69, pp. 604–5 (1910).

TEAL, J. N., *Practical Workings of the Initiative and Referendum in Oregon*, Proceedings of the Cincinnati Conference for Good City Government, 1909, pp. 309-25.

THACHER, G. A., *Initiative and Referendum in Oregon*, Proceedings of the American Political Science Association, vol. 4, pp. 198-221 (1907).

THACHER, G. A., *Initiative and Referendum in Oregon*, Independent, vol. 64, pp. 1191-5 (1908).

THACHER, G. A., *Initiative, Referendum, and Popular Election of Senators in Oregon*, American Political Science Review, vol. 2, pp. 601-5 (1908).

THACHER, G. A., *Oregon Election*, Independent, vol. 64, pp. 1444-7 (1908).

THACHER, G. A., *Interesting Election in Oregon*, Independent, vol. 69, pp. 1434-8 (1910).

THACHER, G. A., *Significance of the Oregon Experiment*, Outlook, vol. 83, pp. 612-4 (1906).

Triumphant Democracy, Arena, vol. 40, pp. 239-41 (1908).

Truth about Oregon, Equity, vol. 16, pp. 73-8 (1914).

U'REN, W. S., *Initiative and Referendum in Oregon*, Arena, vol. 29, pp. 270-5 (1903).

U'REN, W. S., *Operation of the Initiative and Referendum in Oregon*, Arena, vol. 32, pp. 128-31 (1904).

U'REN, W. S., *Oregon's Experience with the Initiative and Referendum*, La Follette's Magazine, Apr. 23, 1910, p. 6.

U'REN, W. S., *Record of Direct Legislation in Oregon*, Equity, vol. 12, pp. 56-7 (1910).

U'REN, W. S., *Results of the Initiative and Referendum in Oregon*, Proceedings of the American Political Science Association, vol. 4, pp. 193-7 (1907).

U'REN, W. S., *State and County Government in Oregon and Proposed Changes*, Annals of the American Academy of Political and Social Science, vol. 47, pp. 271-3 (1913).

U'REN, W. S., *Six Years of the Initiative and Referendum in Oregon*, Chicago City Club Bulletin, vol. 2, pp. 465-78 (1909).

U'REN, W. S., *Second Direct Legislation Amendment Passed*, **Direct Legislation Record**, vol. 6, p. 1 (1899).

U'Ren, W. S., *Symposium, Direct Legislation Record*, vol. 8, p. 60 (1901).

"*W. S. U'Ren*," *Direct Legislation Record*, vol. 5, pp. 19–20 (1898).

Wood, C. E. S., *Oregon Situation in Full, Public*, vol. 11, pp. 320–3 (1908).

Working of the Oregon System, Nation, vol. 98, pp. 451–2 (1914).

Young, F. G., *Oregon History for Oregon System, Quarterly of the Oregon Historical Society*, vol. 12, pp. 264–8 (1911).

II. CONSTITUTIONAL AND STATUTORY PROVISIONS

1. THE INITIATIVE AND REFERENDUM

1. Constitution

Art. 1, sec. 21. Nor shall any law be passed, the taking effect of which shall be made to depend upon any authority, except as provided in this constitution; *provided*, that laws locating the capital of the state, locating county seats, and submitting town and corporate acts, and other local and special laws, may take effect or not, upon a vote of the electors interested (1859).

Art. 4, sec. 1. The legislative authority of the state shall be vested in a legislative assembly, consisting of a senate and house of representatives, but the people reserve to themselves power to propose laws and amendments to the constitution and to enact or reject the same at the polls, independent of the legislative assembly, and also reserve power at their own option to approve or reject at the polls any act of the legislative assembly. The first power reserved by the people is the initiative, and not more than eight per cent of the legal voters shall be required to propose any measure by such petition, and every such petition shall include the full text of the measure so proposed. Initiative petitions shall be filed with the secretary of state not less than four months before the election at which they are to be voted upon. The second power is the referendum, and it may be ordered (except as to laws necessary for the immediate preservation of the public peace, health, or safety), either by the petition signed by five per cent of the legal voters, or by the legislative assembly, as other bills are enacted. Referendum petitions shall be filed with the secretary of state not more than ninety days after the final adjournment of the session of the legislative assembly which passed the bill on which the referendum is demanded. The veto power of the governor shall not extend to measures referred to the people. All elections on measures referred to the people of the state shall be had at the biennial regular general elections, except when the legislative assembly shall order a special election. Any measure referred to the people shall take effect and become the law when it is approved by a majority of the votes cast thereon, and not otherwise. The style of all bills shall be: "Be it enacted by the people of the state of Oregon." This section shall not be construed to deprive any member of the legislative assembly of the right to introduce any measure. The whole number of votes cast for justice of the supreme court at the regular election last preceding the filing of any petition for the initiative or for the referendum shall be the basis on which the number of legal voters necessary to sign such petition shall be counted. Petitions and orders for the initiative and for the referendum shall be filed with the secretary of state, and in submitting the same to the people he, and all other officers, shall be guided by the general laws and the act submitting this amendment, until legislation shall be especially provided therefor (1902).

ART. 4, SEC. 1a. The referendum may be demanded by the people against one or more items, sections, or parts of any act of the legislative assembly in the same manner in which such power may be exercised against a complete act. The filing of a referendum petition against one or more items, sections, or parts of an act shall not delay the remainder of that act from becoming operative. The initiative and referendum powers reserved to the people by this constitution are hereby further reserved to the legal voters of every municipality and district, as to all local, special and municipal legislation, of every character, in or for their respective municipalities and districts. The manner of exercising said powers shall be prescribed by general laws, except that cities and towns may provide for the manner of exercising the initiative and referendum powers as to their municipal legislation. Not more than ten per cent of the legal voters may be required to order the referendum nor more than fifteen per cent to propose any measure, by the initiative, in any city or town (1906).

ART. 4, SEC. 28. No act shall take effect until ninety days from the end of the session at which the same shall have been passed, except in case of emergency; which emergency shall be declared in the preamble or in the body of the law (1859).

ART. 9, SEC. 1a. The legislative assembly shall not declare an emergency in any act regulating taxation or exemption.

ART. 11, SEC. 2. The legislative assembly shall not enact, amend, or repeal any charter or act of incorporation for any municipality, city, or town. The legal voters of every city and town are hereby granted power to enact and amend their municipal charter, subject to the constitution and criminal laws of the state of Oregon (1910).

ART. 14, SEC. 1. At the first regular session after the adoption of this constitution, the legislative assembly shall provide by law for the submission to the electors of this state at the next general election thereafter, the matter of the selection of a place for a permanent seat of government; and no place shall ever be the seat of government under such law, which shall not receive a majority of all the votes cast on the matter of such election (1859).

ART. 14, SEC. 3. The seat of government, when established as provided in section 1, shall not be removed for a term of twenty (20) years from the time of such establishment, nor in any other manner than as provided in the first section of this article. All the public institutions of the state, not located elsewhere prior to January 1, 1907, shall be located in the county where the seat of government is, excepting when otherwise ordered by an act of the legislative assembly and is ratified by the electors of the state at the next general election following such act, by a majority of all the votes cast on the question of whether or not such act shall be ratified (1908).

ART. 17, SEC. 1. Any amendment or amendments to this constitution may be proposed in either branch of the legislative assembly, and if the same shall be agreed to by a majority of all the members elected to each of the two houses, such proposed amendment or amendments shall, with the yeas and nays thereon, be entered in their journals and referred by the secretary of state to the people for their approval or rejection, at the next regular general election, except when the legislative assembly shall order a special election for that purpose. If a majority of the electors voting on any such amendment shall vote in favor thereof, it shall thereby become a part of this constitution. The votes for and against such amendment or amendments, severally, whether proposed by the legislative assembly or by initiative petition, shall be canvassed by the secretary of state in the presence of the governor, and if it shall appear to the governor that the majority of the votes cast at said election on said amendment or amendments, severally, are cast in favor thereof, it shall be his duty forthwith after such canvass, by his proclamation, to declare the said amendment or amendments, severally, having received said majority of votes, to have been adopted by the people of Oregon as part of the constitution thereof, and the same shall be in effect as a part of the constitution from the date of such proclamation. When two or more amendments shall be submitted in the manner aforesaid to the voters of this state, at the same election, they shall be so submitted that each amendment shall be voted on separately. No convention shall be called to amend or propose amendments to this constitution, or to propose a new constitution, unless the law providing for such convention shall first be approved by the people on a referendum vote at a regular general election. This article shall not be construed to impair the right of the people to amend this constitution by vote upon an initiative petition therefor (1906).

2. STATUTES. *Lord's Oregon Laws* AS AMENDED

SEC. 3470. The following shall be substantially the form of petition for the referendum to the people on any act passed by the legislative assembly of the state of Oregon, or by a city council: —

WARNING

It is a felony for any one to sign any initiative or referendum petition with any name other than his own, or to knowingly sign his name more than once for the same measure, or to sign such petition when he is not a legal voter.

PETITION FOR REFERENDUM

To the honorable................ secretary of state for the state of Oregon (or to the honorable .... clerk, auditor, or recorder, as the case may be, of the city of ....)

Appendix

We, the undersigned citizens and legal voters of the state of Oregon (and the district of ...., county of ...., or city of ...., as the case may be), respectfully order that the senate (or house) bill No. .... entitled (title act of, and if the petition is against less than the whole act then set forth here the part or parts on which the referendum is sought), passed by the .... legislative assembly of the state of Oregon at the regular (special) session of said legislative assembly, shall be referred to the people of the state (district of ...., county of ...., or city of.........., as the case may be), for their approval or rejection, at the regular (special) election to be held on the ..... day of .... A.D. 19...., and each for himself says: I have personally signed this petition; I am a legal voter of the state of Oregon, and (district of ...., county of ...., city of ...., as the case may be); my residence and post-office are correctly written after my name.

Name.................Residence...............Post-office ......
(If in a city, street and number.)

(Here follow twenty numbered lines for signatures) (1907).

SEC. 3471. The following shall be substantially the form of petition for any law, amendment to the constitution of the state of Oregon, city ordinance or amendment to a city charter, proposed by the initiative: —

WARNING

It is a felony for any one to sign any initiative or referendum petition with any name other than his own, or to knowingly sign his name more than once for the measure, or to sign such petition when he is not a legal voter.

INITIATIVE PETITION

To the honorable ...., secretary of state for the state of Oregon (or to the honorable ...., clerk, auditor or recorder, as the case may be, for the city of ....):

We, the undersigned citizens and legal voters of the state of Oregon (and of the district of ...., county of ...., or city of ...., as the case may be), respectfully demand that the following proposed law (or amendment to the constitution, ordinance,

or amendment to the city charter, as the case may be), shall be submitted to the legal voters of the state of Oregon (district of ...., county of ...., or city of ...., as the case may be), for their approval or rejection at the regular, general election, or (regular or special city election), to be held on the ..... day of ......, A.D. 19...., and each for himself says: I have personally signed this petition; I am a legal voter of the state of Oregon (and of the district of ......, county of ...., city of .... as the case may be); my residence and post-office are correctly written after my name.
Name .... Residence .... Post-office ......
(If in a city, street and number).

(Here follow twenty numbered lines for signatures) (1907).

SEC. 3472. Before or at the time of beginning to circulate any petition for the referendum to the people on any act passed by the legislative assembly of the state of Oregon, or for any law, amendment to the constitution of the state of Oregon, city ordinance or amendment to a city charter, proposed by the initiative, the person or persons or organization or organizations under whose authority the measure is to be referred or initiated shall send or deliver to the secretary of state, or city clerk, recorder or auditor, as the case may be, a copy of such petition duly signed which shall be filed by said officer in his office, who shall immediately examine the same and specify the form and kind and size of paper on which such petition shall be printed for circulation for signatures.

To every sheet of petitioners' signatures shall be attached a full and correct copy of the measure so proposed by initiative petition; but such petition may be filed by the secretary of state in numbered sections for convenience in handling. Each sheet of petitioners' signatures upon referendum petitions shall be attached to a full and correct copy of the measure on which the referendum is demanded and may be filed in numbered sections in like manner as initiative petitions. Not more than 20 signatures on one sheet shall be counted. When any such initiative or referendum petition shall be offered for filing the secretary of state shall detach the sheets containing the signatures and affidavits and cause them all to be attached to one or more printed copies of the measure so proposed by initiative or referendum petitions; *provided*, all petitions for the initiative and for the referendum and sheets for signatures shall be printed on a good quality of bond or

Appendix

ledger paper on pages 8½ inches in width by 13 inches in length, with a margin of 1¾ inches at the top of binding; if the aforesaid sheets shall be too bulky for convenient binding in one volume, they may be bound in two or more volumes, those in each volume to be attached to a single printed copy of such measure. If any such measure shall, at the ensuing election, be approved by the people, then the copies thereof so preserved, with the sheets and signatures and affidavits, and a certified copy of the Governor's proclamation declaring the same to have been approved by the people, shall be bound together in such form that they may be conveniently identified and preserved. The secretary of state shall cause every such measure so approved by the people to be printed with the general laws enacted by the next ensuing session of the legislative assembly, with the date of the governor's proclamation declaring the same to have been approved by the people. This act shall not apply to the general laws governing the method of determining whether stock of any kind shall be permitted to run at large in any county or portion thereof, nor to the provisions of the local option liquor laws providing methods of determining the sale of intoxicating liquors shall be prohibited in any county, city, precinct, ward or district (As amended by *Laws*, 1913, ch. 359, sec. 1).

SEC. 3473. Each and every sheet of every such petition containing signatures shall be verified on the face thereof, in substantially the following form, by the person who circulated said sheet of said petition, by his or her affidavit thereon and as a part thereof.

STATE OF OREGON } ss.
County of ....

I, ..., being first duly sworn, say: That I am personally acquainted with all the persons who signed this sheet of the foregoing petition, and each of them signed his or her name thereto in my presence; I believe that each has stated his or her name, post-office address and residence correctly, and that each signer is a legal voter of the State of Oregon and county of .... (Or of the city of ...., as the case may be.)

(Signature and post office address of affiant.)

Subscribed and sworn to before me this ..... day of ....,
A.D. 19....

(Signature and title of officer before whom oath is made, and his post office address.)

The forms herein given are not mandatory, and if substantially followed in any petition it shall be sufficient, disregarding clerical and merely technical errors.

(As amended by *Laws*, 1913, ch. 359, sec. 2).

SEC. 3474. If the secretary of state shall refuse to accept and file any petition for the initiative or for the referendum any citizen may apply, within ten days after such refusal, to the circuit court for a writ of mandamus to compel him to do so. If it shall be decided by the court that such petition is legally sufficient, the secretary of state shall then file it, with a certified copy of the judgment attached thereto, as of the date on which it was originally offered for filing in his office. On a showing that any petition filed is not legally sufficient, the court may enjoin the secretary of state and all other officers from certifying or printing on the official ballot for the ensuing election the ballot title and numbers of such measure. All such suits shall be advanced on the court docket and heard and decided by the court as quickly as possible. Either party may appeal to the supreme court within ten days after the decision is rendered. The circuit court of Marion county shall have jurisdiction in all cases of measures to be submitted to the electors of the state at large; in cases of local and special measures, the circuit court of the county, or of one of the counties in which such measures are to be voted upon, shall have jurisdiction; in cases of municipal legislation the circuit court of the county in which the city concerned is situated shall have jurisdiction (1907).

SEC. 3475. When any measure shall be filed with the secretary of state to be referred to the people of the state, or of any county or district composed of one or more counties, either by the legislative assembly or the referendum petition, and when any measure shall be proposed by initiative petition, the secretary of state shall forthwith transmit to the attorney general of the state a copy thereof, and within ten days thereafter the attorney general shall provide and return to the secretary of state a ballot title for said measure. The ballot title shall contain: (1) The name or names of the person or persons, organization, or organizations under whose authority the measure was initiated or referred. (2) A distinctive short title in not exceeding 10 words by which the measure is commonly referred to or spoken of by the public or press, and (3) a general title which may be distinct from the legislative title of the measure, expressing in not more than 100 words the purpose of the measure. The ballot title shall be printed with the numbers of the measure, on the official ballot. In making such ballot title the attorney general shall, to the best of his ability, give a true and impartial statement of the purpose of the measure, and in such language that the ballot title shall not be intentionally an argument, or likely to create prejudice, either for or against the measure. Any person who is dissatisfied with the ballot title provided by the attorney general for any measure may appeal from his decision to the circuit court, as provided by the section 3474, by petition, praying for different title and setting forth the reasons why the title prepared by the attorney general is insufficient or unfair. No appeal shall be allowed from the decision of the attorney general on a ballot title, unless the same is taken within 10 days after said decision is filed. A copy of every such decision shall be served by the secretary of state or the clerk of the court, upon the person offering or filing such initiative or referendum petition, or appeal. Service of such decision may be by mail or telegraph and shall be made forthwith. Said circuit court shall thereupon examine said measure, hear arguments, and in its decision thereon certify to the secretary of state a ballot title for the measure in accord with the intent of this section. The decision of the circuit court shall be final. The secretary of state shall print on the official ballot the title thus certified to him (As amended by *Laws*, 1913, ch. 36, sec. 1).

SEC. 3476. The secretary of state, at the time he furnishes to the county clerks of the several counties certified copies of the names of the candidates for state and district offices, shall furnish to each of said county clerks his certified copy of the ballot titles and numbers of the several measures to be voted upon at the ensuing general election, and he shall use for each measure the ballot title designated in the manner herein provided. Such ballot title shall not resemble, so far as to probably create confusion, any such title previously filed for any measure to be submitted at that election; he shall number such measures and such ballot titles shall be printed on the official ballot in the order in which the acts referred by the legislative assembly and petitions by the people shall be filed in his office. The affirmative of the first measure shall be numbered 300 and the negative 301 in numerals, and the succeeding measures shall be numbered consecutively 302, 303, 304, 305, and so on, at each election. It shall be the duty of the several county clerks to print said ballot titles and numbers upon the official ballot in the order presented to them by the secretary of state and the relative position required by law. Measures referred by the legislative assembly shall be designated by the heading "Referred to the People by the Legislative Assembly"; measures referred by petition shall be designated "Referendum Ordered by Petition of the People"; measures proposed by initiative petition shall be designated and distinguished on the ballot by the heading "Proposed by Initiative Petition." (As amended by *Laws*, 1913, ch. 359, sec. 3).

SEC. 3477. The manner of voting upon measures submitted to the people shall be the same as is now or may be required and provided by law; no measure shall be adopted unless it shall receive an affirmative majority of the total number of respective votes cast on such measure and entitled to be counted under the provisions of this act; that is to say, supposing seventy thousand ballots to be properly marked on any measure, it shall not be adopted unless it shall receive more than thirty-five thousand affirmative votes. If two or more conflicting laws shall be approved by the people at the same election, the law receiving the greatest number of affirmative votes shall be paramount in all particulars as to which there is a conflict, even though such law may not have received the greatest majority of affirmative votes. If two or more conflicting amendments to the constitution shall be approved by the people at the same election, the amendment which receives the greatest number of affirmative votes shall be paramount in all particulars as to which there is a conflict, even though such amendment may not have received the greatest majority of affirmative votes (1907).

SEC. 3478. Not later than the 90th day before any regular general election, nor later than 30 days before any special election, at which any proposed law, part of an act or amendment to the constitution is to be submitted to the people, the secretary of state shall cause to be printed in pamphlet form a true copy of the title and text of each measure to be submitted, with the number and form in which the ballot title thereof will be printed on the official ballot. The person, committee or duly organized officers of any organization filing any petition for the initiative, but no other person or organization, shall have the right to file with the secretary of state for printing and distribution any argument advocating such measure; said argument shall be filed not later than the 115th day before the regular election at which the measure is to be voted upon. Any person, committee or organization may file with the secretary of state, for printing and distribution, any arguments they may desire, opposing any measure, not later than the 105th day immediately preceding such election. Arguments advocating or opposing any measure referred to the people by the legislative assembly, or by referendum petition, at a regular general election, shall be governed by the same rules as to time, but may be filed with the secretary of state by any person, committee or organization; in the case of measures submitted at a special election, all arguments in support of such measure at least 60 days before such election. But in every case the person or persons offering such arguments for printing and distribution shall pay to the secretary of state sufficient money to pay all the expenses for paper and printing to supply one copy with every copy of the measure to be printed by the state; and he shall forthwith notify the persons offering the same of the amount of money necessary. The secretary of state shall cause one copy of each of said arguments to be bound in the pamphlet copy of the measures to be submitted as herein provided, and all such measures and arguments to be submitted at one election shall be bound together in a single pamphlet. All the printing shall be done by the state, and the pages of said pamphlet shall be numbered consecutively from one to the end. The pages of said pamphlet shall be six by nine inches in size and the printed matter therein shall be set in six-point Roman-faced solid type on not to exceed seven-point body, in two columns of 13 ems in width each to the page with six-point dividing rule and with appropriate heads and printed on a good quality of book paper 25 by 38 inches weighing not more than 50 pounds to the ream. The title page of every measure bound in said pamphlet shall show its ballot title and ballot number. The title page of each argument shall show the measure or measures it favors or opposes and by what persons or organization it is issued. When such arguments are printed he shall pay the state printer therefor from the money deposited with him and refund the surplus, if any, to the parties who paid it to him. The cost of printing, binding and distributing the measures proposed and of binding and distributing the arguments, shall be paid by the state as a part of the state printing, it being intended that only the cost of paper and printing the arguments shall be paid by the parties presenting the same, and they shall not be charged any higher rate for such work than is paid by the state for similar work and paper. Not later than the 55th day before the regular general election at which such measures are to be voted upon the secretary of state shall transmit by mail, with postage fully prepaid, to every voter in the state whose address he may have, one copy of such pamphlet; *provided*, that if the secretary shall, at or about the same time be mailing any other pamphlet to every voter, he may, if practicable, bind the matter herein provided for in the first part of said pamphlet, numbering the pages of the entire pamphlet consecutively from one to the end, or he may enclose the pamphlets under one cover. In the case of a special election he shall mail said pamphlet to every voter not less than 20 days before said special election. (As amended by *Laws*, 1913; ch. 359, sec. 4).

SEC. 3483. Every person who is a qualified elector of the state of Oregon may sign a petition for the referendum or for the initiative for any measure which he is legally entitled to vote upon. Any person signing any name other than his own to any petition, or knowingly signing his name more than once for the same measure at one election, or who is not at the time of signing the same a legal voter of this state, or any officer or person willfully violating any provision of this statute, shall, upon conviction thereof, be punished by a fine not exceeding $500, or by imprisonment in the penitentiary not exceeding two years, or by both such fine and imprisonment, in the discretion of the court before which such conviction shall be had (1907).

SEC. 3497. . . . Any person not a candidate for any office or nomination who expends money or value to an amount greater than $50 in any campaign for nomination or election, to aid in the election or defeat of any candidate or candidates, or party ticket, or measure before the people, shall within ten days after the election in which said money or value was expended, file with the secretary of state in the case of a measure voted upon by the people . . . an itemized statement of such receipts and expenditures and vouchers for every sum paid in excess of $5 . . . (1908).

Sec. 3515. Any person shall be guilty of a corrupt practice within the meaning of this act if he expends any money for election purposes contrary to the provisions of any statute of this state, or if he is guilty of treating, undue influence, personation, the giving or promising to give, or offer of any money or valuable thing to any elector with intent to induce such elector to vote or to refrain from voting for any candidate for public office, or the ticket of any political party or organization, or any measure submitted to the people, at any election, or to register or refrain from registering as a voter at any state, district, county, city, town, village, or school district election for public offices or on public measures. Such corrupt practice shall be deemed to be prevalent when instances thereof occur in different election districts similar in character and sufficient in number to convince the court before which any case involving the same may be tried that they were general and common, or were pursuant to a general scheme or plan (1908).

Sec. 3517. No publisher of a newspaper or other periodical shall insert, either in its advertising or reading columns, any paid matter which is designed or tends to aid, injure, or defeat any candidate or political party or organization, or measure before the people, unless it is stated therein that it is a paid advertisement, the name of the chairman or secretary, or the names of the other officers of the political or other organization inserting the same, or the name of some voter who is responsible therefor, with his residence and the street and number thereof, if any, appear in such advertisement in the nature of a signature. . . . Any person who shall violate any of the provisions of this section shall be punished as for a corrupt practice (1908).

Sec. 3518. It shall be unlawful for any person at any place on the day of any election to ask, solicit, or in any manner try to induce or persuade any voter on such election day to vote for or refrain from voting for any candidate, or the candidates or ticket of any political party or organization, or any measure submitted to the people, and upon conviction thereof he shall be punished by a fine of not less than $5 nor more than $100 for the first offense, and for the second and each subsequent offense occurring on the same or different election days, he shall be punished by fine as aforesaid, or by imprisonment in the county jail for not less than five nor more than thirty days, or by both such fine and imprisonment (1908).

SEC. 3519. It shall be unlawful to write, print, or circulate through the mails or otherwise any letter, circular, bill, placard, or poster relating to any election or to any candidate at any election, unless the same shall bear on its face the name and address of the author, and of the printer and publisher thereof; and any person writing, printing, publishing, circulating, posting, or causing to be written, printed, circulated, posted, or published any such letter, bill, placard, circular, or poster as aforesaid, which fails to bear on its face the name and address of the author and of the printer or publisher shall be guilty of an illegal practice, and shall, on conviction thereof, be punished by fine of not less than $10 nor more than $1000 . . . (1908).

2. RECALL

CONSTITUTION

ART. 2, SEC. 18. Every public officer in Oregon is subject, as herein provided, to recall by the legal voters of the state or of the electoral district from which he is elected. There may be required twenty-five per cent, but not more, of the number of electors who voted in his district at the preceding election for justice of the supreme court to file their petition demanding his recall by the people. They shall set forth in said petition the reasons for said demand. If he shall offer his resignation, it shall be accepted and take effect on the day it is offered, and the vacancy shall be filled as may be provided by law. If he shall not resign within five days after the petition is filed, a special election shall be ordered to be held within twenty days in his said electoral district to determine whether the people will recall said officer. On the sample ballot at said election shall be printed in not more than two hundred words, the reasons for demanding the recall of said officer as set forth in the recall petition, and in not more than two hundred words, the officer's justification of his course in office. He shall continue to perform the duties of his office until the result of said special election shall be officially declared. Other candidates for the office may be nominated to be voted for at said special election. The candidate who shall receive the highest number of votes shall be deemed elected for the remainder of the term, whether it be the person against whom the recall petition was filed, or another. The recall petition shall be filed with the officer with whom a petition for nomination to such office should be filed, and the same officer shall order the special election when it is required. No such petition shall be circulated against any officer until he has actually held his office six months, save and except that it may be filed against a senator or representative in the legislative assembly at any time after five days from the beginning of the first session after his election. After one such petition and special election, no further recall petition shall be filed against the same officer during the term for which he was elected unless such further petitioners shall first pay into the public treasury which has paid such special election expenses, the whole amount of its expenses for the preceding special election. Such additional legislation as may aid the operation of this section shall be provided by the legislative assembly, including provision for payment by the public treasury of the reasonable special election campaign expenses of such officer. But the words "the legislative assembly shall provide" or any similar or equivalent words in this constitution or any amendment thereto, shall not be construed to grant to the legislative assembly any exclusive power of law-making nor in any way to limit the initiative and referendum powers reserved by the people (1908).

III. THE VOTE ON INITIATIVE AND REFERENDUM MEASURES

(1) Referred by the Legislative Assembly.
(2) Initiated by Petition.
(3) Referred by Petition.
(*) Adopted at the Election.

GENERAL ELECTION, 1904

Total number of ballots cast, 99,315.

Average percentage vote for state officers, 90.

Number		Yes	No	Percentage of Total Vote Cast Received by Each Measure	Majority-Percentage of Total Vote Cast
—	*Constitutional Amendment* Authorizing the legislative assembly to regulate the office of state printer (2)	45,334 *	14,031	60	46
—	*Bills* Providing for direct primary nominations (2)	56,205 *	16,354	73	57
—	Local option liquor regulation (2)	43,316 *	40,198	84	44

R

GENERAL ELECTION, 1906

Total number of ballots cast, 99,445.

Average percentage vote for state officers, 91.

Number		Yes	No	Percentage of Total Vote Cast Received by Each Measure	Majority-Percentage of Total Vote Cast
—	*Constitutional Amendments* Granting the suffrage to women (2)	36,902	47,075	84	
—	Changing the method applying to constitutional amendments submitted by the legislative assembly, and requiring calls for constitutional conventions to be submitted to the approval of the voters (2)	47,661 *	18,751	67	48
—	Providing for home-rule charters for municipalities (2)	52,567 *	19,852	73	53
—	Authorizing the regulation of the office of state printer by law (2)	63,749 *	9,571	74	64
—	Extending the initiative and referendum to the localities (2)	47,678 *	16,735	65	48
—	*Bills* General appropriation for state institutions (3)	43,918 *	26,758	71	44
—	Amendment of local option liquor law in favor of anti-prohibitionists (2)	35,297	45,144	81	
—	Purchase of Barlow toll road by state (2)	31,525	44,527	77	
—	Prohibiting the issue of free passes and discrimination by railroads and other public service corporations (2)	57,281 *	16,779	74	58
—	Gross-earnings tax on sleeping and refrigerator car companies and oil companies (2)	69,635 *	6,441	77	70
—	Gross-earnings tax on express, telephone, and telegraph companies (2)	70,872 *	6,360	78	71

Appendix

GENERAL ELECTION, 1908

Total number of ballots cast, 116,614.

Average percentage vote for state officers, 89.

Number		Yes	No	Percentage of Total Vote Cast Received by Each Measure	Majority-Percentage of Total Vote Cast
	Constitutional Amendments				
300.	Increasing compensation of members of legislative assembly (1)	19,691	68,892	76	
302.	Permitting the location of state institutions away from the capital by act approved by the people (1)	41,975 *	40,868	71	36
304.	Increasing the number of justices of the supreme court, and authorizing reorganization of the judicial system by law (1)	30,243	50,591	69	
306.	Changing the date of general elections (1)	65,728 *	18,591	72	56
316.	Granting the suffrage to women (2)	36,858	58,670	82	
320.	Giving cities exclusive power to regulate theaters, race tracks, poolrooms, etc., and the sale of liquor, subject to the local option law (2)	39,442	52,346	79	
322.	Providing a modified single tax (2)	32,066	60,871	80	
324.	Permitting the recall of officers (2)	58,381 *	31,002	76	50
328.	Authorizing laws for proportional representation and preferential voting (2)	48,868 *	34,128	71	42
334.	Requiring indictment to be by grand jury (2)	52,214 *	28,487	69	45
	Bills				
308.	Providing for the custody of prisoners in county jails by the sheriff, authorizing the county court to direct the work of prisoners, and regulating the salaries of guards and the prices of prisoners' meals in one county (3)	60,443 *	30,033	78	52

GENERAL ELECTION, 1908 — *Continued*

Number		Yes	No	Percentage of Total Vote Cast Received by Each Measure	Majority-Percentage of Total Vote Cast
310.	Requiring railroads and other common carriers to give certain public officials free passes (3)	28,856	59,406	76	
312.	Appropriation for armories (3)	33,507	54,848	76	
314.	Appropriation for the university (3)	44,115 *	40,535	73	38
318.	Regulating fishing in the Columbia river in favor of the fish-wheel operators (2)	46,582 *	40,720	75	40
326.	Instructing members of the legislature to vote for the people's choice of United States senator (2)	69,668 *	21,162	78	60
330.	Punishing corrupt practices at elections (2)	54,042 *	31,301	73	46
332.	Regulating fishing in the Columbia river in favor of the gill-net operators (2)	56,130 *	30,280	74	48
336.	Creating Hood River county (2)	43,948 *	26,778	61	38

GENERAL ELECTION, 1910

Total number of ballots cast, 120,248.

Average percentage vote for state officers, 87.

Number		Yes	No	Percentage of Total Vote Cast Received by Each Measure	Majority-percentage of Total Vote Cast
	Constitutional Amendments				
300.	Granting the suffrage to women (2)	35,270	59,065	78	
306.	Providing single districts for members of the legislative assembly (1)	24,000	54,252	65	
308.	Repealing the constitutional requirement of equal and uniform taxation (1)	37,619	40,172	65	

Appendix

GENERAL ELECTION, 1910 — *Continued*

Number		Yes	No	Percentage of Total Vote Cast Received by Each Measure	Majority-Percentage of Total Vote Cast
310.	Authorizing the organization of railroad districts and the operation of railroads by the state and localities (1)	32,844	46,070	66	61
312.	Authorizing the levy of state and local taxes on separate classes of property and the apportionment of state taxes among the counties (1)	31,629	41,692	61	
326.	Abolishing the poll tax, requiring all laws regulating taxation or exemption throughout the state to be referred to the people, exempting from constitutional restrictions all measures approved by the people declaring what shall be subject to taxation or exemption and how it shall be taxed or exempted, and authorizing each county to regulate taxation and exemption within its limits, subject to any general laws hereafter enacted (2)	44,171 *	42,127	72	37
328.	Giving cities exclusive power to regulate the liquor traffic within their limits, subject to the local option law (2)	53,321 *	50,779	87	44
342.	State-wide prohibition of the liquor traffic (2)	43,540	61,221	87	
354.	Increasing the maximum limit of county indebtedness for roads and requiring a majority vote for such indebtedness (2)	51,275 *	32,906	70	43
360.	Reorganizing extensively the legislative department (2)	37,031	44,336	68	
362.	Reorganizing extensively the judicial department, changing the system of appeals, and providing for a three-fourths' verdict in civil cases (2)	44,538 *	39,399	70	37

GENERAL ELECTION, 1910 — Continued

Number		Yes	No	Percentage of Total Vote Cast Received by Each Measure	Majority-Percentage of Total Vote Cast
	Bills				
302.	Establishing an insane asylum (1)	50,134 *	41,504	76	42
304.	Calling a constitutional convention (1)	23,143	59,974	69	
314.	Requiring Baker county to add to the salary of the circuit judge (3) . . .	13,161	71,503	70	
316.	Creating Nesmith county (2)	22,866	60,951	69	
318.	Establishing a normal school at Monmouth (2) . . .	50,191 *	40,044	75	42
320.	Creating Otis county (2) .	17,426	62,016	66	
322.	Annexing part of Clackamas county to Multnomah county (2)	16,250	69,002	71	
324.	Creating Williams county (2)	14,508	64,090	65	
330.	Regulating employers' liability (2)	56,258 *	33,943	72	37
332.	Creating Orchard county (2)	15,664	62,712	65	
334.	Creating Clark county (2)	15,613	61,704	64	
336.	Establishing a normal school at Weston (2) . . .	40,898	46,201	72	
338.	Annexing part of Washington county to Multnomah county (2)	14,047	68,221	68	
340.	Establishing a normal school at Ashland (2) . . .	38,473	48,655	72	
344.	State-wide prohibition (2) .	42,651	63,564	·88	
346.	Creating commission on employers' liability (2) . .	32,224	51,719	70	
348.	Regulating fishing in the Rogue river (2)	49,712 *	33,397	69	41
350.	Creating Des Chutes county (2)	17,592	60,486	64	
352.	Providing methods for creating new towns, counties, and municipal districts, and changing county boundaries (2)	37,129	42,327	66	
356.	Providing for presidential primary elections (2) . .	43,353 *	41,624	71	36
358.	Creating a board of people's inspectors of government and providing for an official state gazette (2) . . .	29,955	52,538	69	

Appendix

GENERAL ELECTION, 1912

Total number of ballots cast, 144,113.

Average percentage vote for state officers, 88.

Number		Yes	No	Percentage of Total Vote Cast Received by Each Measure	Majority-Percentage of Total Vote Cast
	Constitutional Amendments				
300.	Granting the suffrage to women (2)	61,265 *	57,104	82	43
302.	Creating the office of lieutenant-governor (1)	59,562	61,644	78	
304.	Authorizing the levy of state and local taxes on separate classes of property and the apportionment of state taxes among the counties (1)	51,852	56,671	75	
306.	Amending the constitutional requirement of equal and uniform taxation (1)	52,045	54,483	74	
308.	Excepting laws regulating taxation or exemption from "emergency" legislation, and repealing the constitutional provisions which required all laws regulating taxation or exemption throughout the state to be referred to the people, exempted from constitutional restrictions all measures approved by the people, declaring what should be subject to taxation or exemption and how it should be taxed or exempted, and authorized each county to regulate taxation and exemption subject to general laws of the state (1)	63,881 *	47,150	77	44
310.	Requiring a majority of the votes cast at the election for the approval of constitutional amendments (1)	32,934	70,325	72	
312.	Providing for double liability of bank stockholders (1)	82,981*	21,738	73	58

GENERAL ELECTION, 1912 — Continued

Number		Yes	No	Percentage of Total Vote Cast Received by Each Measure	Majority-Percentage of Total Vote Cast
322.	Requiring a majority of the votes cast at the election for the approval of initiated measures (2)	35,721	68,861	73	
342.	Exempting indebtedness for roads from the constitutional maximum of state indebtedness, and limiting state indebtedness for roads to a percentage of the valuation of the property in the state. "Harmony" amendment (2)	59,452 *	43,447	71	
346.	Limiting county indebtedness for roads. "Harmony" amendment (2)	57,258 *	43,858	70	40
350.	Permitting taxation of incomes (2)	52,702	52,948	73	
360.	Granting home rule to counties in the matter of indebtedness for roads. "Jackson County" amendment (2)	38,568	63,481	71	
362.	Reorganizing extensively the legislative department (2)	31,020	71,183	71	
364.	Modified single tax	31,534	82,015	79	
	Bills				
314.	Providing for the regulation of public utilities (3)	65,985 *	40,956	74	46
318.	Creating Cascade county (2)	26,463	71,239	68	
320.	Providing a millage tax for the university and the agricultural college and consolidating the government of these institutions (2)	48,701	57,279	74	
324.	Authorizing the issue of county bonds for roads. Grange bill (2)	49,699	56,713	74	
326.	Creating a state highway department. Grange bill (2)	23,872	83,846	75	
328.	Putting into immediate effect the state-printer flat-salary law (2)	34,793	69,542	72	

GENERAL ELECTION, 1912 — *Continued*

Number		Yes	No	Percentage of Total Vote Cast Received by Each Measure	Majority-Percentage of Total Vote Cast
330.	Creating the office of hotel inspector (2)	16,910	91,995	76	
332.	Providing for an eight-hour day on public works (2)	64,508 *	48,078	78	45
334.	Regulating corporations dealing with corporate securities and establishing a corporation department. "Blue-sky" bill (2)	48,765	57,293	74	
336.	Prohibiting the employment of state prisoners by private persons, and authorizing their employment by the state and counties (2)	73,800 *	37,492	77	51
338.	Prohibiting the employment of local prisoners by private persons and authorizing their employment by the counties (2)	71,367 *	37,731	76	50
340.	Creating a state road board and authorizing the issue of state road bonds. "Harmony" bill (2)	30,897	75,590	74	
344.	Authorizing the issue of county bonds for roads. "Harmony" bill (2)	43,611	60,210	72	
348.	Providing methods for the consolidation of cities and the organization of new counties (2)	40,199	56,992	67	
352.	Exempting household goods from taxation (2)	60,357 *	51,826	78	42
354.	Exempting moneys and credits from taxation (2)	42,491	66,540	76	
356.	Revising the inheritance tax laws (2)	38,609	63,839	71	
358.	Regulating freight rates (2)	58,306 *	45,534	72	40
366.	Abolishing capital punishment and regulating the pardoning power (2)	41,951	64,578	74	
368.	Prohibiting boycotting or picketing of shops, etc. (2)	49,826	60,560	77	

GENERAL ELECTION, 1912 — *Continued*

Number		Yes	No	Percentage of Total Vote Cast Received by Each Measure	Majority-Percentage of Total Vote Cast
370.	Prohibiting, in the larger towns, the use of streets, etc., for public meetings or discussions without the consent of the mayor (2)	48,987	62,532	77	
372.	Appropriation for the university (3)	29,437	78,985	75	
374.	Appropriation for the university (3)	27,310	79,376	74	

SPECIAL ELECTION, 1913

Total number of ballots cast, 102,276.

No state officers elected.

Number		Yes	No	Percentage of Total Vote Cast Received by Each Measure	Majority-Percentage of Total Vote Cast
	Bills				
300.	Appropriation for the university (3)	56,659 *	40,600	95	55
302.	Appropriation for the university (3)	53,569 *	43,014	94	52
304.	Providing for the sterilization of habitual criminals and other degenerates (3)	41,767	53,319	93	
306.	Increasing the number of district attorneys (3)	54,179 *	38,159	90	53
308.	Creating an industrial accident commission and regulating workmen's compensation for injuries (3)	67,814 *	28,608	94	66

Appendix

GENERAL ELECTION, 1914

Total number of ballots cast, 259,868.

Average percentage vote for state officers, 82.

Number		Yes	No	Percentage of Total Vote Cast Received by Each Measure	Majority-Percentage of Total Vote Cast
	Constitutional Amendments				
300.	Requiring voters to be citizens of the United States (1)	164,879 *	39,847	79	64
302.	Creating the office of lieutenant-governor (1) . .	52,040	143,804	75	
304.	Permitting the consolidation of large cities with counties (1)	77,392	103,194	70	
306.	Reducing constitutional restrictions upon state indebtedness for irrigation and power projects and development of the untilled lands of the state (1) . .	49,759	135,550	71	
308.	Abolishing the constitutional requirement of equal and uniform taxation (1) . .	59,206	116,490	67	
310.	Permitting the classification of property for taxation, the imposition of income taxes, and reasonable exemptions from taxation (1)	52,362	122,704	67	
314.	Permitting the merger of adjacent cities (1)	96,116 *	77,671	67	37
318.	Increasing the compensation of the members of the legislative assembly (1) . .	41,087	146,278	72	
320.	Establishing a universal eight-hour labor day (2) . . .	49,360	167,888	84	
326.	Providing for the exemption of personal property and improvements on land to the extent of fifteen hundred dollars for each person from taxation (2) . .	65,495	136,193	78	
328.	Prohibiting the sale and authorizing the lease of the beds of navigable waters, and authorizing the construction of municipal docks on such lands (2) .	67,128	114,564	70	

GENERAL ELECTION, 1914 — *Continued*

Number		Yes	No	Percentage of Total Vote Cast Received by Each Measure	Majority-percentage of Total Vote Cast
332.	State-wide prohibition of the liquor traffic (2)	136,842 *	100,362	91	53
334.	Abolishing the death penalty (2)	100,552 *	100,395	77	39
336.	Providing for a specific personal graduated extra tax on owners of land (2)	59,186	124,943	71	
342.	Extending the term of certain county offices from two years to four years (2)	82,841	107,039	73	
348.	Providing for the election of the house of representatives by proportional representation (2)	39,740	137,116	68	
350.	Abolishing the state senate (2)	62,376	123,429	72	
352.	Establishing a department of industry and public works for the unemployed, and imposing an inheritance tax for its maintenance (2)	57,859	126,201	71	
356.	Adding provisions permitting a uniform three-hundred-dollar tax exemption to the section of the constitution which requires equal and uniform taxation and authorizes certain exemptions from taxation, and prohibiting the amendment of this section except by a two-thirds vote of those voting on the issue at the election (2)	43,280	140,507	71	
	Bills				
312.	Providing a millage tax for the Southern Oregon normal school (1)	84,041	109,643	75	
316.	Providing a millage tax for the Eastern Oregon normal school (1)	87,450	105,345	74	
322.	Providing for an eight-hour labor day and room ventilation for female workers (2)	88,480	120,296	80	

GENERAL ELECTION, 1914 — *Continued*

Number		Yes	No	Percentage of Total Vote Cast Received by Each Measure	Majority-percentage of Total Vote Cast
324.	Providing for non-partisan nomination of judicial officers (2)	74,323	107,263	70	
330.	Authorizing cities to construct and operate municipal docks, etc., within the city or within five miles of its limits, and authorizing the lease of submerged lands (2)	67,110	111,113	69	
338.	Consolidating the corporation and insurance departments (2)	55,469	120,154	68	
340.	Regulating the licensing of dentists (2)	92,722	110,404	78	
344.	Providing for a tax-code commission (2)	34,436	143,468	69	
346.	Consolidating the state land board and the desert land board (2)	32,701	143,366	68	
354.	Providing for a pre-primary convention, and amending the presidential primary law (2)	25,058	153,638	69	

IV. A MEASURE AND ARGUMENTS

Referendum Pamphlet, 1912, pp. 209–25

AN AMENDMENT

TO THE

CONSTITUTION OF THE STATE OF OREGON TO BE SUBMITTED TO THE LEGAL VOTERS OF THE STATE OF OREGON FOR THEIR APPROVAL OR REJECTION

AT THE

REGULAR GENERAL ELECTION

TO BE HELD

On the Fifth Day of November, 1912

TO AMEND

Article IV

By initiative petition filed in the office of the Secretary of State, July 3, 1912, in accordance with the provisions of Chapter 226, General Laws of Oregon, 1907.

Printed in pursuance of Section 8 of Chapter 226, Laws of 1907.

SECRETARY OF STATE.

The following is the form and number in which the question will be printed on the official ballot:

PROPOSED BY INITIATIVE PETITION

For amendment of Article IV of the Constitution of Oregon abolishing the State Senate; providing none but registered voters be counted on initiative or referendum petitions; increasing State and municipal referendum powers; House of Representatives to consist of sixty elective members, and the Governor and unsuccessful party candidates for Governor to be *ex-officio* members;

Governor to introduce all appropriation bills, legislature not to increase the amounts thereof, four-year terms, annual sessions; proportional election of members; proxy system of voting on bills, and those introduced after twenty days to go to the next session; control and revocation of franchises. Vote YES or NO.

| 362. | Yes. |
| 363. | No. |

(On Official Ballot, Nos. 362 and 363.)

Article IV of the Constitution of the State of Oregon shall be and the same hereby is amended to read as follows:

ARTICLE IV

SECTION 1. The legislative authority of the State shall be vested in the Legislative Assembly consisting of a House of Representatives, but the people reserve to themselves the power to propose legislative measures, resolutions, laws and amendments to the Constitution, and to enact or reject the same at the polls, independent of the Legislative Assembly, and also reserve power, at their own option, to approve or reject at the polls any act, item, section or part of any resolution, act or measure passed by the Legislative Assembly. The Senate is hereby abolished from and after the adoption of this amendment.

SEC. 1a. The first power reserved by the people is the initiative, and not more than eight per cent, nor in any case more than fifty thousand, of the legal voters shall be required to propose any measure by initiative petition, and every such petition shall include the full text of the measure so proposed. Initiative petitions, except for municipal and wholly local legislation, shall be filed with the Secretary of State not less than four months before the election at which they are to be voted upon. If conflicting measures submitted to the people shall be approved by a majority of the votes severally cast for and against the same, the one receiving the highest number of affirmative votes shall thereby become law as to all conflicting provisions. Proposed amendments to the Constitution shall in all cases be submitted to the people for approval or rejection.

SEC. 1b. The second power is the referendum, and it may be ordered either by petition signed by the required percentage of the legal voters, or by the Legislative Assembly as other bills are enacted. Not more than five per cent, nor in any case more than thirty thousand of the legal voters shall be required to sign and make a valid referendum petition. Only signatures of legal voters whose names are on the registration books and records shall be counted on initiative and on referendum petitions.

SEC. 1c. If it shall be necessary for the immediate preservation of the public peace, health or safety that a measure shall become effective without delay such necessity shall be stated in one section, and if, by a vote of yeas and nays, three-fourths of all the members shall vote, on a separate roll call, in favor of the measure going into instant operation because it is necessary for the immediate preservation of the public peace, health or safety, such measure shall become operative upon being filed in the office of the Secretary of State, or city clerk, as the case may be; provided, that an emergency shall not be declared on any measure creating or abolishing any office, or to change the salary, term or duties of any officer. It shall not be necessary to state in such section the facts which constitute the emergency. If a referendum petition be filed against an emergency measure, such measure shall be a law until it is voted upon by the people, and if it is then rejected by a majority of those voting upon the question, such measure shall be thereby repealed. No statute, ordinance or resolution approved by vote of the people shall be amended or repealed by the Legislative Assembly or any city council except by a three-fourths vote of all the members, taken by yeas and nays. The provisions of this section apply to city councils.

SEC. 1d. The initiative and referendum powers of the people are hereby further reserved to the legal voters of each municipality and district as to all local, special and municipal legislation of every character in or for their respective municipalities and districts. Every extension, enlargement, purchase, grant or conveyance of a franchise, or of any right, property, easement, lease or occupation of or in any road, street, alley or park, or any part thereof, or in any real property or interest in any real property owned by a municipal corporation, whether the same be made by statute, ordinance, resolution or otherwise, shall be subject to referendum by petition. In the case of laws

Appendix

chiefly of local interest, whether submitted by initiative or referendum petition, or by the Legislative Assembly, as for example, the division or creation of counties, or the creation of new or additional offices or officers, the same shall be voted on and approved or rejected only by the people of the locality chiefly interested, except when the Legislative Assembly shall order the measure submitted to the people of the State. Cities and towns may provide for the manner of exercising the initiative and referendum powers as to their municipal legislation, subject to the general laws of the State. Not more than ten per cent of the legal voters may be required to order the referendum nor more than fifteen per cent to propose any measure by the initiative in any city or town.

SEC. 1e. The filing of a referendum petition against one or more items, sections or parts of any act, legislative measure, resolution or ordinance shall not delay the remainder of the measure from becoming operative. Referendum petitions against measures passed by the Legislative Assembly shall be filed with the Secretary of State not later than ninety days after the final adjournment of the session of the Legislative Assembly at which the measure on which the referendum is demanded was passed; except when the Legislative Assembly shall adjourn at any time temporarily for a period longer than ninety days, in which case such referendum petitions shall be filed not later than ninety days after such temporary adjournment. The veto power of the Governor or of a mayor shall not extend to measures initiated by or referred to the people. All elections on general, local and special measures referred to the people of the State or of any locality shall be had at the regular general elections, occurring not less than four months after the petition is filed, except when the Legislative Assembly shall order a special election; but counties, cities and towns may provide for special elections on their municipal legislation proposed by their citizens or local legislative bodies. Any measure initiated by the people or referred to the people as herein provided shall take effect and become the law if it is approved by a majority of the votes cast thereon, and not otherwise. Every such measure shall take effect thirty days after the election at which it is approved. The style of all bills shall be,"Be it enacted by the people of" (the State of Oregon, or name of county or other municipality). The style of charter amendments shall be similar to that used for constitutional amendments. This section shall not be construed to deprive any member of the Legislative Assembly or of a city council of the right to introduce any measure. The whole number of electors who voted for Justice of the Supreme Court at the regular election last preceding the filing of any petition for the initiative or for the referendum shall be the basis on which the number of registered voters necessary to sign such petition shall be computed. Petitions and orders for the initiative and for the referendum shall be filed with the Secretary of State, or in municipal elections with the county or city clerk, auditor, or such other officers as may be provided by law. In submitting the same to the people, he and all other officers shall be guided by the general laws, until additional legislation shall be especially provided therefor.

SEC. 2. The Legislative Assembly shall consist of a House of Representatives of sixty elective members and the ex-officio members herein provided for, and no more. They shall be nominated, apportioned and elected in such manner and from such districts as may be provided by law, but districts shall be composed of contiguous territory. The term of office for Representatives shall be four years, beginning on the day next after the regular general election in November, 1914, at which election sixty elective Representatives shall be elected, and the terms of all Representatives elected prior thereto shall expire. At the first session following the adoption of this amendment it shall be the duty of the Legislative Assembly to divide the State into districts for the election of representatives. No district shall have less than two representatives and no county shall be divided in making a representative district.

SEC. 3. Representatives in the Legislative Assembly shall be chosen by the legal voters, by such method of proportional representation of all the voters that, as nearly as may be practicable, any one sixtieth of all the voters of the State voting for one person for Representative shall insure his election.

SEC. 3a. Until otherwise provided by law, candidates for the office of Representative in the Legislative Assembly shall be nominated in districts in like manner as has been heretofore provided for their election. Each candidate's name shall be printed on the official ballot in the district where he resides, but in no other. Any legal voter in any district may vote for a candidate in any other district by writing or sticking on his ballot the name, and, if necessary to distinguish him from another candidate of the same name, the residence, political party or pledge of the candidate voted for. Every candidate for Representative at the general election shall have the right to have printed with his name on the official ballot not more than twelve words to state his political party or pledges to the people on any questions of public policy. No voter shall vote for more than one candidate for Representative.

SEC. 3*b*. The votes for the election of Representative in the Legislative Assembly shall be counted, canvassed and returned, and certificates of election issued, in like manner as such votes are now counted, canvassed and returned in the election of joint Representatives from districts composed of two or more counties. The certificate shall set forth, by counties, the whole number of votes given in the State for the person to whom it is issued.

SEC. 3*c*. In a district entitled to two Representatives, the two candidates who shall severally receive the highest number of votes shall be thereby elected. In a district entitled to three representatives, the three candidates who shall severally receive the highest number of votes shall be thereby elected, and so on in every district, applying a similar rule, whatever may be the number of Representatives to be elected from the district. Every Representative is the proxy in the Legislative Assembly for all the electors who voted for him. In voting on any bill, resolution, memorial or other roll call each member shall cast for or against the same the number of votes he so represents. A majority of all the votes cast throughout the State for candidates for Representative and represented in the Legislative Assembly as in this article provided shall be necessary to pass any measure in that body, except when voting on emergency sections as provided in section 1*c* of this article.

SEC. 3*d*. The Governor shall be ex-officio a member of the Legislative Assembly. Every candidate for Governor who shall receive a higher number of votes for that office than are cast for any other candidate of his political party for Governor shall be ex-officio a member of the Legislative Assembly; provided, that his political party was entitled to recognition as such by the laws of Oregon at the preceding regular general election. Every such ex-officio member is the proxy in the Legislative Assembly for the total number of electors in the State who voted for unsuccessful candidates of his party for Representative in the Legislative Assembly, and every such ex-officio member shall cast that number of votes for or against any measure on any roll call. This section shall be operative from and after the general election in November, A.D., 1914.

SEC. 3e. The Governor shall have a seat in the Legislative Assembly elected in November, A.D., 1912, and shall be a member of that Assembly for all the purposes of this section; he shall have a member's right to speak and introduce measures. It is the Governor's duty to introduce all bills necessary for the appropriation of public money. No money shall be appropriated by resolution or by any other method than by bill, and no member of the Legislative Assembly other than the Governor shall introduce any bill appropriating public money except for an appropriation to be referred to the people of the State for approval or rejection. The Governor shall not veto any bill passed by the Legislative Assembly. The Legislative Assembly may reduce the amount asked for any purpose by the Governor, but shall not have power to increase any such amount without the consent of the Governor entered in the journal and signed by him. The Governor shall answer all questions that may be put to him in writing by any member concerning the administration of the government or any department thereof, save that when such answers, if made public, might give information that would be prejudicial to the public interest, upon the Governor's statement of that fact, the answer may be withheld until the emergency is past.

SEC. 3f. No money shall ever be appropriated or paid from the public funds to pay all or any part of the cost or expense of making or obtaining initiative or referendum petitions or signatures thereto, either those that have been circulated or that may be circulated hereafter. The Legislative Assembly shall not appoint or create any committee, board or commission to prepare or propose any measure by initiative petition.

SEC. 4. If a vacancy shall occur in any elective legislative office, the Governor shall forthwith order a special election to elect an officer to fill the unexpired term. If the vacancy shall be in the office of a member of the Legislative Assembly the person elected to fill the vacancy shall represent and cast the number of votes on any roll call which were represented by the officer he succeeds. If the vacancy shall be in the office of an ex-officio member of the Legislative Assembly other than the Governor the members of his political party in the

Legislative Assembly shall elect his successor. If the office of Governor shall become vacant for any reason except by recall the Secretary of State shall forthwith order a special general election to be held within sixty days to elect a Governor to fill the unexpired term.

SEC. 5. No person shall be a Representative who is not a citizen of the United States at the time of his election, nor unless he shall be at least twenty-one years of age, and a resident of this State at least five years, and of his district at least one year before his election.

SEC. 6. Appropriations shall be made for the maintenance of the State Government and all existing public institutions, and all institutions aided by State funds. But this section shall not be construed as limiting the power of the Legislative Assembly to change, abolish or refuse aid to any institution created by law or which has heretofore been aided by this State.

SEC. 7. Representatives in all cases, except for treason, felony or breaches of the peace, shall be privileged from arrest during the session of the Legislative Assembly, and in going to and returning from the same; and shall not be subject to any civil process during the session of the Legislative Assembly, nor during the fifteen days next before the commencement thereof. Nor shall a member, for words uttered in debate, be questioned in any other place.

SEC. 8. The sessions of the Legislative Assembly shall be held annually at the capitol of the State, commencing at such dates as may be provided by law.

SEC. 9. The Legislative Assembly, when assembled, shall choose and may discharge its own officers and standing committees, judge of the election, qualifications and returns of its own members, determine its own rules of proceeding, and sit upon its own adjournment. The presiding officer shall not be a member of the Legislative Assembly nor hold any other office at the same time. He shall not appoint standing committees, and shall have no voice or vote on Legislative business. He shall preside over the sessions of the body and have such powers as may be conferred upon him not contrary to the provisions of this article.

SEC. 10. Two thirds of the members elected shall constitute a quorum to do business, but a smaller number may meet, adjourn from day to day, and compel the attendance of absent members. A quorum being in attendance, if the Legislative Assembly fails to effect an organization within the first five days thereafter, the members shall be entitled to no compensation from the end of the said five days until an organization shall have been effected.

SEC. 11. The Legislative Assembly shall keep a journal of its proceedings. The yeas and nays on any question shall, at the request of any two members, be entered, together with the names of the members demanding the same, on the journal; provided, that on a motion to adjourn, it shall require one tenth of the members present to order the yeas and nays.

SEC. 12. The doors of the House and of all committees shall be kept open, except only in such cases as in the opinion of the House require secrecy, but in every such case the yeas and nays shall be entered on the journal. Committees shall be liberal in allowing public hearings on measures; the chairman of every committee shall notify in writing all persons who advise the committee of their desire to be heard on any measure in its charge of the time of such hearing.

SEC. 13. The House may punish its members for disorderly behavior, and may, upon a roll call, with the concurrence of two thirds, expel a member; but not a second time for the same cause.

SEC. 14. The House, during its session, may punish by imprisonment any person not a member, who shall have been guilty of disrespect to the House, by disorderly or contemptuous behavior in its presence, but such imprisonment shall not at any time exceed twenty-four hours.

SEC. 15. The Legislative Assembly shall have all powers necessary for the Legislative department of a free and independent State.

SEC. 16. Every bill shall be read by sections, on three several days, unless in case of emergency, two thirds of the members shall, by a vote of yeas and nays, deem it expedient to dispense with this rule; but the reading of a bill by sections on its final passage shall in no case be dispensed with, and the vote on the passage of every bill or joint resolution shall be taken by yeas and nays.

SEC. 17. Every act shall embrace but one subject, and matters properly connected therewith, which subjects shall be expressed in the title. But if any subject shall be embraced in an act which shall not be expressed in the title, such act shall be void only as to so much thereof as shall not be expressed in the title.

Appendix

SEC. 18. Every act and resolution shall be plainly worded, avoiding, as far as practicable, the use of technical terms.

SEC. 19. No act shall ever be revised or amended by mere reference to its title, but the act revised or section amended shall be set forth and published at full length. All laws may be altered, amended or repealed at any time, and no law shall ever be construed to be a contract on the part of the State or of any municipality therein.

SEC. 20. No grant, franchise, permit, power or privilege given to, purchased by, or conveyed or contracted to any corporation, public or quasi public or private, or to any individual or aggregation of individuals, or in any way whatsoever to serve the public, shall be for a longer period than thirty years. Every such grant, permit, power, franchise and privilege and the use thereof shall always be subject to regulation and control in every and all respects and particulars by the authority granting the same or by its successors, and shall at any time be revocable and terminable at the option of said authority; in the case of such revocation or termination, the plant and property acquired and used in connection with such grant, permit, franchise, power or privilege may be appropriated to the public use on paying to the owners the value thereof with a premium thereon not exceeding twenty per cent of such value; there shall not be included in such reasonable value nor in such premium either all or any part of the value of such grant, permit, franchise, power or privilege. The value so appropriated to be compensated for shall be determined by ascertaining the reasonable value of the plant and property so appropriated for public use in its physical condition at the time of such appropriation. If the State or local government having authority to renew any such grant, permit, franchise [,] power or privilege shall refuse to renew the same and shall refuse to allow the owners of the aforesaid physical property to continue said public service business at and after the expiration of said thirty years, then said government shall pay to the owners the reasonable value of the physical plant and property used by them in conducting said business. This section shall be considered as a part of every such grant, permit, franchise, power and privilege made hereafter.

SEC. 21. The right of eminent domain may be exercised by the State and local governments as to any and all property, whether public, quasi public or private, in the following order of priority except only such property as is owned by the National Government:

First. The right of the State shall be supreme.

Second. The right of any district composed of more than one county.

Third. Any county.

Fourth. Any city or town.

Fifth. Any district composed of less than one county. In case of conflict of interest between two of such public authorities which are equal in the right of priority, the one having the larger population shall have the superior right.

SEC. 22. The Legislative Assembly shall not pass special or local laws in any of the following enumerated cases, that is to say:

1. Regulating the jurisdiction and duties of Justices of the Peace, and of Constables.

2. For the punishment of crimes and misdemeanors.

3. Regulating the practice in courts of justice.

4. Providing for changing the venue in civil and criminal cases.

5. Granting divorces.

6. Changing the names of persons.

7. For laying, opening and working on highways, and for election or appointment of supervisors; but this does not limit the right of the Legislative Assembly to propose, nor the power of the people to approve, any act or appropriation for highways.

8. Vacating roads, town plats, streets, alleys and public squares.

9. Summoning and empaneling grand and petit jurors.

10. For the assessment and collection of taxes for State, county, township or road purposes.

11. Providing for the support of common schools, and for the preservation of school funds.

12. In relation to interest on money.

13. Providing for opening and conducting the elections of State, county or township officers, and designating the places of voting.

14. Providing for the sale of real estate belonging to minors or other persons laboring under legal disabilities, by executors, administrators, guardians or trustees.

15. When a general law can be made applicable.

SEC. 23. Provision may be made by general law for bringing

suit against the State, as to all liabilities originating after or existing at the time of the adoption of this constitution; but no special act authorizing such suit to be brought, or making compensation to any person claiming damages against the State, shall ever be passed.

SEC. 24. A majority of all the electors represented in the Legislative Assembly as in this article provided shall be necessary to pass every bill or resolution; and all bills and resolutions so passed shall be signed by the Speaker and the Chief Clerk and filed forthwith with the Secretary of State.

SEC. 25. Any member shall have the right to protest, and have his protest, with his reasons for dissent, entered on the journal.

SEC. 26. Every statute shall be a public law, unless otherwise declared in the statute itself.

SEC. 27. No act shall take effect until ninety days from the end of the session at which the same shall have been passed, except in cases of emergency, which shall be declared as provided in Section 1c of this article.

SEC. 28. The members of the Legislative Assembly shall receive for their services a sum not exceeding three dollars a day from the commencement of the session; but such pay shall not exceed in the aggregate one hundred and twenty dollars for per diem allowance for any one session. When convened in extra session by the Governor, they shall receive three dollars per day; but no extra session shall continue for a longer period than twenty days. They shall also receive the sum of three dollars for every twenty miles they shall travel in going to and returning from their place of meeting, on the most usual route. The presiding officer of the Legislative Assembly shall, in virtue of his office, receive an additional compensation equal to two-thirds of the per diem allowance of members.

SEC. 29. No Representative shall, during the time for which he may have been elected, be eligible to any office the election to which is vested in the Legislative Assembly; nor shall he be appointed to any civil office of profit which shall have been created or the emoluments of which have been increased during such term, but this latter provision shall not be construed to apply to any officer elective by the people.

SEC. 30. The members of the Legislative Assembly shall, before they enter on the duties of their office, take and subscribe the following oath of office or affirmation:

"I do solemnly swear (or affirm, as the case may be) that I will support the Constitution of the United States and of the State of Oregon, and that I will faithfully discharge the duties of Representative according to the best of my ability." Said oath of office may be administered by any Justice of the Supreme Court.

SEC. 31. When a bill is introduced it shall be placed upon the calendar, and may be acted upon any time during the life of that Legislative Assembly, except that bills introduced after the twentieth day of any session shall not be passed at that session unless they are emergency measures. No measure, except an emergency bill, shall be passed at any session of the Legislative Assembly until it has been printed and in the possession of the members, in its final form, at least five days. No measure shall be altered or amended on its passage so as to change its original purpose.

SEC. 32. A majority of the members, representing also a majority of all the electors in the State who voted for candidates for Representative, may at any time unite in calling a special session of the Legislative Assembly.

SEC. 33. This amendment of Article IV of the Constitution of Oregon is self-executing, but legislation may be enacted to aid and facilitate its operation. All the provisions of the Constitution and laws of Oregon which conflict with this amendment of Article IV or any part hereof, are hereby abrogated and repealed in so far as they conflict herewith.

(On Official Ballot, Nos. 362 and 363.)

ARGUMENT
(affirmative)

SUBMITTED BY

THE PEOPLE'S POWER LEAGUE OF OREGON

in favor of the measure designated on the official ballot as follows:

PROPOSED BY INITIATIVE PETITION

For amendment of Article IV of the Constitution of Oregon abolishing the State Senate; providing none but registered voters be counted on initiative or referendum petitions; increasing State and municipal referendum powers; House of Representatives to consist of sixty elective members, and the Governor and unsuccessful party candidates for governor to be ex-officio members; Governor to introduce all appropriation bills, legislature not to increase the amounts thereof, four year terms, annual sessions; proportional election of members; proxy system of voting on bills, and those introduced after twenty days to go to the next session; control and revocation of franchises. **Vote YES or NO.**

| 362. | Yes. |
| 363. | No. |

THE PEOPLE'S POWER LEAGUE OF OREGON

Offers this argument to explain and advocate the approval of the proposed amendment of Article IV of the Constitution of Oregon. From year to year the members of this league have prepared and proposed to the people the measures commonly known as the "Oregon System," including the Initiative, Referendum, Direct Primary, Recall, Corrupt Practices Act, Statement No. 1 method of electing United States Senators, Three Fourths Jury Verdict in Civil Cases, Abolition of Technicalities on Appeal to the Supreme Court, the Presidential Primary, and City Home Rule laws and Constitutional Amendments.

Every measure offered by the People's Power League of Oregon and approved by the people is producing better results than were promised by the League. The official ballot number of this amendment is Number 362 Yes, Number 363 No.

1. The adoption of this amendment will result in saving nearly a million dollars a year in the State appropriations, and some of the members of the League believe the saving will be much greater. In support of this statement we call your attention to the following letter from Governor West:

STATE OF OREGON, Executive Department, Salem.
June 26, 1912.
Hon. W. S. U'Ren, Oregon City, Or.

Dear Sir: I am in receipt of yours of recent date in which you ask as to what reduction, if any, could be had in appropriations for the years 1913–1914, over those of 1911 and 1912 if this office was given the control of all appropriation bills.

In reply will say the amount required for the expenses of the State Government for 1911 and 1912 was in round numbers $5,670,000. If this office had control of the appropriation bills I believe the 1913 and 1914 appropriations could easily be kept down to $4,000,000, and without crippling in any manner our State institutions or denying them anything to which they are justly entitled in the way of maintenance or improvements.   Yours very truly,

(Signed) Oswald West.

This amendment gives the Governor the right to introduce any measure in the Legislature, and gives him sole power to introduce bills appropriating public money. The Legislature may reduce any appropriation recommended by the Governor, but cannot increase the amount without the Governor's consent. The Governor, being thus a member of the Legislature, will not be able to veto bills. (Please read Section 3c of the amendment.)

2. The amendment abolishes the State Senate, which is a useless and unnecessary expense. By abolishing the State Senate, the people will concentrate all legislative responsibility on the Representative alone, and thus destroy the habit of politicians and pledge breakers of passing a bill in the House and "killing it in the Senate," or passing a bill in the Senate and "killing it in the House."

The Senate is an imitation of the British House of Lords, and the imitation was copied by all the American states and most American cities. During the last thirty years most of the cities have abolished the imitation half of their city councils with good results. Every one knows what the British people have done to their House of Lords within the last two years. (See Section 1 of the amendment.)

3. Sections 1c and 1d of the amendment greatly strengthen and extend the people's State and local referendum powers by requiring a three-fourths majority of the Legislature, or of a city council, to amend

Appendix

or repeal any measure enacted by vote of the people, or to declare an emergency on any bill or ordinance to prevent the people from rejecting it before it goes into operation.

The initiative and referendum are further safeguarded by requiring that none except registered voters shall sign initiative or referendum petitions.

4. The amendment establishes the proxy system of proportional representation of all the voters for electing members of the Legislature and passing bills. If this amendment is adopted, every political party at the election in 1914 and thereafter will have representation in the Legislature in proportion to the number of its voters at the ballot box.

This will make the Legislature as progressive as the people of the State, and that will greatly reduce the necessity for constant use of the initiative in order to get progressive laws.

This amendment will make it impossible for a few more than one-half of the voters to elect 59 of the 60 Representatives, as was done by one party in 1906, or to elect 58 of the 60 Representatives as happened in 1910. This proxy system of proportional representation will take effect at the election in November, 1914. (See Sections 3 to 3b and Section 24.)

5. By Section 20, every franchise or permit hereafter granted to a railroad or other public service corporation may always be regulated or revoked by the town, city, county or district granting the same, or it may be purchased by the town, city, county or district at an advance of not more than 20 per cent over its physical value or cost, but nothing is to be paid or allowed for the franchise. The amendment will make it impossible to turn future special privileges into private property in Oregon.

6. Section 21 defines and increases the power of eminent domain which may be used by State and local governments to obtain property for public use by paying the reasonable value thereof.

There are other and less important provisions, intended to strengthen those already mentioned. The Speaker of the House is to be only a presiding officer, without a vote and without power to appoint standing committees.

The Legislature will meet annually, and ample provision is made to prevent hasty legislation. (See Sections 8, 9, 31 and 32.)

Under this amendment no law can be construed to be a contract.

The members of the People's Power League believe that if this amendment is adopted by the people it will result in a great saving of money and in a very great decrease in the number of laws. The British Parliament holds a session of from five to seven months, and it considers that fifty laws is a large number to be passed at one session. The Oregon Legislature holds a session of forty days, and at the session of 1911 that body passed 277 laws and 41 resolutions and memorials. Respectfully submitted,

PEOPLE'S POWER LEAGUE OF OREGON.

For members and officers of this League, see the negative argument for amendment of Section 1 of Article XVII of the Constitution on page 35 of this book.

(On Official Ballot, Nos. 362 and 363.)

ARGUMENT
(negative)

SUBMITTED BY

MARION COUNTY TAXPAYERS' LEAGUE

opposing the measure designated on the official ballot as follows:

PROPOSED BY INITIATIVE PETITION

For amendment of Article IV of the Constitution of Oregon abolishing the State Senate; providing none but registered voters be counted on initiative or referendum petitions; increasing State and municipal referendum powers; House of Representatives to consist of sixty elective members, and the Governor and unsuccessful party candidates for Governor to be *ex-officio* members; Governor to introduce all appropriation bills, legislature not to increase the amounts thereof, four-year terms, annual sessions; proportional election of members; proxy system of voting on bills, and those introduced after twenty days to go to the next session; control and revocation of franchises. Vote YES or NO.

362.	Yes.
363.	No.

Appendix

To the Voters of Oregon:

The proposed amendment to Article IV of the State Constitution is the most drastic measure ever submitted to the people of the State. It provides for the abolishment of the State Senate and the creation of a legislative body consisting of a single branch. The experience of this and other countries has established the wisdom of legislative bodies with two branches, one branch acting as a check or balance upon the other and thereby preventing the enactment of hasty, selfish and ill-advised legislation. This measure also proposes to abolish the veto power of the Governor — a power generally recognized throughout civilized nations. With a one-chamber legislature, unrestrained by the executive veto power, much legislation extremely hostile to the best interests of the body politic and the taxpayers would be certain of enactment.

The system of proportional representation contemplated by Section 2 of the proposed measure, would mean that large areas of territory would practically be unrepresented in the legislature, as representatives would be apportioned strictly according to population with a large majority coming from Multnomah and other thickly populated counties in Western Oregon. Under the proposed arrangement, Multnomah County would have more representation than the combined representation of the counties of Baker, Crook, Curry, Gilliam, Grant, Harney, Hood River, Jackson, Josephine, Klamath, Lake, Malheur, Morrow, Sherman, Umatilla, Union, Wallowa, Wasco and Wheeler. Large counties in Eastern Oregon would necessarily be grouped into legislative districts and a sparsely populated county, such as Sherman, united with a thickly populated county, such as Wasco, for legislative purposes, would be unrepresented, as the representatives would undoubtedly be chosen from the more thickly populated county of the district. In other words, such counties as Grant, Harney, Lake, Gilliam, Morrow, Sherman, Wheeler and Wallowa could not expect to secure representation in the Oregon legislature.

In stating its indictment against George III, the Declaration of Independence charges:

"He has refused to pass other laws for the accommodation of large districts of people unless those people would relinquish the right of representation in the legislature — a right inestimable to them and formidable to tyrants only."

Our forefathers understood by the right of representation in the legislature, the right of the people of each legislative district to choose, by a majority vote, certain men to sit in the legislature as representatives of that district, and to whom the people of that district had a right to look for protection. The proposed measure destroys this right. What the State of Oregon needs is an amendment to the Constitution providing that each county, regardless of size or population, shall have at least one representative in the lower house of the legislature, and that additional representation be apportioned according to population.

The system of proportional representation which is proposed in the pending measure means minority instead of majority representation. Thus, an elector in Multnomah County would vote for one representative, although that county would be entitled to 18 representatives. This is the plan followed in the selection of delegates to the recent national conventions at Chicago and Baltimore. It did not work satisfactorily as it disfranchised the elector from voting for the full quota of his party delegates. The proposed plan of selecting legislators would not work satisfactorily as it would disfranchise the elector from voting for his district's full quota of legislators.

The proxy system of voting in the legislature would result in great confusion and would enable a few men representing a large number of voters to combine and defeat legislation emanating from less popular men who had received a similar number of votes.

The proposed measure also provides that the Governor and certain defeated candidates for Governor shall have seats and votes in the legislature, and that they shall hold the proxies of all those electors who voted for the unsuccessful candidates for the legislature in their several parties. This ridiculous proposition would enable the ex-officio members to combine with a few regular members and defeat all legislation not meeting with their approval. Successful and defeated candidates for Governor might, on the other hand, prolong their campaign warfare and transform the legislature into a clearing house for political grievances.

The proposal to place in the hands of the Governor the sole right to introduce appropriation bills would clothe the chief executive with altogether too much power and permit him to exercise undue influence over other legislation. This is a government of, by and for the people, and the representative of the people should enjoy all the rights and privileges of representatives of a sovereign state. They should be permitted to meet and legislate without executive interference except through the constitutional veto power. The Governor should attend to the duties of the executive department and not interfere with legislative matters until the acts are finally presented to him for approval or disapproval. Our forefathers recognized the three coördinate branches of the government — the executive, the legislative and the judicial. The distinction between these branches has been recognized and maintained since the institution of the government. The recent Democratic convention at Baltimore reaffirmed its faith in this distinction by the adoption of the following plank in its platform:

"We believe in the preservation and maintenance in their full strength and integrity of the three coördinate branches of the federal government — the executive, the legislative and the judicial — each keeping within its own bounds and not encroaching upon the just powers of each of the others."

Section 4 of the proposed measure provides that if the office of Governor shall become vacant for any cause except by the recall, the Secretary of State shall forthwith call a special election, to be held within sixty days, to elect a Governor for the unexpired term. Courts have held that when a Governor goes over the State line he ceases to be Governor until his return to the State; so, in the event of the absence of the Governor from Oregon, or of his ill health or inability to perform his duties, the taxpayers will be called upon to defray the expenses of a special election. This feature of the proposed measure is altogether unnecessary, inasmuch as there is now pending a constitutional amendment providing for the election of a Lieutenant Governor, and of an automatic succession to the Governor's office in case of the death, resignation or inability of the chief executive to perform his duties.

The proposed amendment provides for annual sessions of the legislature. Experience has taught that biennial sessions are adequate to the needs of the State. We have at present too many elections, too much legislation and too many boards, commissions and offices, and it is time for a policy of retrenchment rather than the adoption of a provision for annual sessions with their consequent extravagance, demoralization of general business and political excitement. The proposal whereby a majority of the legislators may unite in calling a special session is altogether wrong, for it would enable a few men to continue the legislature in session almost indefinitely and thereby greatly increase the burden of taxation.

There is no assurance that this amendment will, if enacted, decrease the burden of taxation or minimize the use of the initiative or referendum.

This whole measure is a crude experiment and the public good demands its defeat. You are, therefore, urged to vote "No."

Respectfully submitted,

MARION COUNTY TAXPAYERS' LEAGUE,

By A. M. LaFOLLETT, *President.*

V. AN INITIATIVE PETITION

WARNING

It is a felony for any one to sign any initiative or referendum petition with any other name than his own, or to knowingly sign his name more than once for the measure, or to sign such petition when he is not a legal voter.

INITIATIVE PETITION

To the Honorable Ben. W. Olcott,
Secretary of State for the State of Oregon:

We, *the undersigned citizens and legal voters of the State of Oregon, respectfully demand that the following proposed law shall be submitted to the legal voters of the State of Oregon, for their approval or rejection, at the regular general election to be held on the fifth day of November* A.D. *1912, and each for himself says: I have personally signed this petition; I am a legal voter of the State of Oregon; my residence and postoffice are correctly written after my name.*

NAME	RESIDENCE (If in a city, street and number)	POSTOFFICE

[Here follow twenty numbered lines.]

Appendix 275

STATE OF OREGON, } ss.
  County of......................
I,...
being first duly sworn, say: ... *signed this sheet of the foregoing petition, and each of them signed his name thereto in my presence; I believe that each has stated his name, postoffice address, and residence correctly, and that each signer is a legal voter of the State of Oregon and County of* ....

....
Postoffice address:................
Subscribed and sworn to before me this......day of........, A. D. *1912.*
....
Notary Public for Oregon.
Postoffice address:................

A BILL

For an Act to exempt certain property from taxation.

Be it enacted by the people of the State of Oregon:

SECTION 1. The following property shall be exempt from taxation: All debts due or to become due, whether on account, contract, note, mortgage, bond or otherwise, either within or without this State; all public stocks and securities; all bonds, warrants and moneys due or to become due from this State, or any county or other municipal subdivision thereof; all stocks and shares in incorporated companies; *provided,* that this act does not exempt bank stocks, shares and banking capital from assessment and taxation.

VI. NEWSPAPER ADVICE ON DIRECT LEGISLATION

Eugene *Register,* Oct. 29, 1914, p. 4

The Measures Summarized

From day to day during the past month The Register has discussed the measures to be voted on this fall, taking them up in order as they appear in the official pamphlet. They are presented herewith in summarized form, together with advice as to how to vote on them. This advice is based upon the discussions that have already appeared.

Nos. 300–301. Requires voters to be citizens of the United States. Excellent measure and should be approved. Vote yes.

Nos. 302–303. Creates office of lieutenant governor. Already defeated once. Not needed. Vote no.

Nos. 304–305. Permits consolidation of city and county governments when county contains city of 100,000 inhabitants. Applies only to Portland and Multnomah county and is intended to promote economy there. Vote yes.

Nos. 306–307. Permits the state to incur indebtedness or lend its credit up to four per cent of its assessed valuation for road construction and irrigation, power and development projects. Opens the way for the state to incur heavy bonded indebtedness. Vote no.

Nos. 308–309. Clears the way for much needed tax reform. Makes possible the abolishment of the tax on mortgages. Vote yes.

Nos. 310–311. Permits much needed tax reform. Complementary measure to Nos. 308–309. Vote yes.

Nos. 312–313. Provides for re-establishment of Southern Oregon Normal school at Ashland and levies one fortieth of a mill for maintenance. More normal schools needed for the training of teachers in common schools. Vote yes.

Nos. 314–315. Permits the consolidation of cities when voters concerned so desire. If two towns wish to consolidate, they should be permitted to do so. Vote yes.

Nos. 316–317. Provides for the re-establishment of Eastern Oregon Normal school at Weston, and levies tax of one fortieth of a mill for maintenance. Same reasons apply as to 312–313. Vote yes.

Nos. 318–319. Increases pay of legislators from three to five dollars a day and increases maximum length of legislative session from 40 to 60 days. Provides added inducement for good men to go to the legislature. Vote yes.

Nos. 320–321. Universal eight hour law. Most vicious measure ever proposed in Oregon. Would ruin every industry in the state. Vote no.

Nos. 322–323. Eight hour law for women workers. Not needed. Already covered by industrial welfare commission. Vote no.

Nos. 324–325. Non-partisan judiciary bill. Not needed. Same results can be achieved without changing election laws if voters wish. Vote no.

Nos. 326–327. $1500 exemption amendment. Single tax with a sugar coating. Purpose is to increase tax on land. Vote no.

Nos. 328–329. Public docks and water frontage amendment. Locks up all land between low and high water mark of navigable rivers from development. Menaces all industrial concerns and factories that need water frontage. A tinkerer's scheme. Vote no.

Nos. 330–331. Municipal wharves

Appendix

and docks bill. Companion measure to Nos. 328-329. Tinkerer's scheme. Vote no.

Nos. 332-333. Prohibition amendment. No explanation needed. Vote yes.

Nos. 334-335. Abolishes death penalty. If murderers will stop murdering the death penalty will be automatically abolished. Leave it to them. Vote no.

Nos. 336-337. Graduated extra tax amendment. Imposes additional tax on land above a certain value. Single tax in a slightly modified form. Vote no.

Nos. 338-339. Consolidating corporation and insurance departments. Spite measure, designed to legislate the corporation commissioner out of office. Vote no.

Nos. 340-341. Dentistry bill. Spite measure, initiated because one individual failed to pass the state dental examination. Vote no.

Nos. 342-343. County officers' term amendment. One of the few measures on the ballot that provide for real economy. Vote yes.

Nos. 344-345. Tax code commission bill. Not needed. We already have a state tax commission that is sufficient for all purposes. Vote no.

Nos. 346-347. Purports to abolish desert land board. Spite measure designed to legislate State Engineer Lewis out of office because of political disagreements. Destroys present excellent water code. Vote no.

Nos. 348-349. Proportional representation amendment. Tinkerer's scheme. If adopted would lead to endless confusion. Vote no.

Nos. 350-351. Abolishing state senate. Tinkerer's scheme. Vote no.

Nos. 352-353. Public employment amendment. Tinkerer's scheme. Would swamp the state with unemployed from everywhere. Vote no.

Nos. 354-355. Primary delegate election bill. Would reëstablish convention system and provide an additional election at heavy cost. A tinkerer's scheme. Vote no.

Nos. 356-357. Equal assessment and taxation and $300 exemption amendment. Tax measure whose need is not apparent. Vote no.

Oregonian, Nov. 2, 1914, p. 13

RECOMMENDATIONS OFFERED ON MEASURES

The Oregonian again presents herewith its list of recommendations on initiated bills and amendments.

For an amendment of section 2, article 2 of the constitution, relative to voting qualifications. 300 yes, 301 no.
Vote 300 yes.

For constitutional amendment to create office of Lieutenant Governor. 302 yes, 303 no.
Vote 303 no.

For an amendment to section 6, article 15 of the constitution, to permit city and county governments to be consolidated upon vote of the people interested. 304 yes, 305 no.
Vote 304 yes.

For amendment to section 7, article 9 of the constitution, authorizing state indebtedness for irrigation and power projects. 306 yes, 307 no.
Vote 307 no.

For amendment of section 22, article 1 of the constitution, modifying the uniform rule of taxation. 308 yes, 309 no.
Vote 309 no.

For amendment of section 1, article 9 of the constitution. 310 yes, 311 no.
Vote 311 no.

A bill for an act to levy annually a tax to reëstablish the Southern Oregon Normal School at Ashland. 312 yes, 313 no.
No recommendation.

For amendment of article 9 of the constitution permitting enactment of a general tax law authorizing adjoining cities to consolidate on vote of their electors. 314 yes, 315 no.
Vote 314 yes.

A bill for an act to levy annually a tax to reëstablish the State Normal School at Weston, Umatilla County. 316 yes, 317 no.
No recommendation.

For an amendment of section 29, article 4 of the constitution, raising pay of legislators. 318 yes, 319 no.
Vote 319 no.

Universal constitutional eight-hour day amendment. 320 yes, 321 no.
Vote 321 no.

Eight-hour day for female workers. 322 yes, 323 no.
Vote 323 no.

Non-partisan judiciary bill. 324 yes, 325 no.
Vote 324 yes.

$1500 tax exemption. 326 yes, 327 no.
Vote 327 no.

Public docks and waterfront amendment. 328 yes, 329 no.
Vote 329 no.

Municipal wharves and docks bill. 330 yes, 331 no.
Vote 331 no.

Prohibition constitutional amendment. 332 yes, 333 no.
No recommendation.

Constitutional amendment abolishing death penalty. 334 yes, 335 no.
Vote 335 no.

Specific graduated extra-tax amendment. 336 yes, 337 no.
Vote 337 no.

Consolidating corporation and insurance departments. 338 yes, 339 no.
Vote 339 no.

Dentistry bill. 340 yes, 341 no.
Vote 341 no.

County officers' term amendment. 342 yes, 343 no.
Vote 342 yes.

Tax code commission bill. 344 yes, 345 no.
Vote 345 no.

Measure abolishing Desert Land Board and merging certain offices. 346 yes, 347 no.
Vote 347 no.

Proportional representation amendment. 348 yes, 349 no.
Vote 349 no.

State Senate constitutional amendment, abolishing that body. 350 yes, 351 no.
Vote 351 no.

Constitutional amendment establishing department of industry and public works. 352 yes, 353 no.
Vote 353 no.

Primary delegate election bill. 354 yes, 355 no.
Vote 355 no.

Equal assessment and taxations and $300 exemption amendment. 356 yes, 357 no.
Vote 357 no.

Eugene *Register*, Nov. 3, 1914, p. 1.

CONDENSED ADVICE ON THE MEASURES

Vote yes.	Vote no.
No. 300.	No. 303.
No. 304.	No. 306.
No. 308.	No. 321.
No. 310.	No. 323.
No. 314.	No. 325.
No. 316.	No. 327.
No. 318.	No. 329.
No. 332.	No. 331.
No. 342.	No. 335.
	No. 337.
	No. 339.
	No. 341.
	No. 345.
	No. 347.
	No. 349.
	No. 351.
	No. 353.
	No. 355.
	No. 357.

These recommendations are the same as have appeared in more amplified form in The Register in previous issues.

VII. RECOMMENDATIONS OF THE TAXPAYERS' LEAGUE
November 3, 1914

The Taxpayers' League was organized many years ago. It has always taken an active interest in public affairs. Since the adoption of the initiative and referendum it has at each election made recommendations to the voters on the measures proposed.

As an earnest and consistent friend of the initiative and referendum The League protests against their indiscriminate use as a means of advancing some individual's peculiar views, or some special interest, or as a weapon to "get even" with some official who may perchance disagree with some one in the conduct of the affairs of his office. The initiative and referendum "were intended and can only be used as a safeguard by the public against misrepresentation by the legislature and not as an original source of general legislation."

Twenty-nine measures appear on the ballot. Of these fifteen are constitutional amendments and fourteen are bills for proposed laws. The character and purpose of some of the measures merit most careful consideration.

The League would feel it were derelict in its duty if it did not emphasize the fact that this is not the time for revolutionary or experimental legislation. Worldwide as well as local conditions should warn us to be on our guard. The constant submission of half-baked, illy considered and often radical measures is unquestionably beginning to create distrust abroad with the result, whether they pass or not, that every one is a sufferer from it. The laborer, the mechanic, the merchant, the banker and the property holder alike are interested. In the interest of this state there is but one attitude for the citizen to take and that is to be sure he is right and that he understands a measure before he votes. At a 1913 city election every measure proposed was defeated. Such a result is far better than to inadvertently pass some law that will cause the people of this state untold loss before it can be repealed. Measures of far reaching consequence are on the ballot. The single and graduated tax, although defeated by a vote of more than two to one two years ago, appear in a different guise but for the same purpose and backed by the same interests.

Eight hour laws that would make even the conduct of a farm or the household impossible are submitted; a bill levying a confiscatory tax on estates of not less than ten per cent and as much more as may be provided by law, and to create a department of industry and public works to furnish work for the unemployed is also proposed. State-wide prohibition is to be voted on. Abolishment of the senate and proportional representation are also proposed.

These are but a few of the important measures upon which the people are called to take action. Under existing conditions we submit to the wage earner, the home owner and the capitalist alike that due consideration should be given before embarking upon experimental legislation and revolutionary changes. WE URGE THE VOTER WHEN IN DOUBT TO VOTE "NO." The League has studied the different measures proposed and submits the following advice and suggestions to voters for their consideration.

1. VOTE ON EVERY MEASURE.
2. WHEN IN DOUBT — VOTE "NO."
3. BETTER BE SURE THAN SORRY.

TAXPAYERS' LEAGUE,
By L. J. GOLDSMITH,
Secretary.

VOTERS TO BE CITIZENS
300 **YES**.
301 **NO**.

A constitutional amendment prescribing citizenship as a qualification for voting. An immigrant with first papers can vote now. In view of the important duties of a voter in this state, full citizenship is not too high a requirement.

Voters are advised to vote " Yes."

LIEUTENANT GOVERNOR
302 **YES**.
303 **NO**.

To act as president of the senate and to receive $10 a day during legislative session. To succeed the governor in case the latter dies or is disqualified. Would prevent log-rolling for presidency of the senate, and would provide a substitute for the governor on board of control. The secretary of state in case he succeeds, as at present, has two votes, an absolute control.

Voters are advised to vote " Yes."

CONSOLIDATION OF CITY AND COUNTY GOVERNMENT
304 **YES**.
305 **NO**.

Gives the legislature, or the people by the initiative, power to consolidate city and county government where a city has over 100,000 inhabitants. This would eliminate a large amount of

duplication and needless expense and simplify government very materially.
Voters are advised to vote " Yes."

INCREASE OF STATE DEBT LIMIT
306 **YES.**
307 **NO.**

Prescribing a debt limit of not to exceed 2 per cent of assessed valuation for road building, and a like amount for the construction of irrigation, power projects and agricultural development. Appropriates no money but authorizes it to be done if deemed advisable. It would authorize the state to issue bonds up to $38,000,000. This is excessive.
Voters are advised to vote " No."

ABOLISHING UNIFORM TAXATION RULE
308 **YES.**
309 **NO.**

A constitutional amendment eliminating the present requirement that all taxation be equal and uniform. Briefly stated, the purpose of these proposed amendments is to authorize classification of property for taxation. A necessary change if we expect ever to have fair and equitable taxation in this state. Recommended by State Tax commission.
Voters are advised to vote " Yes."

CLASSIFICATION FOR TAXATION PURPOSES
310 **YES.**
311 **NO.**

Providing for general laws to govern the levy of taxes; permitting classification of property for taxation purposes, and also income and proportional or graduated taxes, and authorizing reasonable exemptions. This, and the preceding measure go together and form a constitutional basis for rational and equitable tax reform in this state. This and the foregoing amendment are both sound and progressive and should not be confused with any other tax measure or measures.
Voters are advised to vote " Yes."

THE ASHLAND NORMAL
312 **YES.**
313 **NO.**

Levying $\frac{1}{20}$ of a mill on all taxable property in the state for the construction and support of a normal school at Ashland. This presents a clear issue of whether the voters want more normal schools or not.
No recommendation.

MERGER OF CITIES
314 **YES.**
315 **NO.**

A constitutional amendment authorizing a general law to allow a city to surrender its charter and be merged into an adjoining city, on vote of a majority of the electors of each of the cities affected. There being no way to affect such consolidation now, this measure is advisable.
Voters are advised to vote " Yes."

EASTERN OREGON STATE NORMAL
316 **YES.**
317 **NO.**

Levying $\frac{1}{20}$ of a mill tax for a Normal School at Weston in Umatilla County. A measure similar to 312–313 above.
No recommendation.

INCREASING PAY TO MEMBERS OF THE LEGISLATURE
318 **YES.**
319 **NO.**

Legislative pay is $3 a day, with a

forty-day limit. This increases it to $5 a day for sixty days. It is not apparent that a small increase in pay would secure higher-class men, or that lengthening the session without providing for a divided session, would be beneficial. The League believes legislative reform should go deeper and be more radical.

Voters are advised to vote " No."

UNIVERSAL EIGHT-HOUR LAW
330 YES.
321 NO.

This measure provides that no one shall work more than eight hours per day in any employment whatsoever. It would disorganize and make impossible much of the business and work carried on in the state. Domestic help and farm labor would be particularly hard hit under it.

Voters are advised to vote " No."

EIGHT-HOUR LAW FOR WOMEN
322 YES.
323 NO.

This prescribes an eight-hour day in most of the occupations in which women are employed. The State Industrial Welfare Commission is now in charge of the work, with ample authority to enforce any provisions of the sort it finds advisable. This law is superfluous, would needlessly complicate and confuse the situation, and would work a positive hardship on many women at present employed. It is inflexible, and exceptions could not be made, as is now possible under the supervision of the Welfare Commission.

Voters are advised to vote " No."

NON-PARTISAN JUDICIARY
324 YES.
325 NO.

This bill prohibits party nominations for judicial offices, and provides for nominations by petition of 1 per cent of the legal voters in the district. Would prevent political designation on the ballot. Would make possible a choice of judges on the basis of fitness, rather than party affiliations and party services. The legislature or the people can provide for preferential voting, if they desire. A non-partisan election should do much to keep the judiciary out of politics.

Voters are advised to vote " Yes."

$1500 TAX EXEMPTION
326 YES.
327 NO.

Exempting from taxation all personal property, dwelling houses, buildings, and improvements on land, livestock, etc., up to $1500, belonging to any one person, the land itself to be taxed. This is one of Mr. U'Ren's measures, and is partial single tax. Single tax has been repudiated very decisively in this state. It is not working satisfactorily anywhere else, and this [is] a poor time for Oregon to experiment with it.

Voters are advised to vote " No."

PUBLIC DOCKS AND WATER-FRONTAGE
328 YES.
329 NO.

An amendment prohibiting the sale of beds of navigable waters, and subjecting the same to public use. Providing for leasing to private parties for constructing wharves, docks, etc. Would revoke valuable wharfage rights, claimed by riparian owners, on which taxes have long been paid, and in which the state has acquiesced. Adoption of the amendment would be followed by long litigation and uncertainty as to titles. Would remove much property from the tax rolls, and unsettle conditions to an extent the state can ill afford at this time.

Voters are advised to vote " No."

MUNICIPAL WHARVES AND DOCKS
330 **YES.**
331 **NO.**

This measure follows the preceding one, and authorizes the building of municipal wharves and docks on the land covered by that amendment. It should stand or fall with the preceding one.

Voters are advised to vote " No."

PROHIBITION
332 **YES.**
333 **NO.**

This is a clear issue, on which the people are well advised, and on which it appears that any recommendation would be superfluous.

No recommendation.

ABOLISHING DEATH PENALTY
334 **YES.**
335 **NO.**

This is another clear issue, on which opinion is already well formed.

No recommendation.

SUR-TAX
336 **YES.**
337 **NO.**

This levies a confiscatory tax on all owners of realty assessed at more than $25,000. No argument is possible in support of this sort of provision. Is an attempt to impose burdensome taxation on lands and to reach single tax by indirection. Would ruin the market for land, and do inestimable harm to the state. It is in substance the same bill as was proposed and overwhelmingly defeated two years ago as part of the single tax program.

Voters are advised to vote " No."

CONSOLIDATING CORPORATION AND INSURANCE DEPARTMENTS
338 **YES.**
339 **NO.**

This is a spite measure and an obvious abuse of the initiative. An attempt to legislate an officer out of office on personal grounds. It should be decisively defeated.

Voters are advised to vote " No."

DENTISTRY BILL
340 **YES.**
341 **NO.**

Another personal measure, obviously initiated for advertising purposes. Would put the standard of efficiency in the practice of dentistry lower than in almost any other state. An abuse of the initiative.

Voters are advised to vote " No."

INCREASING TERM OF COUNTY OFFICERS
342 **YES.**
343 **NO.**

Would give four-year terms to the officers elected at this election. If an officer has made good at the end of two years, he will be reëlected. If not, the two-year term gives the people an opportunity to get rid of him, without the expense of a recall. This measure would not reduce the number of elections, and would not cut down expenses.

Voters are advised to vote " NO."

TAX CODE COMMISSION
344 **YES.**
345 **NO.**

The State now has a **Tax Commis-**

Appendix

sion, and has heretofore had various special ones. No real tax reform is possible unless the constitutional amendments No. 308-309 and No. 310-311 are carried. The proposed Commission is superfluous.

Voters are Advised to Vote " No."

ABOLISHING DESERT LAND BOARD
346 YES.
347 NO.

This measure abolishes the office of State Engineer and abolishes the Desert Land Board. The measure is ill-advised and would largely nullify the present Water Code and hamper very seriously the coöperative work with the Federal Government in stream measurement, topographic map making, etc. The State Engineer is a necessary officer, and the office is doing excellent work. No reason appears why it should be stopped.

Voters are Advised to Vote " No."

PROPORTIONAL REPRESENTATION
348 YES.
349 NO.

Provides that each voter vote for one candidate for representative and the sixty in the state receiving the highest number be elected. Questionable if this would give us as representative legislators as we now have. A large proportion of votes would be wasted on very popular candidates, who would be elected anyhow, or others with no chance. With no eliminating process a large proportion would be elected with only a small plurality. Each legislator having one vote, a man elected by 25,000 votes and another by 1000 would have equal authority. A majority in the legislature would not necessarily in any way represent the majority of the voters. And unless that condition is to be attained, no change is justified.

Voters are advised to vote " No."

ABOLISHING STATE SENATE
350 YES.
351 NO.

Experience has shown that some check on legislative action is wise. The two house system is approved by the experience of all parts of the world. This measure proposes to abolish the Senate, usually composed of the older and more experienced legislators, and to turn the whole work over to the House of Representatives.

Voters are advised to vote " No."

DEPARTMENT OF INDUSTRY AND PUBLIC WORKS
352 YES.
353 NO.

This is a measure initiated by the Socialist party providing for a tax of not less than ten per cent, and as much more as the legislature may name, on all estates of deceased persons, amounting to $50,000 or over, and for appropriations to be made for the support of a department to take care of the unemployed. It would draw the unemployed of the whole United States to Oregon to be supported by the people of this state.

Voters are advised to vote " No."

PRIMARY DELEGATE ELECTION BILL
354 YES.
355 NO.

This measure would add one election to the number we now have, with the effect of getting us back to the old convention system. It is an attempt to knock out the present direct primary in a very expensive and cumbersome way.

Voters are advised to vote " No."

TAXATION: TWO-THIRDS VOTE TO AMEND OR REPEAL
356 YES.
357 NO.

This measure, if carried, would make permanent the present defective and inadequate taxation system in this state by requiring a two-thirds vote to modify it. It is the more dangerous in that it would perpetuate any of the illy-considered or confiscatory tax measures that may pass at this election. It is strictly a "gag" measure.

Voters are advised to vote " No."

COUPON

CUT OUT AND TAKE WITH YOU

Voters to be citizens	Vote Yes 300
Lieutenant Governor	Vote Yes 302
Consolidation City and County	Vote Yes 304
Increase State Debt Limit	Vote No 307
Abolishing Uniform Taxation Rule	Vote Yes 308
Classification for Taxation Purposes	Vote Yes 310
Ashland Normal School	No Recommendation
Merger of Cities	Vote Yes 314
Eastern Oregon State Normal	No Recommendation
Increasing Legislative Pay	Vote No 319
Universal Eight-hour Law	Vote No 321
Eight-hour Law for Women	Vote No 323
Non-partisan Judiciary	Vote Yes 324
$1500 Tax Exemption	Vote No 327
Public Docks and Water Frontage	Vote No 329
Municipal Wharves and Docks	Vote No 331
Prohibition	No Recommendation
Abolishing Death Penalty	No Recommendation
Sur-tax	Vote No 337
Consolidating Corporation and Insurance Departments	Vote No 339
Dentistry Bill	Vote No 341
Increasing Term of County Officers	Vote No 343
Tax Code Commission	Vote No 345
Abolishing Desert Land Board	Vote No 347
Proportional Representation	Vote No 349
Abolishing State Senate	Vote No 351
Department of Industry and Public Works	Vote No 353
Primary Delegate Election Bill	Vote No 355
Two-thirds Vote on Taxation Measures	Vote No 357

(Paid advertisement Taxpayers' League, L. J. Goldsmith, Secy., 321 Corbett Bldg.)

Oregon Journal, Nov. 2, 1914, p. 12.

VIII. ADVERTISEMENTS

SINGLE TAX==KILL IT

Single Tax Is Again on the Ballot Cleverly Disguised. There Are Seven Tax Bills on the Ballot and Two of Them Are Single Tax in Effect

TO BEAT SINGLE TAX
Vote 327 No and 337 No

There are thousands of people in the City of Portland who are striving to pay for their lots and get a home. If this measure is carried their property will be absolutely confiscated and they will be compelled to sacrifice what they have paid on the property. It is unquestionably the most unjust measure that was ever offered.

The best citizens in a community are those who own real property and this is a direct blow to that class of citizens and if you wish to be square with lot owners be sure to defeat these two measures.

These measures, if carried, will increase the taxes on your lots over 40 per cent. It is one of the most vicious and cunningly disguised measures on the ballot.

Bear in mind there is

NO EXEMPTION WHATEVER ON LOTS OR LAND

but on the contrary the taxes on your land is greatly increased.

The Realty Board of Portland most earnestly ask your complete coöperation in defeating this most unjust increase in taxes.

F. N. CLARKE, Chairman,
FRED A. JACOBS,
A. C. CALLAN.

(Paid Advertisement.)

Oregonian, Nov. 2, 1914, p. 6.

WORKINGMEN VOTE 309 X — NO

After a hard struggle against the money of the Employer's Association, the people, in November, 1910, passed the Employers' Liability Law. This has been tried and has given entire satisfaction. It requires protection rather than compensation, and that is what we want. Under the Compensation Act of Washington, in seven months, accidents increased from $25\frac{1}{3}$ per cent to $59\frac{5}{18}$ per cent. (See *Oregonian*, Aug. 17.) The Washington Commission, however, tries to lay this at the door of Mr. John Barleycorn, which is ridiculous.

The lumber interests of this state, who have the "human butcher shops," opposed the Employers' Liability Law with large sums of money. In 1911, they raised another "slush" fund, and went to the Legislature by the trainloads to pass a compensation act. The labor unions of Portland succeeded in defeating the bill. Again, at the last Legislature, they raised a large sum of money, and went in trainloads to the Legislature, and succeeded in passing the present bill. These efforts were all made, and this bill was passed to defeat the Employers' Liability Law.

Under the present Compensation Act, a man with both arms or both legs or both eyes removed, which would be permanent disability, would receive $25.00 per month. Multnomah County pays at the rate of $26.70 per month to keep paupers. Who would keep any man with both of his legs off for $25.00 per month?

Again, the Employers' Association succeeded in having Harvey Beckwith appointed a Commissioner. The only thing to recommend him was the fact that he was forty years with big express companies.

The *Oregonian* of October 25 has an article stating the Industrial Insurance Commission of Washington won a victory because it defeated a widow from recovering when her husband was killed as a result of a rock flying from a blast, striking him while he was eating his meal at the company's boarding table. Mr. Beckwith will always have some excuse to keep from paying the pitiful amounts mentioned in his Compensation Act.

The laboring people do not want this act.

F. L. GIFFORD, *Business Manager*,
International Brotherhood of Electrical Workers.

(Paid Advertisement.)

Oregonian, Nov. 1, 1913, p. 2.

Appendix

X. A RECALL PETITION
Hood River County, 1913

RECALL PETITION
WARNING

It is a felony for any one to sign any initiative or referendum petition with any name other than his own, or to knowingly sign his name more than once for the same measure, or to sign such petition when he is not a legal voter.

To the Honorable W. E. Hanson, County Clerk of Hood River County, State of Oregon.

We, the undersigned, citizens and legal voters and qualified electors of the State of Oregon and County of Hood River, by this petition respectively demand the immediate resignation and recall of Geo. R. Castner from the office of County Judge, Geo. A. McCurdy and J. R. Putnam from the offices of County Commissioners, all of Hood River County, Oregon, which offices they now hold and have held for a period of more than six months prior to the circulation of this petition.

That no recall petition has been filed against said officers or either of them, nor any special recall election held against said officers or either of them during their term of office.

We further respectfully demand, that if the said Geo. R. Castner, Geo. A. McCurdy and J. R. Putnam do not resign from the offices of County Judge and Commissioners of Hood River County, Oregon, within five (5) days after the date of the filing of this petition, you call a special election in said County of Hood River, State of Oregon, within twenty (20) days thereafter in accordance with the provisions of the Constitution and the General Laws of the State of Oregon, and each for himself says: "I have personally signed this petition; I am a legal voter of the state of Oregon, and County of Hood River; my residence and postoffice are correctly written after my name."

The following are the reasons for demanding the immediate resignation and recall of the said Geo. R. Castner, Geo. A. McCurdy and J. R. Putnam from the offices of Judge and Commissioners of Hood River County, Oregon.

That the said Geo. R. Castner, Geo. A. McCurdy and J. R. Putnam in the conduct of their said offices as Judge and Commissioners of

Hood River County, Oregon, have been unwise and inefficient, careless and extravagant in the management of the County business, and in proof we cite the following facts:

(1)

On the 7th day of February, 1913, the said Judge and Commissioners appointed C. K. Marshall Road Master of Hood River County, Oregon, for one (1) year at a salary of $5.00 per day and from $2.50 to $7.50 per day additional for the use of his automobile while working for the county as a Road Master. (The record shows C. K. Marshall was paid $40.00 for inspecting the Tucker Bridge, $33.85 for viewing roads, $471.25 for services and automobile as Road Master in five months. No Bills presented and no salary for the months of July and August have been paid to Mr. Marshall.)

(2)

Unnecessarily expending heavy sums of money for improperly oiling roads.

(3)

Allowing and paying unitemized claims against the county (Extract from grand jury report under date July, 1913) "We find that the bills presented against the county are not as a rule itemized as to articles, labor performed, time or dates, and we therefore recommend that all bills presented against the county be itemized."

(4)

Permitting a wagon bridge to be improperly constructed across Hood River (near Winan's place) and paying $1730.28 for the construction of the bridge, which was built in a grossly negligent and careless manner and is dangerous and unsafe for traffic.

[Here follow signatures of electors accompanied by the verification prescribed by statute.]

Appendix

XI. A RECALL BALLOT

Stub	Stub
To be torn off by the chairman	To be torn off by the first clerk

SAMPLE BALLOT

SPECIAL MUNICIPAL ELECTION, CITY OF FLORENCE
FRIDAY, NOVEMBER 13, 1914

Make a cross (X) between the number and name of each candidate or answer voted for.

REASONS FOR DEMANDING RECALL OF GEORGE W. EVANS, MAYOR. — That on or about May 16, 1914, the said George W. Evans as Mayor of the City of Florence, did authorize and direct the destruction of a building belonging to Al Ready; which act was contrary to law and in excess of the authority of said Mayor.

That Al Ready did subsequently obtain a judgment against George W. Evans, in an action in the Justice Court, Florence Precinct, for damages occasioned by said wrongful act; and that on or about August 3, 1914, said George W. Evans, Mayor, did, in a session of the Council of the City of Florence, authorize and vote for the payment of said judgment and costs, amounting to about $81.70, out of funds belonging to the City of Florence; which act constituted a wrongful conversion of the funds of said city.

We assert that on account of these and sundry other illegal acts the said George W. Evans is an unfit person to hold the office of Mayor of the City of Florence.

MAYOR GEORGE W. EVANS' JUSTIFICATION OF HIS COURSE IN OFFICE. — "That no action for damages has ever been brought against George W. Evans in his private capacity, but in fact, against George W. Evans as Mayor, and against another officer, and against both in their official capacity, and that the improvement made by the destruction of the building mentioned was greatly in excess of this amount; that the City Council of the City of Florence in regular session authorized the payment of said judgment, it being absolutely impossible for the Mayor or any other officer of the City to pay this amount without the Council's action, and that the allegation that the Mayor authorized the payment of the same is made only to misrepresent the facts; that I am willing to leave my other acts, both as to this matter and to all other things, to the consideration of the voters."

Shall George W. Evans be recalled from the office of Mayor?	
12	Yes
13	No

For Mayor	Vote for one.
15	C. D. MOREY.
14	GEORGE W. EVANS.

INDEX

INITIATIVE AND REFERENDUM.
Abolition of legislature, 129–30, 159–61.
Adoption, 3–5.
Advertisements, 287–8.
Amendment of constitution. *See* constitutional amendment.
Amendment of direct legislation by legislature, 145–56.
Amendment of initiative measures before submission to vote, 28–9.
Associations as authors, 18; as educators of voters, 97, 266–74, 280–8.
Authors of measures, 9–20. *See* Motives.

Ballot, length, 78–80; sample, 288.
Ballot titles, 8, 29, 43–4, 45, 52–3, 107–11.
Bibliography, 221–7.
Burden on voters, 78–85.

Campaign organization, 86; methods, 93–9. *See* Finance.
Combination of subjects in measures, 42, 43–6, 112–3.
Competition with legislature, 159–65.
Concealment of authorship, 13–6. *See* Fraud.
Conflict of measures, 7, 47–9, 115–7.
Conservatives. *See* Radicals.
Constitution, stability, 180–4.
Constitutional amendments, 6, 177–8, 180–4.
Constitutional convention, 177–9.
Constitutional limitations, applicable to direct legislation, 180–1; absence in legislation by initiative, 180–3; referendum as a substitute for constitutional limitations on legislature, 171–2.
Constitutionality of provisions for initiative and referendum, 128, note 2; constitutionality of measures determined by courts, 173–4.

INITIATIVE AND REFERENDUM — *Cont.*
Courts, relation to direct legislation, 173–6; interpretation, 173–4; declare unconstitutional, 173–4; "recall" of decisions, 174–6.

Deception. *See* Fraud.
Definitions, 5.
Division of statutes as check on referendum, 144.
Drafting measures. *See* Preparation.

Education of voters, 91–100.
Elections, interest, 101–3.
Emergency legislation, 132–44.
Executive, author of measures, 12–3, 126–7; veto of referendum measures, 10, 126; veto as protection against abuse of emergency clause, 135–9, 141; as protection against abuse in amendment and repeal of direct legislation by legislature, 146, 150, 152, 156; as cause of use of direct legislation, 163; influence of direct legislation on executive, 127.
Expenses, 87–90.

Federal matters, 187.
Finance, 87–90.
Form of measures, 50–3.
Fraud, 13–6, 29, 42–4, 65–74.

Governor. *See* Executive.

History, 3–5.

Individuals as authors, 16–8.
Information for voters, 93–9, 254–74, 275–9, 287–8.
Intelligence in voting, 99–100, 107–25.
Interest in elections, 101–3.
Interests, 21–5, 113–5.
Interpretation of measures by courts, 173–4.

INITIATIVE AND REFERENDUM — *Cont.*
Law, 5-8, 227-40.
Legislature, faults as cause of adoption of initiative and referendum, 4; author of measures, 6-7, 9-12, 30, 85, 164-5; nullify veto by referendum, 10; resubmission of measures defeated at election, 11, 146, 155; public opinion bills, 157-8; powers shared with voters, 128-30; abolition of legislature, 129-30, 159-61; regulation of initiative and referendum, 131-2, 149; emergency legislation, 132-44; division of statutes, 144; amendment and repeal of direct legislation, 145-56; competition of direct legislation with legislature, 28-9, 78-85, 159-66; faults of legislature as cause of direct legislation, 82-5, 159-63, 167-8; effect of direct legislation on legislature, 9-11, 167-70; constitutional restrictions removable on account of referendum, 171-2.
Local initiative and referendum, not considered, v.
Local interests, 22-5, 113.
Log-rolling, 22-5, 44-6.

Majority vote required, 6-7, 103-5, 180. *See* Minority.
Measures, preparation, 26-30; classified, 31-41; number proposed, 78-80, 241-53; enacted, 105-7, 241-53.
Minority rights, 103-5, 182-3. *See* Majority.
Motives, 21-5, 113-5.

Number of measures proposed, 78-80, 241-53; enacted, 105-7, 241-53.

Pamphlet for voters, 8, 93-5, 254-74.
People, authors of measures, 13-20.
People's Power League, 3, 18, 254-70.
Petitions, percentage required, 6, 54-8; form, 7, 274-5; verification of signatures, 7-8, 70-1, 275; geographical distribution of signatures, 58-9; payment of circulators, 59-64; methods of circulators, 64-74; substitutes for circulation, 74-7; an initiative petition, 274-5.

INITIATIVE AND REFERENDUM — *Cont.*
Political parties, 185-6.
Popularity of initiative and referendum, 3-5, 178-9, 188.
Preparation of measures, 26-30.
Press, influence in direct legislation, 96-7, 98-9, 275-9.
Progressives. *See* Radicals.
Public opinion bills, 157-8.

Radicals, progressives, and conservatives, 18-20, 31-2, 117-20.
Recall of judicial decisions, 174-6.
Regulation of initiative and referendum by legislature, 131-2, 149.
Repeal of direct legislation by legislature, 145-56.
Representative government, 98-9, 128-30, 159.
Republican form of government, 128.

Separate items subject to referendum, 6.
Special interests, 21-5, 113-5.
Stability of government, 180-4.
Subjects of measures, 31-41, 241-53; suitable and unsuitable, 37-41, 112-3.

U'Ren, W. S., 3, 4-5, note, 17-8.

Vote on measures, 101-25, 241-53; interest in elections, 101-3; minority v. majority, 103-5; amount of legislation enacted, 105-7; rationality of the vote, 107-25; confusion of the measure with the referendum, 107; identification of measures, 107-8; knowledge of contents of measures, 108-12; attention to legal technicalities, 112; vote on subjects unsuitable to direct legislation, 112-3; on measures submitted by selfish interests, 113-5; on conflicting measures, 115-7; conservatism and progressivism in the vote, 117-20; vote of the uncertain voter, 121-3; vote as protest, 123; intelligence of the vote in general, 123-5.

RECALL.
  Adoption, 191.
  Authors, 200, 211-2.

  Ballot, 192, 215, 291-2.
  Bibliography, 221-7.

  Campaign, 211-2.
  Checks on recall movements, 213-4.
  Concealment of authorship, 200, 212.

  Definition, 191.

  Effects, 194, 217-8.
  Elections attempted, 202-7; held, 194-202; interest, 216.

  Federal officers, 193.
  Finance, 193, 213.
  Fraud, 212.

  History, 191.

  Impeachment and recall, 216-7.
  Interest in elections, 216.
  Issues confused, 214-6.

RECALL — *Cont.*
  Judges, 202, 205-6, 208-10.

  Law, 191-4, 240-1.

  Majority. *See* Plurality.
  Motives, 207-11, 216-7.

  Officers subject, 191, 193-4; effect on officers, 217-8; term lengthened, 217.

  Petition, sample, 289-90.
  Petition making, 191-3, 211-3.
  Plurality election, 192, 215-6.

  Referendum as substitute for recall, 213-4.

  Short ballot, relation to recall, 217-8.

  Threats of recall, 207.

  U'Ren, W. S., 191.

Printed in the United States of America.

THE following pages contain advertisements of a few of the Macmillan books on kindred subjects

The New American Government and Its Work

By JAMES T. YOUNG
Professor of Public Administration in the University of Pennsylvania

Cloth, 8vo, $2.25

This book, intended for that growing circle of readers who are interested not only in political form and structure, but also more especially in *What the Government Is Doing and Why*, is characterized by the following features:

1. It places greater emphasis than usual on the *work* of the government.

2. It pays more attention to present problems, especially to the *Public Regulation of Business*.

3. It applies to every aspect of government the test of *Results*—whether the subject be the powers of the President, the election laws, or the Sherman Act—for the value of a court, a statute, or a political institution should be known by its output.

4. It depicts the *Government As It Is*, and as it has developed. Our system is not a finished crystal, nor an ancient historical manuscript, but a growth. And it is still growing.

5. It includes the interpretation of the Constitution and the chief regulative laws, in the most recent *Decisions of the Supreme Court*. It is this that gives clear, definite meaning to the discussion of government forms and activities.

6. It presents an *Ideal*. It does not hesitate to point out the moral defects, and the social cost of political weakness and inefficiency but its *Tone* is *Optimistic*.

THE MACMILLAN COMPANY
Publishers   64-66 Fifth Avenue   **New York**

Documents on the State-wide Initiative, Referendum and Recall

By CHARLES A. BEARD, Associate Professor of Politics in Columbia University; and BIRL E. SHULTZ, Indiana Scholar in Political Science in Columbia University.

Cloth, 12mo, $2.00

This volume includes all of the constitutional amendments providing for a state-wide system of initiative and referendum now in force, several of the most significant statutes elaborating the constitutional provisions, all of the constitutional amendments now pending adoption, six important judicial decisions, and certain materials relative to the state-wide recall. While no attempt has been made to go into the subject of the initiative, referendum, and recall as applied to local and municipal government, some illustrative papers showing the system in ordinary municipalities and commission-governed cities have been included.

* * * * * * * * * * *

In the introductory note Professor Beard presents a keen analysis and scholarly discussion of the documents contained in this volume. His conclusions will be found intensely stimulating and suggestive to every student of political science who is interested in the present-day movement toward popular reform.

Furthermore, the book will be found the most convenient source upon which to base a course on this subject. It will also be a valuable supplementary text for use in courses on State Legislation, Party Government, etc.

THE MACMILLAN COMPANY
64–66 Fifth Avenue, New York

A NEW STUDY OF SOCIOLOGY

Outlines of Sociology

By FRANK W. BLACKMAR

Professor of Sociology in the University of Kansas

AND

JOHN L. GILLIN

Associate Professor of Sociology in the University of Wisconsin

8vo, $2.00

A unified survey of the entire field of sociology. Theoretical phases of the subject are fully treated, and its practical bearings developed in chapters on social pathology and the methods of social investigation. The inclusion of the latter serves to vitalize the study of sociology by giving the reader an opportunity to make a first hand study of society, while supplying him with a few simple principles to guide him in the work.

The subject is treated under the following main headings:

Part I, The Nature and Import of Sociology. II, Social Evolution. III, Socialization and Social Control. IV, Social Ideals and Social Control. V, Social Pathology. VI, Methods of Social Investigations. VII, The History of Sociology.

Conspicuous for the broad scope of its treatment, its up-to-dateness on the newer lines of sociological thinking, and the simple direct method of presentation, the "Outlines of Sociology" offers an admirable book for club and individual reading.

THE MACMILLAN COMPANY

Publishers   64–66 Fifth Avenue   New York

The Government of American Cities

By Professor WILLIAM B. MUNRO
Of Harvard University

Cloth, 8vo, $2.00

Here Professor Munro presents with fairness and impartiality all the aspects of such subjects as Commission Government, The Initiative, The Referendum, The Recall. Other phases of municipal government in this country are also considered, so that the work may be described as a comprehensive survey of present conditions in our cities. The book is found even more interesting and stimulating than the author's "The Government of European Cities."

By the Same Author

The Government of European Cities

Cloth, 8vo, $2.00

"On the whole Professor Munro's book may be fairly characterized as the most useful of its kind thus far published, because it furnishes the material for making comparisons which must inevitably disclose the true course of numerous American municipal shortcomings." — *San Francisco Chronicle.*

"This book is distinctly an addition to our text-books on municipal administration, despite the fact that we have several very good ones already. It is a book which will prove of great benefit to the serious-minded reader interested in municipal governments; but it will probably be used mostly as a reference or text-book in colleges and universities." — *The American Journal of Sociology.*

"Cette étude est très fructueuse pour tous ceux qu'intéressent les questions de droit public comparé." — *Société Belge d'Etudes Coloniales.*

"Dr. Munro's book is an indispensable one to the student of municipal government who would acquaint himself with the experience of the world. He modestly disclaims any assumption of exhaustiveness, but it certainly gives us an admirably clear picture alike valuable from its analytical, comparative, and historical aspects." — *The Argonaut*, San Francisco.

THE MACMILLAN COMPANY
Publishers   64-66 Fifth Avenue   **New York**

American Municipal Progress

By CHARLES ZUEBLIN

New Edition, Entirely Rewritten and Greatly Enlarged

Professor Zueblin's work has a message for all who live in either a great metropolis or a small, progressive town. It is not so much a new and revised edition of Mr. Zueblin's earlier work as it is a new volume. The development of the cities and the growth of the social conscience in the past decade have made necessary a larger treatment, and the author, although using the earlier work as a nucleus for the new, has almost doubled its pages, and at the same time has added to its value with many illustrations.

The book takes up in detail such problems as public utilities, schools, libraries, children's playgrounds, parks, public baths and public gymnasiums; also such questions as those of rapid transit, sanitation and the care of streets; the latest experiments in municipal ownership and municipal administration are recorded. The discussion is from the standpoint of public welfare, and is based on repeated personal investigations in the leading cities of the United States. Despite its large interest for the general reader, its comprehensiveness makes it valuable to the research student as well, and its exhaustive bibliography is invaluable to the specialist. The work is unique and will be found a complete guide in many unfamiliar paths.

THE MACMILLAN COMPANY
Publishers   64-66 Fifth Avenue   New York

The American City: A Problem in Democracy

By DELOS F. WILCOX, Ph.D.

New edition. Cloth, 12mo, $1.25

The problem of city government is a live one to-day. Dr. Wilcox believes that the great political and social reforms of the future will come through the city. By tracing the causes of city growth, the peculiarities of life in the city and its ideals of democracy, he has tried to make plain to all the breadth of a city's influence, the foundations of its organization, the extent of its responsibility and the sources of its revenue in this country.

"This book will commend itself as a study of the municipal problem in our larger and more important cities. Mr. Wilcox has brought together a large amount of expert information." — *New York Call.*

"The book will instruct the citizen interested in clean politics, and especially the voter wishing to find the best forward step to promote civic decency and justice."— *Chicago Examiner.*

Voting Trusts: Chapters in Recent Corporate History

By HARRY A. CUSHING
Of the New York Bar

Cloth, 8vo, $1.50

This is a concisely written volume of real interest to investigators and business men as well as to trust company officials and lawyers. It is the first book on the subject and covers the early history of voting trusts and the details of their more recent development. The facts have been gathered and collated with substantial thoroughness as illustrations of the discussion under the three heads of the significance, the contents, and the law of voting trusts. A selection of important documents is also included.

THE MACMILLAN COMPANY
Publishers   64-66 Fifth Avenue   New York

STORAGE LIBRARY
DATE DUE

DARTMOUTH COLLEGE
3 3311 00520 2066